NTE
NATIONAL TEACHER EXAMINATIONS

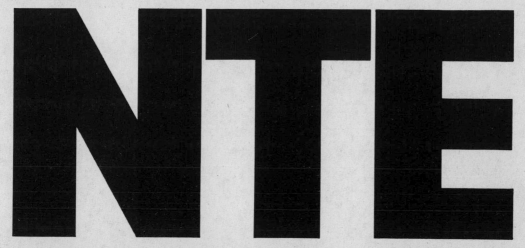

NTE

NATIONAL TEACHER EXAMINATIONS

David J. Fox, Ph.D.

Professor of Education
Director of Research and Graduate Studies
School of Education
City College, City University of New York

ARCO PUBLISHING, INC.
NEW YORK

Eighth Edition, Third Printing, 1985

Published by Arco Publishing, Inc.
215 Park Avenue South, New York, N.Y., 10003

Library of Congress Cataloging in Publication Data

Fox, David J.
  NTE, national teacher examinations
  1. National teacher examinations—Study guides.
  I. Title   II. Title: N.T.E., national teacher examinations.
LB1762.F72   1984   379.1'57   83-19722
ISBN O-668-05783-1 (pbk.)

Printed in the United States of America

For Louise—a constant inspiration

CONTENTS

PART FOUR: UNDERSTANDING YOUR EXAMINATION SCORES

PART FIVE: DIAGNOSTIC CORE BATTERY I

PART SIX: REVIEW EXAMINATION IN PROFESSIONAL KNOWLEDGE

PART SEVEN: DIAGNOSTIC CORE BATTERY II

PART EIGHT: WRITING ABILITY DIAGNOSTIC SCORE SHEET

PART NINE: REVIEW TESTS FOR SPECIALTY AREAS

THE GOALS OF THIS BOOK

This book is intended to help you score as high as you possibly can on the National Teacher Examinations (NTE), objective tests of your knowledge of education and related areas. To help you achieve the highest score you can we have set out to accomplish four goals:

1. To make you familiar with the content of the examinations, so that you have some sense of what the questions are about and the areas they cover.

2. To make you familiar with the different types of questions asked on the examinations. Although all questions are objective, many different types of questions are used, including some you probably have not seen before, such as questions testing your ability to listen.

3. To give you the opportunity to diagnose your strengths and weaknesses, so that you can use your review and study time most effectively.

4. To enable you to do your best when you finally take the examinations, so that your score reflects your full knowledge after effective studying and is not lowered by test anxiety or inefficient test-taking behavior.

In order to reach these goals, the following special features have been provided:

1. Two complete diagnostic examinations. Both diagnostic examinations are slightly longer in some areas than the actual NTE in order to cover all subject areas and question types that may appear on the actual test.

2. A special section on answering the different types of objective questions.

3. Newly developed questions to provide practice in responding to questions testing your listening skills and your reading ability.

4. Unique answer tables for each of the Diagnostic Professional Examinations that indicate how well you have answered the questions in each of the different areas, such as Developmental Psychology, Learning Theory, Curriculum Development, Evaluation, Teaching Practices, and the special curriculum areas.

5. A special section on effective studying that provides you with a detailed plan for taking the examination.

Format Chart and Timetable
for Diagnostic Core Batteries I and II

Section of Examination/ Sub-test	Number of Questions	Time to Allow
I. Professional Knowledge	130	95 min.
Psychological Foundations		
Social, Cultural, Philosophical Foundations		
Teaching Principles, Curriculum Development, Supervision		
Professional Awareness		
II. General Knowledge	135	95 min.
Humanities		
Social Studies	(35)	
Literature	(25)	
Art and Music	(20)	
Science and Mathematics		
Science	(32)	
Mathematics	(23)	
III. Communication Skills	86	110 min.
Listening Ability	(28)	
Reading Ability	(23)	
Writing Ability*	(35)	
Total		

*(Essay not included in Diagnostic Core Batteries)

The number of questions on the Diagnostic Examinations are similar to the number on the National Teacher Examinations, but the number and percentage of questions on each sub-test may vary from examination to examination.

Part One

ABOUT THE NATIONAL TEACHER EXAMINATIONS

WHAT THE NTE ARE USED FOR

The National Teacher Examinations (to be referred to as the NTE) are a series of objective examinations given by the Educational Testing Service of Princeton, New Jersey. The NTE are described in the official *Bulletin of Information* as " . . . standardized, secure tests that provide objective measures of academic achievement for college seniors completing teacher-education programs, and for advanced candidates who have received additional training in specific fields."

Candidates most often take one or more of the examinations as one piece of information to supply to school systems when they seek a job. In some instances the school system requires applicants to take the NTE; in other instances the candidate decides to take the examination in the expectation that a strong performance will increase the likelihood of obtaining a teaching position. Remember, your performance on the NTE is *one* piece of information about your academic performance. Your college transcript is another piece of information, as are letters of reference and the impression you make in a personal interview. Thus, while the NTE scores can be an important part of your professional resume, they are only one piece of information, and so should be taken in that context.

THE NATURE OF
THE EXAMINATIONS

The NTE consists of a three-part Core Battery given in one day, and a series of Specialty Area Examinations given on a separate morning. The Core Battery consists of an examination in Communication Skills followed by one in General Knowledge, given in the morning, and an examination in Professional Knowledge given in the afternoon. The Specialty Area Examinations cover different areas, and you select the one in which you choose to be examined.

The Communication Skills Examination has three major sections. Since the first section is intended to test your ability to listen, it presents its basic information through a tape recording. You listen to the material on the tape, and then respond by choosing among possible answers which are printed in your question booklet. A second section tests your ability to read by presenting you with printed informational material after which there are questions about the material. The other section of the Communication Skills Examination is intended to test your understanding of the rules for writing, as well as your ability to write. It consists of questions on English usage as well as a short essay.

The second examination, the General Knowledge Examination, consists of two sub-tests. One covers the Humanities, specifically Literature, Social Studies, and the Fine Arts. The second covers Science and Mathematics.

The Professional Knowledge Examination is a broadly based test covering all of the areas in a typical teacher-education program. Thus, it includes questions based on courses in psychological foundations as well as in social foundations; also, to a lesser extent, in historical and philosophical foundations. It emphasizes material covered in courses in methods of teaching, classroom management, and curriculum development, and has a new emphasis on professional issues such as teacher and student rights and the teacher's professional responsibilities.

The typical NTE examination session is a full and long day. The morning session begins at 8:00 A.M. and concludes at 1:15 P.M. After 45 minutes for lunch, the afternoon session begins at 2:00 and concludes at 4:45. The Specialty Area Examinations run from 8:30 to 11:15 A.M.

All of the questions are objective; that is, some kind of a question is posed, and you are given four or five possible answers and asked to choose the one that best answers the question. As we shall discuss in Part Three, several different types of objective questions are used. For example, you are sometimes asked to identify the best answer, sometimes the one that is least sensible. But in every case you will be able to indicate your choice of the possible answers by blackening an answer space on the familiar machine-scored answer sheet. You will not have to respond to true-false questions, nor write any kind of fill-in answers or essays, other than the one in the Writing Examination.

Content of the Core Battery

Professional Knowledge. Questions in this section may be drawn from any of the areas covered in your Education sequence. In its informational booklet on the Core Battery, ETS notes that the items are derived from ". . . the core of knowledge and those cognitive processes that are of direct relevance to teaching."[1]

The questions relate to what ETS considers to be two large dimensions of the teacher's role: (1) the process of teaching; and (2) the context of teaching.

The process of teaching means the series of steps or roles, from planning your instruction, including the selection of appropriate techniques and materials; implementing your plan in the classroom; evaluating the outcome of your instructional efforts; and your ability to do all this in a professional manner.

The first of these roles, planning instruction, tests information you should have covered in courses on methods and materials and on curriculum planning and development. It includes questions on objectives, needs assessment, grouping, and material development. In addition, it includes material on recognizing the characteristics in children which relate to instruction, and so draws on materials usually covered in courses on child development.

The second role, related to implementation, tests your understanding of the process of learning and achievement, your use of such dynamics as reinforcement, setting standards and limits, instructional design, practice and feedback, and your use of evaluative data to rethink and replan the instructional process itself. Most of this material would be covered in courses related to the theories of human learning and/or courses in instructional design.

The third role involves the teacher as a measurer and evaluator of learning. This role includes material you would have covered in courses concerned with assessment and evaluation, tests, and measurement. Interpreting test scores, simple statistical interpretations, and aspects of measurement such as reliability and validity are covered in the questions related to this role, as are other aspects of evaluation, such as reporting pupil progress and evaluating the effectiveness of the teacher's instructional efforts in a unit or in a total program.

The last aspect of the process of teaching involves materials on the teacher's professional behavior. Much of this area overlaps some of the others to some extent, for it concerns student feelings (which should also be considered in implementing instruction) handling controversial issues (also considered in planning instruction), the rights and responsibilities of teachers — in brief, many of the concerns which are covered in a thorough course on the social foundations of education, or a course on the school in society.

The context of teaching refers to your understanding of student rights and your ability to recognize the implications of both federal policies and legal decisions for classroom practices, as well as your recognition of the forces and factors beyond the classroom which affect the student, the teacher, and the school.

This dimension focuses on the increasingly important area of student rights a the impact of federal policy and legal decisions on the school and even the classro The movement for equality of educational opportunity which highlighted the 19 and the bilingual educational emphasis of the 1970's, as well as the concern proper class placement for the handicapped of the late 1970's, all came into nence in education from federal policy or legal decisions. This area highlights cern with these areas, as well as with the out-of-school influences on educat as the movement for community involvement and control, the concern wi for education, and the policies and practices of professional organizatio this material is covered in social foundations courses and in professiona classes. Some of the material, realistically, is *not* directly covered in the education program. Thus, you may have to do some extra reading to prepared in this area.

The context of teaching also considers the out-of-school factors

---

[1]"NTE Programs, Core Battery Tests." Educational Testing Servic 1982.

Media Specialist — Library and Audiovisual Services

Music Education

Physical Education

Reading Specialist

Social Studies

Spanish

Speech Communication

Speech — Communications and Theater

Speech Pathology

In addition, an Area Examination in Agriculture is offered only at a few test centers. Read the official bulletin of information carefully.

Selecting a Specialty Area Examination. When deciding upon a Specialty Area Examination, most candidates usually select the area in which they majored in Education. In some instances, usually when candidates are seeking specific jobs outside their Education major, they may take a second Area Examination, or even take only the Area Examination needed for the job. If you are taking the NTE for a specific job or to meet the request of a specific school system, ask that school system which Area Examination they would prefer you to take. The Educational Testing Service sets no minimum number of courses or credits you must have completed to take a special Area Examination (except in Audiology and Speech Pathology), so the responsibility is yours to take only those specialized examinations for which you are reasonably prepared. In Audiology and Speech Pathology, the *Bulletin of Information* indicates the kind of advanced preparation the Specialty Area Examination assumes you have.

HOW TO APPLY

The NTE are given by the Educational Testing Service (ETS). Applications can be obtained by writing or phoning:

National Teacher Examinations
Educational Testing Service
Box 911
Princeton, NJ 08541
Telephone No. (609) 921-9000

The cost for any of the three tests in the Core Battery is $20; two tests on the same test date cost $32.50; and all three Core Battery tests on the same test date cost $45. Each Specialty Area Test costs $30. The late registration fee has been raised to $12. After you send in your application and check to ETS, you will receive a response card or ticket admitting you to the examination and indicating the test center to which you have been assigned.

The following are two new policies announced in relationship to fees:

A. If you are a college senior receiving financial aid, and you cannot pay the required fees for the NTE, a fee waiver may be available. Income guidelines and procedures are described in the informational booklet on the examination.

B. If you live in California or New York, you will now be able to pay your fees through Ticketron or Tele-Tron. Again, procedures are described in detail in the informational booklet.

Although the only certain way to be permitted to take the examination is to register in advance and receive the admission ticket, ETS does permit "walk-in" testing, for which you go to a test center on the date of the test with a completed registration form. If they should have space and sufficient extra test materials, you will be permitted to take the test. You will later be billed for the test plus a $15 extra charge. There is no guarantee that there will be space or extra materials available. This is an emergency last resort, if for some reason you have not registered in advance.

The examination is given at three- to five-month intervals. Check the bulletin for all test dates. The NTE are given on Saturdays at selected test centers. Not all test centers are used at each administration, so you may be assigned to one other than your first choice, particularly in large cities with more than one center. If your religious convictions prohibit your taking the test on a Saturday, you may ask to take the test on the Monday following its regular administration. If you live more than 100 miles from one of the test centers listed, you may ask that ETS arrange for the NTE to be given at a supplementary test center. Disabled persons who cannot take the test under normal conditions may ask to have the NTE given under conditions that make it possible for them to complete it. For each instance, the bulletin of information explains these special application procedures.

The regular registration period for the examination closes about three weeks prior to the examination date, and you can register for one week thereafter by paying a late-registration fee. Registration closes two to three weeks earlier if you require one of the special arrangements for testing, such as a Monday test date.

TEST CENTERS

The National Teacher Examinations are given in each of the fifty states, as well as in the District of Columbia and Puerto Rico. For your convenience, the centers in each of these areas are listed here.

Alabama
  Birmingham, Birmingham Southern College
  Florence, University of North Alabama
  Jacksonville, State University
  Livingston, Livingston University
  Mobile, Mobile College
  Mobile, University of South Alabama
  Montgomery, Alabama State University
  Norman, Alabama A & M University
  Troy, State University
  Tuskegee Institute, Tuskegee Institute
  University, University of Alabama

Arizona
  Tempe, Arizona State University

Arkansas
  Arkadelphia, Henderson State University
  Arkadelphia, Ouachita Baptist University
  Conway, University of Central Arkansas
  Fayetteville, University of Arkansas
  Harrison, North Arkansas Community College
  Little Rock, Philander Smith College
  Little Rock, University of Arkansas
  Magnolia, Southern Arkansas University
  Monticello, University of Arkansas
  Pine Bluff, University of Arkansas
  Russellville, Arkansas Tech. University
  Searcy, Harding College
  State University, Arkansas State University

California
  Arcata, Humboldt State University
  Bakersfield, California State College
  Berkeley, University of California
  Carson, Dominguez Hills, California State University
  Chico, California State University
  Edwards, Air Force Base
  Fresno, California State University
  Fullerton, California State University

Irvine, University of California
Long Beach, California State University
Los Angeles, University of California
Los Angeles, University of Southern California
Riverside, University of California
Rohnert Park, Sonoma State University
Sacramento, California State University
San Bernardino, California State College
San Diego, San Diego State University
San Francisco, San Francisco State University
San Francisco, University of San Francisco
San Luis Obispo, California State Polytechnic University
Santa Barbara, University of California
Santa Clara, University of Santa Clara
Stockton, University of the Pacific
Turlock, California State College, Stanislaus

Colorado
  Boulder, University of Colorado
  Colorado Springs, Colorado College

Connecticut
  Storrs, University of Connecticut
  West Hartford, University of Hartford

Delaware
  Dover, Delaware State College

District of Columbia
  Washington, University of District of Columbia
  Washington, Howard University

Florida
  Gainesville, University of Florida
  Lakeland, Florida Southern College
  Miami, Miami Dade Community College
  Orlando, Orange County Public Schools
  Tallahassee, Florida State University

12

Georgia
  Albany, State College
  Americus, Georgia Southwestern College
  Athens, University of Georgia
  Atlanta, Emory University
  Atlanta, Georgia State University
  Augusta, Augusta College
  Augusta, Paine College
  Brunswick, Junior College
  Carrollton, West Georgia College
  Columbus, Columbus College
  Dahlonega, North Georgia College
  Demorest, Piedmont College
  Ft. Valley, State College
  Gainesville, Junior College
  Macon, Mercer University
  Milledgeville, Georgia College
  Mt. Berry, Berry College
  Rome, Shorter College
  Savannah, Armstrong State College
  Savannah, State College
  Statesboro, Georgia Southern College
  Valdosta, State College

Hawaii
  Honolulu, University of Hawaii

Illinois
  Carbondale, Southern Illinois University
  Champaign, University of Illinois
  Chicago, Chicago State University
  Chicago, Loyola University
  DeKalb, Northern Illinois University
  Evanston, National College of Education
  Evanston, Northwestern University
  Peoria, Bradley University
  River Forest, Concordia Teachers College

Indiana
  Bloomington, Indiana University
  Evansville, University of Evansville
  Indianapolis, Butler University
  Muncie, Ball State University
  Terre Haute, Indiana State University
  West Lafayette, Purdue University

Iowa
  Des Moines, Drake University
  Dubuque, University of Dubuque
  Iowa City, University of Iowa

Kansas
  Topeka, Washburn University
  Wichita, State University

Kentucky
  Barbourville, Union College
  Berea, Berea College
  Georgetown, Georgetown College
  Lexington, University of Kentucky
  Louisville, University of Louisville
  Murray, State University

Louisiana
  Alexandria, Louisiana State University
  Baton Rouge, Louisiana State University
  Baton Rouge, Southern University
  Grambling, Grambling State University
  Hammond, Southeastern Louisiana University
  Lafayette, University of Southwestern Louisiana
  Lake Charles, McNeese State University
  Monroe, Northeast Louisiana State University
  Natchitoches, Northwestern State University
  New Orleans, Loyola University
  New Orleans, St. Mary's Dominican College
  New Orleans, Tulane University
  New Orleans, University of New Orleans
  Pineville, Louisiana College
  Ruston, Louisiana State Technical University
  Shreveport, Centenary College
  Shreveport, Louisiana State College
  Thibodaux, Nicholls State University

Maine
  Orono, University of Maine
  Portland, University of Southern Maine

Maryland
  Baltimore, Morgan State University
  College Park, University of Maryland
  Frostburg, State College
  Towson, State College

Massachusetts
  Amherst, University of Massachusetts
  Boston, State College
  Cambridge, Lesley College
  Fall River, Fall River Public Schools
  Fitchburg, State College

Lowell, University of Lowell—South Campus
North Adams, State College
Pittsfield, Pittsfield Public Schools
Salem, State College

Michigan
Detroit, University of Detroit
East Lansing, Michigan State University
Marquette, North Michigan University
Mt. Pleasant, Central Michigan University
Olivet, Olivet College

Minnesota
St. Paul, Concordia College

Mississippi
Blue Mountain, Blue Mountain College
Cleveland, Delta State University
Clinton, Mississippi College
Columbus, Mississippi University for Women
Hattiesburg, University of Southern Mississippi
Holly Springs, Rust College
Itta Bena, Mississippi Valley State University
Jackson, State University
Jackson, Millsaps College
Lorman, Alcorn State University
Meridian, Meridian Junior College
Mississippi State, Mississippi State University
Natchez, University of Southern Mississippi
University (Oxford), University of Mississippi

Missouri
Jefferson City, Lincoln University
Joplin, Missouri Southern State College
Kansas City, Avila College
Kansas City, University of Missouri
Kirksville, Northeast Missouri State University
St. Louis, St. Louis University
Warrensberg, Central Missouri State University

Montana
Butte, Montana Technical College
Missoula, University of Montana

Nebraska
Hastings, Hastings College
Kearney, State College
Lincoln, University of Nebraska
Peru, Peru State College
Scottsbluff, Nebraska Western College

New Hampshire
Manchester, St. Anselm's College

New Jersey
Glassboro, State College
Jersey City, St. Peter's Preparatory School
Lakewood, Georgian Court College
New Brunswick, Rutgers–The State University
South Orange, Seton Hall University
Trenton, State College
Union, Kean College
Upper Montclair, State College
Wayne, William Paterson College

New Mexico
Albuquerque, University of Albuquerque
Albuquerque, University of New Mexico

New York
Bronx, Fordham University
Brooklyn, Brooklyn College
Buffalo, State University of New York
Cortland, State University College
Hempstead, Hofstra University
Jamaica, St. John's University
New York, Columbia University
Oneonta, State University College
Rochester, University of Rochester
St. Bonaventure, St. Bonaventure University
Staten Island, St. John's University
Stony Brook, State University of New York
Syracuse, Syracuse University

North Carolina
Asheville, Asheville City Schools
Boiling Springs, Gardner-Webb College
Boone, Appalachian State University
Buie Creek, Campbell College
Chapel Hill, University of North Carolina
Charlotte, Charlotte-Mecklenburg Board of
  Education
Cullowhee, Western Carolina University
Durham, Duke University
Durham, North Carolina Central University
Elizabeth City, Elizabeth City State University
Fayetteville, Terry Sanford Senior High School
Greensboro, North Carolina A & T State
  University

Greensboro, University of North Carolina
Greenville, East Carolina University
Hickory, Lenoir Rhyne College
Laurinburg, St. Andrews Presbyterian College
Mars Hill, Mars Hill College
New Bern, New Bern Senior High School
Raleigh, William Enloe High School
Rocky Mount, North Carolina Wesleyan
    College
Salisbury, Catawba College
Wilmington, University of North Carolina
Wilson, Atlantic Christian College
Winston-Salem, Winston-Salem City Schools

North Dakota
Grand Forks, University of North Dakota
Minot, State College

Ohio
Athens, Ohio University
Berea, Baldwin-Wallace College
Bowling Green, State University
Cincinnati, University of Cincinnati
Cleveland, John Carroll University
Columbus, Ohio State University
Dayton, University of Dayton
Kent, State University
Youngstown, Youngstown State University

Oklahoma
Alva, Northwestern Oklahoma State
    University
Durant, Southeastern State University
Langston, Langston State University
Oklahoma City, Oklahoma City University
Shawnee, Oklahoma Baptist University
Stillwater, Oklahoma State University

Oregon
Ashland, Southern Oregon State College
Eugene, University of Oregon
Portland, State University

Pennsylvania
Allentown, Cedar Crest College
Bloomsburg, State College
Cheyney, State College
Clarion, State College
Dallas, College Misericordia
Grove City, Grove City College

Indiana, Indiana University of Pennsylvania
Kutztown, State College
Mansfield, State College
Millersville, State College
Philadelphia, Temple University
Philadelphia, University of Pennsylvania
Pittsburgh, Duquesne University
Pittsburgh, University of Pittsburgh
Scranton, Marywood College
Scranton, Scranton Public Schools
Slippery Rock, State College
University Park, Pennsylvania State University
West Chester, State College

Rhode Island
Providence, Providence Public Schools

South Carolina
Aiken, Aiken Senior High School
Charleston, College of Charleston
Clemson, Clemson University
Columbia, Richland Northeast High School
Conway, Coastal Carolina College
Florence, South Florence High School
Greenville, Greenville Senior High School
Greenwood, Greenwood High School
Kingstree, Kingstree Senior High School
Newberry, Newberry College
Orangeburg, Orangeburg Wilkinson High
    School
Rock Hill, Winthrop College
Spartanburg, Spartanburg Senior High School
Sumter, School District 17
Walterboro, Walterboro Senior High School

South Dakota
Rapid City, South Dakota School of Mines
Yankton, Mount Marty College

Tennessee
Chattanooga, University of Tennessee
Clarksville, Austin Peay State University
Cleveland, Lee College
Cookeville, Tennessee Technical University
Jackson, Union University
Jefferson City, Carson-Newman College
Johnson City, East Tennessee State University
Knoxville, University of Tennessee
Martin, University of Tennessee
Memphis, LeMoyne-Owen College

Memphis, State University
Milligan College, Milligan College
Murfreesboro, Middle Tennessee State University
Nashville, Vanderbilt University

Texas
Abilene, Abilene Christian College
Austin, University of Texas
Dallas, Southern Methodist University
Denton, North Texas State University
El Paso, University of Texas
Houston, University of Houston
Lubbock, Texas Tech University
Marshall, East Texas Baptist College
Marshall, Wiley College
Prairie View, A & M University
San Antonio, St. Mary's University
Tyler, Texas College
Waco, Baylor University

Utah
Salt Lake City, University of Utah

Vermont
Burlington, University of Vermont

Virginia
Blacksburg, Virginia Polytechnic Institute and State University
Charlottesville, University of Virginia
Danville, Averett College
Emory, Emory & Henry College
Fairfax, George Mason University
Farmville, Longwood College
Fredericksburg, Mary Washington College
Hampton, Hampton Institution
Harrisonburg, Madison University
Lawrenceville, St. Paul's College
Lynchburg, Lynchburg College
Lynchburg, Randolph-Macon Woman's College
Norfolk, State College
Norfolk, Old Dominion University
Petersburg, Virginia State College

Radford, Radford College
Richmond, Virginia Commonwealth University
Richmond, Virginia Union University
Williamsburg, College of William & Mary
Winchester, Shenandoah College
Wise, Cinch Valley College

Washington
Pullman, Washington State University
Seattle, Seattle Pacific University
Spokane, Gonzaga University

West Virginia
Athens, Concord College
Bluefield, Bluefield State College
Buckhannon, West Virginia Wesleyan College
Charleston, University of Charleston
Elkins, Davis & Elkins College
Fairmont, State College
Glenville, State College
Huntington, Marshall University
Institute, West Virginia State College
Montgomery, West Virginia Institute of Technology
Morgantown, West Virginia University
Romney, Hampshire County Board of Education
Salem, Salem College
Shepherdstown, Shepherd College
West Liberty, State College

Wisconsin
Eau Claire, University of Wisconsin
Green Bay, University of Wisconsin
Kenosha, University of Wisconsin-Parkside
Madison, University of Wisconsin
Milwaukee, University of Wisconsin
Stevens Point, University of Wisconsin
Whitewater, University of Wisconsin

Wyoming
Laramie, University of Wyoming

Commonwealth of Puerto Rico
Rio Piedras, University of Puerto Rico

Part Two

HOW TO PREPARE FOR THE EXAMINATIONS

STUDYING FOR THE EXAMINATIONS

The NTE cover an enormous range of material; there are relatively few items on any one specific topic. This combination means that normal studying techniques will not work.

These are not examinations for which you can cram the night before, or even the entire week before. Instead, these are examinations requiring a period of careful preparation using the materials in this book for diagnosing strengths and weaknesses, with ample time for corrective reading in areas of weakness.

The usual intensive approach to studying, by which you try to learn every significant detail of the subject, is also not useful. Only a handful of these details in any area will be covered on the NTE. Instead, you need a studying approach by which you broadly survey each major area and review the key names and concepts and their interrelationships, so that you can apply and interpret concepts as well as recognize the names and ideas.

Best Study Methods

You should establish a cycle in which you alternate periods of study with a testing session with this book. The emphasis during the second period of study should be on those areas that the testing sessions indicate need additional work.

Your first resource for studying should be the notes you have and the texts you have used in the education courses you have taken. This is material you have already studied once, and it must be the foundation on which you build your test performance. It is the material most readily recalled through review, and even if it must be relearned, it is material you should be able to relearn relatively easily.

The roles described in the informational booklet on the Core Battery, which we discussed earlier in the section, "The Nature of the Examinations," will not be particularly helpful in guiding your studying because they represent a reorganization of the material in most teacher education programs. Rather than try to regroup all of your notes, it is better to study under the course structure you had.

Course Material For Review

Begin by reviewing your notes and texts in any of the several courses generally grouped as cultural or social foundations, including courses in the history of education, philosophy of education, and educational sociology. How much time you need depends, of course, upon how recently you have taken the courses, how thorough your notes are, and how well you remember the material. Since your intent is to cover as much information as possible, this review should be relatively superficial rather than intensive. One specific piece of advice: Pay attention to names and the concepts or theories associated with the names.

Move on to child development (childhood and adolescence), and the area related to how learning takes place (theories of learning, or instruction). Devote your next block of time to reviewing these materials.

For the third area of review—the teacher as manager of the environment and of learning and instruction—study notes and materials from the courses in methods and materials, teaching practices, and special methods. Review also from any other courses you've taken related to the teaching process—from the moment when you organize your classes, considering the social, psychological, and cognitive characteristics of the children, through the periods when you plan your lessons, not only with these characteristics in mind but also the range of their skills and abilities and their individual differences.

While reviewing these areas, you should be conscious that some of the questions on the NTE related to this role involve applying the concepts and theories you have reviewed in the previous roles, particularly concepts in the psychological foundations of education. Thus, when you come upon specific suggestions for organizing materials or for considering student behavior or learning, you should get in the habit of trying to associate that teaching practice with the concept in child development or in learning theory from which it derives. Not only will this prepare you for the specific questions associated with these roles, but it will also be a useful re-review of the materials from the earlier areas.

The role of the teacher as measurer and evaluator of learning calls for a consideration of your course materials related to assessment, tests and measurement, and evaluation. Here you should be concerned with reviewing the basic functions of these processes, the names and uses of the major tests used in the schools, and the basic concepts. But unlike the other areas, in which the concepts involved are so numerous it is hard to predict what will be on any one test, in this area you can be reasonably certain that there will be questions testing your understanding of reliability and/or validity, the percentile system, and particularly the median or fiftieth percentile, the moment system with its mean and standard deviation, and the concept of the normal curve.

The review process we suggest is one during which you review, use the practice questions in this book to test your understanding, use the special answer tables to see how well you did in each special area, and use these results to decide what materials to review the second time. When you complete the second review, take the next test and once again use the answer tables to diagnose your strengths and weaknesses.

But remember that the basic material for the study process must be your course notes and your texts, *not* the questions in this book. These questions are not intended to teach you concepts or teaching practices; they are intended to test your understanding and your ability to apply these concepts and ideas. Moreover, the range of content in the materials related to these five roles of the teacher is so huge that you may know the answers to all of the questions in this book and yet find that only a small proportion of these questions, or questions related to them, will appear on any one version of the NTE.

The only circumstances under which the questions in this book should be your basic study materials are if you have decided to take the NTE at the last minute or if for personal or professional reasons you have had no time to study notes and course materials. Ideally, you will have time to study properly and complete your studies a few days before you are scheduled to take the NTE. Let us turn, then, to being certain that you are prepared to perform at your highest level.

Physically Preparing for the Examinations

Should you choose to take all three Core Battery Examinations on the same day, you will have a day of intensive intellectual activity, from 8:00 A.M. until 4:00 P.M. To obtain your best score on each of these examinations, you must maintain a high level of effective test-taking behavior throughout each testing session. If you are to be able to do this, you must approach the testing day as a gruelling physical chore, and prepare accordingly.

Rule One. Be well rested as you enter the room where the examination is to be given. Do not spend the night before cramming for the examination until the early hours of the morning. You will risk losing more points through fatigue than you stand to gain even by covering some items that are, in fact, on the examination you take. It is wise to plan your schedule for the week before the examination to provide the maximum rest you can, so that you can really work at full attention for the entire examination.

Rule Two. Enter the examination as relaxed and free of tension as possible. You undoubtedly know what makes you tense; if so, avoid it in the days before the examination. Similarly, if you know what makes you relax—a movie the night before the test, a leisurely breakfast the morning of the examination—do it. This can be a most significant day in your professional development, so indulge yourself to make relaxation as likely as possible.

Rule Three. Maintain your level of fitness throughout the day. This means that you should also analyze what lunch does to you. If you're the kind of person who wants nothing more than to curl up and take a nap after a heavy lunch, then settle for tea and toast the day of the NTE, since neither curling up nor a nap will do much for your score on the Professional Education Examination in the afternoon.

Psychologically Preparing for the Examinations

In addition to being physically prepared for the NTE, you should also spend a few minutes to be certain that you are psychologically prepared. The basic aspect of psychological preparation is to enter the examination as relaxed and calm as possible and to remain calm throughout the test. A key to maintaining calm is to realize that these are not the kind of examinations on which you are expected to know all of the items, nor is it necessary to know all or almost all to do well on the examinations. Even the best-prepared person who takes these examinations will miss several questions. Remember this as you work through each examination. Avoid the experience of many people, who begin to lose confidence as they realize that they don't have a clear answer to some of the first questions they encounter. Then, as they continue on and meet some more questions that are difficult or about which they are uncertain, anxiety begins to build, and each new problem increases their anxiety until their anxiety itself interferes with their test performance.

Deliberately and consciously set out to prevent this. Try to treat each question as a separate problem and, once past it, move on afresh to the next. Avoid "keeping score" yourself as you work through.

Remember, too, that the examination "score" you receive is not an absolute score based on the percentage of items you answered correctly, but is a percentile based on how your performance compared to the performance of other people with comparable educational backgrounds who took the test. Thus, it is possible to miss several items and still achieve a respectable percentile.

Examination Day Procedures

The NTE sessions will begin and end on time, so plan your schedule for the day of the examination to be there early. The last thing you need is to begin the examination tensely, after rushing to the test center or beginning late and losing working time, so do leave yourself ample time to arrive comfortably. If the test center is on a college campus, leave an extra fifteen minutes to find the specific building, since many campuses are poorly marked.

Bring along your ETS admission ticket, several sharp No. 2 pencils, and an eraser. Identification with a picture is required. Also remember to bring the *Critical Information form* that is printed in the information booklet. Complete it at home before you come to the test center.

There is no need to bring anything else for the examinations. You will not be permitted to use, or even to keep close to you, books, notes, scratch paper, or any such equipment as a calculator, compass, protractor, or ruler.

Once all candidates are seated by the proctor, the examination materials will be distributed. From that point on you should observe strict silence, even if you are taking the examination with some friends. The proctor is responsible for maintaining strict security, so do nothing to cause distraction or lose time. If something seems wrong with your materials or you have a question, raise your hand, and the proctor will come to you.

Be certain that you listen attentively to all directions, particularly those for putting the identification numbers on your examination, for those numbers will form the basis for reporting your score.

The identification information requested before the examination begins is to be recorded by filling in the appropriate letters or numbers on forms such as the one below. You enter information on this form in the same way that you enter answers on a traditional machine-scored answer sheet: by blacking in the appropriate space. Thus, in the completed example below, the fact that the candidate was born on January 24, 1946 has been entered by blacking in the spaces *01* for January, *24* for the date, and *46* for the year. Note that the first month is entered as *01*, with the zero used to place the significant digit at the right. This is a rule whenever entering information on forms like this.

Date of Birth						
0	1		2	4		4	6

Part Three

HOW TO TAKE THE EXAMINATIONS SUCCESSFULLY

HOW TO INDICATE YOUR ANSWERS

All parts of the NTE are scored using automatic data processing equipment, with the exception of the Essay Examination. Thus, except for the essay, all of your answers are entered onto an answer sheet.

Most of you have had ample experience with entering answers on answer sheets that are to be scored by automatic data processing equipment. If not, the answer sheets consist of a series of spaces like that below, in which the question number appears with five letters (corresponding to the five possible options) to the right. You are to blacken the oval space beneath the letter that indicates your answer. Thus, in the example below, the candidate has chosen (C) as the answer to question 57.

$$\begin{array}{ccccc} A & B & C & D & E \\ \end{array}$$

57. ○ ○ ● ○ ○

If you want to change an answer, be certain that you completely erase the original answer. The data processing equipment will pick up the original answer unless it is completely erased, and if it senses two marks for a question, it will mark the question wrong. For this same reason, be certain that you make no stray marks on the answer sheet, for these too may be picked up as incorrect answers. If you need scratch paper for writing, use the margins of the question booklet. Put nothing on the answer sheet but the answers you want to have counted.

ANSWERING CONTENT QUESTIONS

The Professional Knowledge and the General Knowledge sections consist of content questions—that is, questions which test your store of information.

The Kinds of Questions Asked

The content questions on the NTE are all multiple-choice questions in which there is a stem that poses the question and then four or five possible answers. Typical of this kind of question are the examples below.

1. Experiments on the level of aspiration demonstrate that people generally

   (A) raise their level of aspiration after success
   (B) maintain a level of aspiration based on their self-concept, independent of success or failure in a particular situation
   (C) raise their level of aspiration after experiencing failure
   (D) set their level of aspiration to the demands of the situation without reference to success or failure
   (E) do not change their level of aspiration

2. The Lutheran revolt profoundly affected the conduct of education by

   (A) introducing secular curricula into elementary and secondary schools
   (B) encouraging universal education
   (C) separating school regulation from other civil authority
   (D) removing schools from church domination
   (E) stressing teaching of philosophy

Lengthy Questions

Note that some questions like this are wordier than others; in fact, on the NTE some of the stems are longer than those you usually encounter in multiple-choice tests. Thus, although many items on the NTE are relatively brief and ask a clear, pointed question, many others involve a considerable amount of reading, as in the example here.

1. Kandel, discussing the democratic ideal in secondary education in *The New Era in Education,* makes the following statement:
   ". . . There is unfortunately a tendency to confuse the political aspect of democracy with other aspects, such as the intellectual and the economic. Such equalitarianism would reduce equality of educational opportunity to identity of opportunity. . . ."
   The following five statements deal with the area of school administration. It would be most consistent with the point of view expressed in Kandel's quotation above to propose that schools

   (A) establish a single diploma for satisfactory work in any one of the courses—academic, general, or vocational

(B) eliminate special schools, which are socially divisive, in favor of high schools that include all kinds of courses and students

(C) strengthen student self-government machinery so that it can play a real part in school management

(D) create more honor classes to serve the special needs of gifted students

(E) establish autocratic classes, dominated by teachers

Questions like these are difficult for several reasons. The first, of course, is that, rather than posing a question of information or association, they demand interpretation. The second is that in a pressure situation they require a moment of studied and serious reading, which many candidates do not expect. Hoping to fly along from question to question, they are suddenly stopped cold by a long reading passage, and then the next difficulty sets in: anxiety. The question becomes a blur as you grope for understanding and an answer.

A simple way to cope with a lengthy reading passage is to reverse the usual order of business: Usually you read the stem and then confront the question, and often go back to the passage to search for a clue to the answer. Instead, reverse that order: Read the question first, and also look over the possible answers offered, and *then* read the passage. This gives you a context in which to read, and guides your reading of the material. Knowing the options also provides you with a sense of the kind of distinctions you will have to make to answer the question, and this too is useful as you read.

Remember, there will be such questions and that there is sufficient time to consider them.

Varieties of Multiple-Choice Questions

In addition to questions requiring lengthy reading, there are other variations of the simple multiple-choice format with one correct answer. One frequent variation of the single-right-answer procedure is to ask you to identify the answer choice that is *not* correct, *not* true, or *least* correct, or that does *not* apply. For example, consider the questions below.

1. Which of the following is *not* among the basic principles of programmed instruction?

   (A) principle of small steps
   (B) principle of self-pacing
   (C) principle of immediate confirmation
   (D) principle of affective set
   (E) principle of sequencing

2. Which one of the following terms is *not* correctly matched with the illustrative definition?

   (A) projection—attributing one's own motives or thoughts to others
   (B) conversion—developing a physical symptom to avoid a difficult situation
   (C) sublimation—making one's faults seem like advantages
   (D) suppression—using self-control to prevent the overt expression of impulses and tendencies to action
   (E) regression—exhibiting behavior typical of earlier maturational levels

You must be alert to these questions, since otherwise your eye will be attracted to the first correct answer and you will choose that. Negative questions should be attacked in the same way as other single-answer questions: Read over all of the answer choices and see if any one strikes you as wrong or out-of-place. If it does, select it. If not, then use the regular process of cutting down the number of choices by ruling out the one or more answers that you are reasonably certain are correct. Having done this, you should have narrowed the problem to deciding which one of two or three is wrong, and then you can simply rely on your intuitive response to the choices, or guessing.

Example 2 above also illustrates another variation of the item-type, one in which the question posed is simply to decide which of five pairs of answers is correct or incorrect. This kind of item is particularly popular in the Literature section when authors and their works are listed, as in example 1 below, and in the questions on Fine Art when artists and their works are listed, as in example 2 below. But in any subject area, your task is to identify the one pair that meets the criterion, either by being correct or incorrect.

1. Which author is correctly matched with a novel that he wrote?

    (A) Twain .... *A Tale of Two Cities*
    (B) Dickens .... *Ivanhoe*
    (C) Wolfe .... *Look Homeward, Angel*
    (D) Jones .... *Hawaii*
    (E) Michener .... *Breaking Away*

2. Which artist is incorrectly matched with the work of art he or she created?

    (A) Da Vinci .... ''Mona Lisa''
    (B) Michaelangelo .... ''Sistine Chapel''
    (C) Bonheur .... ''Self-Portrait''
    (D) Copley .... ''Portrait of George Washington''
    (E) Van Gogh .... ''Sunflowers''

If you know the answer, particularly if you are asked which one is correct, then obviously you make the choice and move on. If you do not know the answer, or if you have narrowed it down to two or three of the five choices, one helpful technique is to treat each choice as a fill-in question. For example, suppose that for example 1, above, you had eliminated choices ''B'' and ''E'' but weren't certain which of the other three was correct. Take the book title in ''A'' and ask yourself who wrote *A Tale of Two Cities*. Possibly the correct association will pop into mind, and then if it does use the association to decide if ''A'' is correct. If not repeat the process with ''C'' and ''D.''

A more complex variation of this format occurs when a question is followed by several possible answers. More than one answer is correct, and you are given several combinations of answers and asked to select the combination that includes only correct answers. An example of this kind of question follows.

1. The following are possible causes of the American Revolution:
    1. the colonists' resentment of the imposition of taxes by Parliament
    2. the objection of settlers in the South to British laws against extending slavery
    3. the resistance to supporting and sheltering a British standing army

4. the limits Britain set on settling land in the West
5. the colonists' resentment of the impressment of colonial sailors

The correct answers are

(A) 1, 2, and 3
(B) 2, 4, and 5
(C) 2, 3, and 5
(D) 3 and 4 only
(E) 1, 2, and 4

The way to tackle this kind of question is to begin work with the single answers and use your information to eliminate as many choices as you can. If you can, with reasonable certainty, eliminate one or two choices, then you can also eliminate any combination that includes them. One specific cue to remember is that if a possible answer appears in three or more combinations, it is probably correct. If it appears in only one combination, it is probably wrong.

Another variation of this format occurs when the problem posed for you is to consider three, four, or five listed answers, and put them in order by some rationale given in the question. For example, you may be asked to put them in order according to some psychological or educational rationale, as in example 1 below, or in chronological order, as in example 2.

1. Three terms used in discussing various stages of physiological development of the human organism are (1) embryo, (2) neonate, and (3) fetus. The correct *developmental* order for these terms is

(A) 2, 1, 3
(B) 1, 2, 3
(C) 3, 1, 2
(D) 1, 3, 2
(E) 2, 3, 1

2. The following battles were all important during the American Revolution: (1) the battle of Yorktown, (2) the battle of Saratoga, (3) the battle of Trenton, and (4) the battle of Bunker (or Breed's) Hill. Which is the correct chronological order?

(A) 4, 1, 3, 2
(B) 1, 2, 4, 3
(C) 4, 2, 3, 1
(D) 3, 1, 4, 2
(E) 4, 3, 2, 1

In answering questions like these, the technique is to try to identify the extremes, that is, the first and the last in order. Ideally, you have done this, because you read the question and knew which came first or last. If not, see if the test-maker provided any help, by looking over the options to see if any one appears more often than another. In example 2, you would find such a clue: the fact that battle number 4 appears in first position in three of the five options. Even if you can only identify one end of the set, first or last, it will help, for you can now review the answers and eliminate any that do not agree with your first or last choice. This will always reduce the number of options you must consider to no more than two or three. Then it is a matter of checking out the middle positions for these few choices, and pinning down the best answer you can. Even if you must guess, you have increased your chances of guessing correctly to an acceptable level.

Rules for Answering
Content Questions

Rule 1. *After reading a question, answer it yourself without reading the options.* Let your associations to the question work to produce an answer. Then, after you have made every association you can and have as complete an answer in your head as possible, and only then, should you read over the answers offered. But now you are looking for the answer you have formed, or for an answer as close to it as you can find. If you find such an answer, that is the one you select. Trust your associations and yourself, and build as many of your answers around these associations as you can.

Rule 2. *Do not change an answer without a specific reason.* This is particularly true when you have completed the examination and are reading through it to check your work. Candidates too often change answers at this point, and statistics indicate that a majority of these changes make a correct answer into a wrong answer. Why? Because after taking the entire examination your associations may be blurred and confused by all that you have read, and particularly confused by all of the wrong answers you have been reading. Therefore, as you read through a second time, answers that seemed right the first time now look a little less desirable, and options you quickly rejected the first time seem to have more to offer.

Rule 3. *Do not spend a great deal of time on any one question.* Every question on the NTE counts as much, and no more, than every other question. Therefore, no one question is worth a lot of your time. It is simply silly to spend several minutes determinedly working through question 64 and then run short of time. Guess or come back to it later.

Rule 4. *Go through the entire examination once, answering only those questions for which you make associations.* But what if there is no association as you read a question, or if the association that you make doesn't match any answer on the test? Apply Rule Four: Don't answer the question on your first run-through. Simply leave it and go on to the next question. If you do this, you will work your way through the whole test once, answering only those questions that do produce clear associations that match one of the answers.

Rule 5. *Go through the entire examination a second time, answering those questions for which you now have an association.* Having gone through the entire examination once, you now go back to questions omitted and try again, by reading the question a second time and seeing if you have any greater success in generating an answer matching one of the options given. Why should you have any better success this second time? Because taking the examination itself is a kind of learning experience, and later questions will often trigger an association, shake loose some forgotten piece of information, or even provide a piece of information you can use in answering these questions. It is not at all unusual to find a later question stated in such a way that it clears up the confusion that led you to pass by an earlier question without answering it.

Rule 6. *Try to answer the questions left by eliminating options you know are wrong.* There will probably be some questions still unanswered. As you return to these, you will find they are of two kinds. Some cover familiar material, from which you simply couldn't put an answer together. You know you were exposed to the material at some time, but haven't been able to pull it together. The other kind of question is the kind to which you drew an absolute blank, neither an association nor even the vaguest idea when you were ever exposed to the information or where you were supposed to have learned it. The first kind can be tackled by using Rule Six: Examine each of the possible answers to try to eliminate one or more, using information you do have. For it is possible, even probable, that even if you do not know the right answer, you can recognize that one or two options are clearly wrong. And this can be a help in guessing. For if you have to choose from among five answers by guessing, the probability of being correct is only 20 percent—one in five. If you can eliminate two of those answers, knowing they are wrong, you improve your chance of guessing correctly to 33 percent—one of the three possible answers left.

Rule 7. *Guess on the Core Battery.* There is no penalty for guessing on the Core Battery. If you cannot arrive at an answer choice or draw a complete blank, guess and go on to the next unanswered question. However, on the Specialty Area Review Tests there is a penalty for answering a question incorrectly. Therefore, for the Specialty Area Tests do not answer any item if you cannot reduce the options to at least three. And do not answer any item on a Specialty Area Test if you draw an absolute blank.

ANSWERING LISTENING ABILITY QUESTIONS

For most of you, the section testing your ability to listen will be a new testing experience. In one part, you will have information presented to you by a tape recording with questions and possible answers printed in your test booklet. Thus, you will have to listen to the material, and, you will have to coordinate that listening experience with the printed questions and answers. In another section of the listening test, both the information and the questions are tape recorded, with only the possible answers printed, so here you must listen to the material and continue to listen carefully so that you hear the questions, for they will not be repeated.

Before the actual testing part of the Listening Ability section begins, the examiner will play an introductory part of the tape recording so that you can get used to the voices on the tape and the speed with which they will speak the test material. Obviously, if you have any difficulty hearing the material where you are sitting, raise your hand and tell this to the examiner so that he or she can either adjust the volume or permit you to move to a seat where you can hear everything clearly.

Because of the addition of the Listening Ability test to the Core Battery, some readers with hearing impediments will now be considered eligible for the special testing provisions made for disabled persons. On earlier versions of the NTE, without this Listening component, your hearing loss might not have been a serious problem, as long as you could understand the examiner. However, now you must be able to hear fully and precisely. If you have significant hearing loss, you should read the section of the NTE *Bulletin of Information* on "Handicapped Individuals," and decide which testing circumstances are most appropriate for you.

Before discussing the specifics of the Listening Ability test, let us make one rule very clear: *No material on this test is repeated.* Neither the conversations nor the questions will be said more than once, so you must begin to listen carefully from the first word on.

The Listening Ability component of the Core Battery consists of three different sections:

The first section consists of single sentences, either statements or questions, and your task is to select an option which is consistent with the statement or which answers the question sensibly. Examples A and B are illustrations of the questions in the section. Example A illustrates the type of question where you must select the option which is the most reasonable answer to the question asked. Example B illustrates the type of question where you must select the answer which is most consistent with the statement read.

EXAMPLE A: **Listening to a question**

You hear on the tape: *What would you like for dessert?*

You will see in your question booklet

(A) A roast beef sandwich please
(B) A copy of the *Times*

(C)   Ice cream would be nice

(D)   The green jacket

EXAMPLE B: **Interpreting what you hear**

You hear on the tape: *John was so confident, he couldn't under-stand how he got that grade on the test.*

(A)   John did well on the test.

(B)   John's confidence was destroyed.

(C)   John didn't know a test was sched-uled.

(D)   John's grade was lower than he ex-pected.

For Example A, you would choose option (C) as the answer, since it is the only option that sensibly answers the question, "What would you like for dessert?" Ex-ample B is more complex. The statement you hear indicates that John had been confi-dent, and couldn't understand his grade. The implication is that John did not do as well as he expected to do, and so you would choose option (D).

The second section of the Listening component presents brief conversations be-tween two people — a conversation of two to several sentences — followed by a question you will hear *on the tape*. Be alert to the fact that you cannot relax your concentration when the conversation is apparently complete. You must stay alert to hear the ques-tion. As we noted earlier, nothing is ever repeated in the Listening Ability Test. Your task here is to choose the option which best answers the question. Sometimes, as in the reading passages, the answer will have been directly specified in the conversation (see Example C below); at other times it will require an inference on your part from some aspect of the conversation. For example, in the first question of Example D, while the conversation does not directly state the time of day, the fact that one person referred to "having breakfast" indicates that it is taking place in the morning, and so option (C) is correct.

EXAMPLE C: **Listening to a brief conversation and to a question**

You will hear:

Man: Which sections in English I are still open?

Woman: There's one open on Monday and Wednesday at 10:00.

Questioner: What is the man trying to do?

You will see in your question booklet:

(A)   register for an English course

(B)   travel to London

(C)   rent a new home

(D)   buy a book

EXAMPLE D: **Listening to an extended conversation and to a question**

You will hear:

The next two questions refer to the following conversation:

Man: How heavy a schedule do you have today?

Woman: My first appointment is at 9:15, my last at 6:00.

Man: It's good we have breakfast together these days.
Woman: Actually tomorrow will be an early day, we'll have the evening together.

Questioner: What time of day is it?

You will see in your question booklet:

(A) noon
(B) evening
(C) morning
(D) cannot be determined

Then you will hear the tape again.

Questioner: What can you say about this couple?

You will see in your booklet:

(A) They work together.
(B) The man prepared breakfast.
(C) They haven't been together much recently.
(D) The woman has been promoted recently.

This last question again calls for an inference. You should remember the conversation well enough to realize that the couple have been so busy that they have not been able to spend time together. Thus option (C) is correct.

The third section of the Listening Ability test is the most challenging. In this section you will hear a longer passage read aloud, and then will be *asked* one or more questions about the passage. The questions will be on the tape, as they were in the dialogues. Here again the sequence will be: Listen to the question; choose an answer; listen to the next question; choose an answer.

Obviously the most important strategy in all sections of the Listening Ability test is to pay total attention to what is being said. Questions relate only to content. Do not devote attention to whether the speaker is male or female, sounds old or young, friendly or angry. Listen to what is being said, and try and put the speaker or speakers into a context of time and place, based on what is being said.

Another strategy is to scan the question options that are printed in your test booklet beforehand; they will provide some structure for your listening and give you a notion of what the choices are about. However, since in most cases the questions will not be printed, this device might not be suitable for everyone. Therefore in the practice Listening Ability items, try some each way and decide if knowing the choices does or does not help you structure your listening and make it more effective.

What makes the Listening Ability test particularly difficult is the fact that the material is read only once. There is no chance to review, or to listen again to any item. Remember: To succeed on this test, you must pay full attention from the first word to the last, without permitting anything or anyone to distract you.

ANSWERING READING ABILITY QUESTIONS

The techniques for answering the reading questions are different from those required on the content questions. These are self-contained questions—the answers to each set of questions based on a reading passage lie within that passage itself. Thus they present an opportunity to score well.

The best rule for responding to the reading passages is to be calm and methodical. Your basic approach here is, in many respects, exactly opposite to the approach discussed earlier for answering content questions. (For content questions, we advised reading the question carefully *before* looking over the possible answers to make your own association to the question. We also advised scanning the entire set of questions once, answering only those where you had firm associations, since the other questions themselves might help.)

For reading passages, you should scan the questions about each passage before you read the passage, in order to understand the kinds of information being called for. Instead of scanning the entire examination, scan each passage separately, and complete it before moving on. Unlike content questions, there is nothing in later passages to help you with earlier passages.

The reading passages vary in length from one or two sentences of under 100 words to longer multiple-sentence passages of 200 words or more as in the examples below.

PASSAGE A: *Brief passage*

Every computer has two kinds of memory: memory cells called ROM (read only memory), the contents of which are accessible only to the machine, and the memory cells called RAM (random access memory).

PASSAGE B: *Passage of about 100 words*

Unlike a tape recorder, which plays music while the tape is running, a computer runs an entire tape and stores the contents in memory before it starts "playing" the program. Every piece of software is labeled with the number of K required to run it on the computer. If your computer has only 4K and you want to use a program that requires 16K, you must buy a memory expansion device. An advantage of cartridges is that they become part of the computer when plugged in and do not need to transfer their program to the computer's memory. Nevertheless, even software purchased in cartridge form may require more memory than your machine has.

PASSAGE C: *Passage of 200 or more words*

The age of personal computers is upon us—and unavoidable during this season of gift buying and selling. Advertisements urge us to buy computers for the home, for business, for school. These electronic marvels apparently can educate us, do our taxes, play games with us, and make us better bridge players. Computers have not yet appeared that can walk the dog, but from the barrage of ads, you do get the sense that owning a computer somehow makes you a better person. Suppose that you decide to take the plunge and buy a computer for the family—or for yourself. Just what do you need, and what can it do for you? It would be nice to be able to answer those questions quickly and clearly, and to be able to add that the major home computers can be rated A, B, C, and D, and that the obvious one for you to buy is X. Unfortunately, a multitude of things must be considered before you can make a sensible choice.

A computer is a tool used to perform tasks that people could perform for themselves if they had the time. (The calculations necessary to steer a spaceship to the moon could have been done with a pencil and paper over several million years.) Because of the high speeds at which they operate, computers make practical certain previously inconceivable tasks. A computer also allows high-speed access to various kinds of information on demand, and can be interactive, relating your queries or responses to preprogrammed sequences of questions and answers. Lastly, a computer can be a medium for creative endeavor. This potential, accessible more often to the young than to those of us who are set in our ways, is probably the most important, for we do not know all the ways these machines can be put to use.

A reading passage will be concerned with one and only one topic, and all the questions will relate only to the material presented in the passage. You will be asked to make generalizations beyond the passage, and you will be asked to make inferences about the author's intent, or purpose. You will not be asked to provide any other information about the topic, or to use other information in choosing your answer to any reading questions.

Each reading question will focus on one specific aspect of the passage, such as the meaning of a specific phrase or sentence, the reason the author wrote the material, the probable events which led up to some aspect of the passage, or the strength of the author's arguments. Some questions will be direct, but most will be indirect. A direct reading question is one where the answer can be found by searching the passage. An indirect question, in contrast, is one where you must use the information in the passage to make some generalization beyond the passage.

An example of the direct question is provided by question 1 below, which refers back to Passage A.

Question 1.   How many kinds of memory does a computer have?

    (A) random
    (B) depends on the memory cells
    (C) two
    (D) one

This is a direct question; the answer is directly given in the phrase, "Every computer has two kinds of memory . . ."

Questions 2 and 3 below, based on Passages B and C, are the types of questions you should expect. While the passage provides a basis for answering these questions, you cannot go directly to a word or phrase to pinpoint the answer. Rather, you must read the passage and from your understanding of what is being said, identify the most sensible option or choice.

Question 2.   In Passage B, the author is alerting the reader that

    (A) a tape recorder is preferable to a computer for playing music
    (B) it is important to always read labels on software
    (C) computers won't work without memory expansion devices
    (D) all computers cannot process all software

Question 3.   In Passage C, the author implies that

(A) computers make excellent gifts
(B) it's simple to decide which computer is best for you
(C) you should decide what you want the computer to do, before buying
(D) people could do everything computers do, if they weren't lazy

For question 2, in the context of Passage B, options (A), (B), and (D) make sense. The author does imply that the tape recorder plays music, whereas a computer would store it, and also suggests that you should read labels. (D) is stated in the last sentence. Option (C) can be dismissed, since it is wrong. The author notes that memory expansion is only necessary if the program exceeds the memory of the computer. Thus you have three possible options which are at least consistent with the passage, and there is nothing in the passage which would eliminate any of the three directly. You must have enough interpretive ability to recognize that (A) and (B), while consistent with the passage, are not what the author is seeking to "alert" the reader about. Thus you would settle on (D) as the author's intent.

Similarly, in reading question 3, based on Passage C, you might be attracted to (A), since the implication of the introductory remarks is that computers are attractive gifts. You should reject (B). The implication in the latter part of the second paragraph is that while it would be nice to select simply, it cannot be done. (C) is never dealt with directly, but the entire intent of the third paragraph is that understanding of needed tasks is necessary if a person is to select a computer sensibly. (D) would be attractive if your eye caught the first sentence of the third paragraph, but if you read the parenthetical insert you would realize the author is not talking about laziness, but about incredible time savings using the computer. Considering all this reduces the choices to (A) and (C), and once again, even if both are true, the relative importance of the two choices makes it clear that the major implication involved is expressed in (C).

You should be particularly careful to verify all of your answers to the direct questions by a quick reference back to the passage. These are items which can be considered "sure" points for your score. Do not lose any of them. For example, in question 1, it takes but a second to refer back to the passage to verify that indeed, "Every computer has two kinds of memory. . . ."

When your choice cannot be directly verified by finding the exact words in the original passage, you should make a quick overview of the material to see if your choice is consistent with the passage and its content.

Indirect questions may ask you to make an inference beyond the material in the passage; or, to evaluate the soundness of the author's arguments and/or the strength and relevance of the evidence produced, if the passage is arguing for a particular point of view. These are the most difficult reading questions for they not only call on your ability to read the material, but also on your ability to reason and evaluate. Moreover, they cannot be verified at any useful level by referring back to the passage.

The best way, therefore, to answer these questions is to ask yourself whether "the argument is sound," or "the evidence is sensible," or "the inference follows." If you draw a blank on any of these aspects, omit the question. Do not guess on this type of indirect question.

You can be certain that the reading passages will not test your store of knowledge or memory for facts. All the information you need to answer each question will be presented in the reading passages. Do *not* try to use other information you may have as the basis for answering any of the reading questions. For example, do not say an author's evidence is weak just because you know of some other information that is not presented in the reading passage. The author's evidence is strong or weak based only on what is presented in the passage, or what is implied in the passage.

ANSWERING WRITING ABILITY QUESTIONS

The writing examination has two parts. The first part contains two question types testing your ability to recognize good English usage. The first question type, English Usage, presents you with a sentence with four different underlined parts. You are to check each part and see if it is correct, using the familiar rules of capitalization, punctuation, use of pronouns, agreement of verb and subject, etc. If one of the four is wrong, indicate it on your answer sheet. If all four underlined parts are correct, you indicate this by choosing (E), which always means "no error."

The second question type is called Sentence Correction. You are given a sentence with an underlined phrase, then you are given five options. (A) always repeats the underlined phrase. Choose (A) if you think the phrase is correct. The other four options change some aspect of the phrase.

Both types of questions call for your ability to recognize and apply the rules of English usage. If your scores are low in this area on the Diagnostic Exams, review the rules of English usage in a high school-level English usage review book, paying particular attention to verb and subject agreement, capitalization, punctuation, and the use of tenses. Since this is material you have studied in high school, trust your associations to what sounds correct. But if you draw a blank, do not guess unless you can reduce the possible options to two or three.

The Essay

In this section of the examination, candidates are given a topic and asked to prepare and write an essay on it during a thirty-minute testing period. All candidates receive the same topic. Topics are of a general nature, and do not require you to know any specific aspect of education, such as child development or philosophy. Instead, they are planned to enable each candidate to use his or her own personal experiences, either in their professional or personal life. Thus you would not be asked to compare and contrast Piaget's and Skinner's ideas about human development, but you might be asked to write about the most interesting child you have met in a classroom, or about the most exciting day you ever spent.

The writing ability examination is scored as a total piece of work; that is, you receive one overall score for both parts. However, ETS has listed the criteria they use in evaluating the essay. They note that they consider "quality of insight or central idea; evidence that the writer knows why the piece is being written and for whom; consistency of point of view; cohesiveness; strength and logic of supporting information;

---

[1]*NTE Core Battery.* Educational Testing Service, Princeton, N.J., 1982, p. 21.

rhetorical force; appropriateness of diction, syntax, and paragraphing; and correctness of mechanics and usage. Examinees should be sure to write on the topic assigned, to address all the points presented in the topic assignment, and to support generalizations with specific examples."[1]

Note that the specific content of what you say is not important. You will not lose credit if the rater does not agree that the child you write about is interesting . . . or if the examiner didn't think your day sounded very exciting. Rather, the criteria make clear that the key to a successful essay is to present your ideas in a clear, logically organized way, with appropriate and correct use of language. Therefore, do not spend too many minutes trying to think of a sensational way to write about the topic. Instead, save as much time as possible for the organization of your ideas, and for the actual writing of the essay.

There are two keys to successful writing. The first is organization. Few people can sit down and write a successful essay off the top of their head. Most of us first need to think through the topic and jot down our ideas as they come to mind—a kind of personal brainstorming session. The next step is to organize the ideas into a sensible outline so that they can be presented in a logical sequence, with all the material relevant to each idea presented together.

Once the outline is written, you can begin to write. Now you can concentrate on the mechanics of writing since the creative part is complete and outlined for you. You can pay attention to sentence structure, spelling, paragraphing, and grammatical precision.

Part Four

UNDERSTANDING YOUR EXAMINATION SCORES

HOW THE NTE ARE SCORED AND HOW THE SCORES ARE REPORTED

Since the new version of the NTE was first given in November of 1982, ETS has relatively little data on which to base interpretation of the scores. The percentile ranks for the Communication Skills Examination, for example, which were used in January of 1983, were based on 7,265 persons.

The NTE now reports scores for each test separately, without the composite score previously reported. You, as the examinee, will receive a report indicating the number of items which you answered correctly on each test. For the Professional Knowledge Test this is your final score, since no other computations are performed by ETS. However, for the tests of Communication Skills and of General Knowledge, a weighted score is also derived, so that each of the separate components of the test (such as Literature, Social Studies, or Science in General Knowledge) can be given equal weight even if they did not have the same number of items or difficulty levels.

These weighted scores in General Knowledge and Communication Skills and the raw score (number correct) in Professional Knowledge are then transformed to scaled scores, so that all three can be reported on a scale from 600 (representing no items answered correctly) to 690, representing the highest possible score. The informational bulletin explaining this process notes that each question counts about one point, although there will be fractional differences in question value from test to test and from edition to edition. For your purposes, each question is as important to your score as each other question.

ETS is also sending examinees a set of three percentile tables through which they, and an interested potential employer, can derive a percentile rank, using their scaled score. Thus a scaled score of 661 is needed on the Communication Skills Test to reach the median, or 50th percentile. The median for General Knowledge is a scaled score of 657, and for Professional Knowledge, 658.

Scores on Specialty Area Examinations are reported as percentile ranks also, and these percentiles, too, are derived from the number of items answered correctly. On your score report for the General Knowledge Test and the Communications Skills Test you will also see reported the number of items you answered incorrectly, the number of questions you omitted, and the number you did not answer, presumably because you did not reach them.

Undoubtedly, as the amount of data on the new NTE increase, some changes and/or additions to the score report will be made, so you should carefully read all of the interpretive information provided by Educational Testing Service.

Part Five

DIAGNOSTIC CORE BATTERY I

DIAGNOSTIC CORE BATTERY I

The first Diagnostic Core Battery consists of three sections. The first, Professional Knowledge, involves questions about Professional Education, including questions on the psychological and social foundations of education and the application of these principles in the classroom, as well as general teaching principles and practices. The second, General Knowledge, includes questions on the Humanities (Social Studies, Literature, and the Fine Arts), and on Science and Mathematics. The third, Communication Skills, includes practice items in Listening and in Reading, as well as questions applying the rules of standard written English.

On the Diagnostic Core Battery, each question is followed by four or five answers. You are to consider the answers and choose the one answer that is correct or most nearly correct, and then blacken the answer space for that question number on the Answer Sheet. Be certain to blacken only one space for each question. If you want to change an answer, carefully and thoroughly erase your first answer before entering your new answer. On the actual NTE, you will have to follow this procedure if you want to change an answer. Also, adhere to the time restrictions allowed for each section of the Diagnostic Core Battery, since this will prepare you for actual NTE procedures.

Answer Sheet
Section 1: Professional Knowledge

1 Ⓐ Ⓑ Ⓒ Ⓓ Ⓔ	27 Ⓐ Ⓑ Ⓒ Ⓓ Ⓔ	53 Ⓐ Ⓑ Ⓒ Ⓓ Ⓔ	79 Ⓐ Ⓑ Ⓒ Ⓓ Ⓔ	105 Ⓐ Ⓑ Ⓒ Ⓓ Ⓔ
2 Ⓐ Ⓑ Ⓒ Ⓓ Ⓔ	28 Ⓐ Ⓑ Ⓒ Ⓓ Ⓔ	54 Ⓐ Ⓑ Ⓒ Ⓓ Ⓔ	80 Ⓐ Ⓑ Ⓒ Ⓓ Ⓔ	106 Ⓐ Ⓑ Ⓒ Ⓓ Ⓔ
3 Ⓐ Ⓑ Ⓒ Ⓓ Ⓔ	29 Ⓐ Ⓑ Ⓒ Ⓓ Ⓔ	55 Ⓐ Ⓑ Ⓒ Ⓓ Ⓔ	81 Ⓐ Ⓑ Ⓒ Ⓓ Ⓔ	107 Ⓐ Ⓑ Ⓒ Ⓓ Ⓔ
4 Ⓐ Ⓑ Ⓒ Ⓓ Ⓔ	30 Ⓐ Ⓑ Ⓒ Ⓓ Ⓔ	56 Ⓐ Ⓑ Ⓒ Ⓓ Ⓔ	82 Ⓐ Ⓑ Ⓒ Ⓓ Ⓔ	108 Ⓐ Ⓑ Ⓒ Ⓓ Ⓔ
5 Ⓐ Ⓑ Ⓒ Ⓓ Ⓔ	31 Ⓐ Ⓑ Ⓒ Ⓓ Ⓔ	57 Ⓐ Ⓑ Ⓒ Ⓓ Ⓔ	83 Ⓐ Ⓑ Ⓒ Ⓓ Ⓔ	109 Ⓐ Ⓑ Ⓒ Ⓓ Ⓔ
6 Ⓐ Ⓑ Ⓒ Ⓓ Ⓔ	32 Ⓐ Ⓑ Ⓒ Ⓓ Ⓔ	58 Ⓐ Ⓑ Ⓒ Ⓓ Ⓔ	84 Ⓐ Ⓑ Ⓒ Ⓓ Ⓔ	110 Ⓐ Ⓑ Ⓒ Ⓓ Ⓔ
7 Ⓐ Ⓑ Ⓒ Ⓓ Ⓔ	33 Ⓐ Ⓑ Ⓒ Ⓓ Ⓔ	59 Ⓐ Ⓑ Ⓒ Ⓓ Ⓔ	85 Ⓐ Ⓑ Ⓒ Ⓓ Ⓔ	111 Ⓐ Ⓑ Ⓒ Ⓓ Ⓔ
8 Ⓐ Ⓑ Ⓒ Ⓓ Ⓔ	34 Ⓐ Ⓑ Ⓒ Ⓓ Ⓔ	60 Ⓐ Ⓑ Ⓒ Ⓓ Ⓔ	86 Ⓐ Ⓑ Ⓒ Ⓓ Ⓔ	112 Ⓐ Ⓑ Ⓒ Ⓓ Ⓔ
9 Ⓐ Ⓑ Ⓒ Ⓓ Ⓔ	35 Ⓐ Ⓑ Ⓒ Ⓓ Ⓔ	61 Ⓐ Ⓑ Ⓒ Ⓓ Ⓔ	87 Ⓐ Ⓑ Ⓒ Ⓓ Ⓔ	113 Ⓐ Ⓑ Ⓒ Ⓓ Ⓔ
10 Ⓐ Ⓑ Ⓒ Ⓓ Ⓔ	36 Ⓐ Ⓑ Ⓒ Ⓓ Ⓔ	62 Ⓐ Ⓑ Ⓒ Ⓓ Ⓔ	88 Ⓐ Ⓑ Ⓒ Ⓓ Ⓔ	114 Ⓐ Ⓑ Ⓒ Ⓓ Ⓔ
11 Ⓐ Ⓑ Ⓒ Ⓓ Ⓔ	37 Ⓐ Ⓑ Ⓒ Ⓓ Ⓔ	63 Ⓐ Ⓑ Ⓒ Ⓓ Ⓔ	89 Ⓐ Ⓑ Ⓒ Ⓓ Ⓔ	115 Ⓐ Ⓑ Ⓒ Ⓓ Ⓔ
12 Ⓐ Ⓑ Ⓒ Ⓓ Ⓔ	38 Ⓐ Ⓑ Ⓒ Ⓓ Ⓔ	64 Ⓐ Ⓑ Ⓒ Ⓓ Ⓔ	90 Ⓐ Ⓑ Ⓒ Ⓓ Ⓔ	116 Ⓐ Ⓑ Ⓒ Ⓓ Ⓔ
13 Ⓐ Ⓑ Ⓒ Ⓓ Ⓔ	39 Ⓐ Ⓑ Ⓒ Ⓓ Ⓔ	65 Ⓐ Ⓑ Ⓒ Ⓓ Ⓔ	91 Ⓐ Ⓑ Ⓒ Ⓓ Ⓔ	117 Ⓐ Ⓑ Ⓒ Ⓓ Ⓔ
14 Ⓐ Ⓑ Ⓒ Ⓓ Ⓔ	40 Ⓐ Ⓑ Ⓒ Ⓓ Ⓔ	66 Ⓐ Ⓑ Ⓒ Ⓓ Ⓔ	92 Ⓐ Ⓑ Ⓒ Ⓓ Ⓔ	118 Ⓐ Ⓑ Ⓒ Ⓓ Ⓔ
15 Ⓐ Ⓑ Ⓒ Ⓓ Ⓔ	41 Ⓐ Ⓑ Ⓒ Ⓓ Ⓔ	67 Ⓐ Ⓑ Ⓒ Ⓓ Ⓔ	93 Ⓐ Ⓑ Ⓒ Ⓓ Ⓔ	119 Ⓐ Ⓑ Ⓒ Ⓓ Ⓔ
16 Ⓐ Ⓑ Ⓒ Ⓓ Ⓔ	42 Ⓐ Ⓑ Ⓒ Ⓓ Ⓔ	68 Ⓐ Ⓑ Ⓒ Ⓓ Ⓔ	94 Ⓐ Ⓑ Ⓒ Ⓓ Ⓔ	120 Ⓐ Ⓑ Ⓒ Ⓓ Ⓔ
17 Ⓐ Ⓑ Ⓒ Ⓓ Ⓔ	43 Ⓐ Ⓑ Ⓒ Ⓓ Ⓔ	69 Ⓐ Ⓑ Ⓒ Ⓓ Ⓔ	95 Ⓐ Ⓑ Ⓒ Ⓓ Ⓔ	121 Ⓐ Ⓑ Ⓒ Ⓓ Ⓔ
18 Ⓐ Ⓑ Ⓒ Ⓓ Ⓔ	44 Ⓐ Ⓑ Ⓒ Ⓓ Ⓔ	70 Ⓐ Ⓑ Ⓒ Ⓓ Ⓔ	96 Ⓐ Ⓑ Ⓒ Ⓓ Ⓔ	122 Ⓐ Ⓑ Ⓒ Ⓓ Ⓔ
19 Ⓐ Ⓑ Ⓒ Ⓓ Ⓔ	45 Ⓐ Ⓑ Ⓒ Ⓓ Ⓔ	71 Ⓐ Ⓑ Ⓒ Ⓓ Ⓔ	97 Ⓐ Ⓑ Ⓒ Ⓓ Ⓔ	123 Ⓐ Ⓑ Ⓒ Ⓓ Ⓔ
20 Ⓐ Ⓑ Ⓒ Ⓓ Ⓔ	46 Ⓐ Ⓑ Ⓒ Ⓓ Ⓔ	72 Ⓐ Ⓑ Ⓒ Ⓓ Ⓔ	98 Ⓐ Ⓑ Ⓒ Ⓓ Ⓔ	124 Ⓐ Ⓑ Ⓒ Ⓓ Ⓔ
21 Ⓐ Ⓑ Ⓒ Ⓓ Ⓔ	47 Ⓐ Ⓑ Ⓒ Ⓓ Ⓔ	73 Ⓐ Ⓑ Ⓒ Ⓓ Ⓔ	99 Ⓐ Ⓑ Ⓒ Ⓓ Ⓔ	125 Ⓐ Ⓑ Ⓒ Ⓓ Ⓔ
22 Ⓐ Ⓑ Ⓒ Ⓓ Ⓔ	48 Ⓐ Ⓑ Ⓒ Ⓓ Ⓔ	74 Ⓐ Ⓑ Ⓒ Ⓓ Ⓔ	100 Ⓐ Ⓑ Ⓒ Ⓓ Ⓔ	126 Ⓐ Ⓑ Ⓒ Ⓓ Ⓔ
23 Ⓐ Ⓑ Ⓒ Ⓓ Ⓔ	49 Ⓐ Ⓑ Ⓒ Ⓓ Ⓔ	75 Ⓐ Ⓑ Ⓒ Ⓓ Ⓔ	101 Ⓐ Ⓑ Ⓒ Ⓓ Ⓔ	127 Ⓐ Ⓑ Ⓒ Ⓓ Ⓔ
24 Ⓐ Ⓑ Ⓒ Ⓓ Ⓔ	50 Ⓐ Ⓑ Ⓒ Ⓓ Ⓔ	76 Ⓐ Ⓑ Ⓒ Ⓓ Ⓔ	102 Ⓐ Ⓑ Ⓒ Ⓓ Ⓔ	128 Ⓐ Ⓑ Ⓒ Ⓓ Ⓔ
25 Ⓐ Ⓑ Ⓒ Ⓓ Ⓔ	51 Ⓐ Ⓑ Ⓒ Ⓓ Ⓔ	77 Ⓐ Ⓑ Ⓒ Ⓓ Ⓔ	103 Ⓐ Ⓑ Ⓒ Ⓓ Ⓔ	129 Ⓐ Ⓑ Ⓒ Ⓓ Ⓔ
26 Ⓐ Ⓑ Ⓒ Ⓓ Ⓔ	52 Ⓐ Ⓑ Ⓒ Ⓓ Ⓔ	78 Ⓐ Ⓑ Ⓒ Ⓓ Ⓔ	104 Ⓐ Ⓑ Ⓒ Ⓓ Ⓔ	130 Ⓐ Ⓑ Ⓒ Ⓓ Ⓔ

Diagnostic Core Battery I
Section 1: Professional Knowledge

100 Minutes—130 Questions

Directions: For each of the following questions, select the choice that best answers the question or completes the statement.

1. How many of the fifty states in the United States have tenure laws which cover all public schools in the state?

    (A) all fifty
    (B) the forty-eight contiguous states, excepting Alaska and Hawaii
    (C) about half, mostly in the East and Far West
    (D) all but a few in the South
    (E) about three-fourths of the states

2. A very young child learns that the small, furry, purring object in his house is a "kitty." While visiting another house, this child points to a small dog there and says, "Kitty." This illustrates

    (A) immediate reinforcement
    (B) simultaneous discrimination
    (C) an unconditioned response
    (D) primary stimulus generalization
    (E) secondary stimulus generalization

3. It has been found that intellectually gifted children tend to surpass average children in

    (A) personal and social adjustment
    (B) physical size and health
    (C) social maturity and poise
    (D) all of the above
    (E) none of the above

4. The recommendation that a poem be read over in its entirety before memorizing individual lines illustrates an awareness of the principles of

    (A) proactive inhibition
    (B) gestalt organization
    (C) massed practice
    (D) secondary reinforcement
    (E) retroactive inhibition

5. An author made the following statement:
    "Objective tests in history are superior to essay tests because they test understanding of history rather than ability in English composition."
    In this quotation, the author is indicating his belief that short-answer history tests are more

    (A) objective

(B) reliable
(C) ambiguous
(D) comprehensive
(E) valid

6. Ms. Jackson, the Principal, announces over the intercom speaker that it is time to stand and salute the flag. Harry does not wish to participate. He has the right to

   I. stand but remain silent
   II. stay seated at his desk
   III. chat with a friend, if he stands

   (A) I only
   (B) II only
   (C) III only
   (D) I and II only
   (E) none of the above

7. The typical pattern of a generalized learning curve would show

   (A) a slow initial rise followed by a more rapid rise and then a gradual flattening
   (B) a rapid initial rise followed by a gradual decline in rate of learning
   (C) a rapid initial rise followed by a plateau
   (D) a slow initial rise followed by an acceleration in rate of learning
   (E) a rapid initial rise followed by a rapid decline in rate of learning

8. A report of a classroom observation in a sixth-grade class noted that there was a "high degree of disorganization, boredom, quarrelsomeness, and inefficiency." If one had to assess the teacher's style of leadership in the class from this evidence, it would seem most likely that control is

   (A) benevolent authoritarian
   (B) rigid authoritarian
   (C) student-centered
   (D) laissez-faire
   (E) liberation

9. Within learning theorists' frame of reference, probably the best way of approaching the organization of subject matter is to move from the

   (A) familiar to the unfamiliar
   (B) general to the particular
   (C) logical to the psychological
   (D) societal to the individual
   (E) complex to the simple

10. Which instrument would be most desirable for testing the general mental ability of a second-grade pupil, aged seven years three months?

    (A) Lorge-Thorndike Intelligence Test
    (B) Goodenough Intelligence Test
    (C) Vineland Social Maturity Test
    (D) Wechsler Intelligence Scale for Children (Revised)
    (E) Wechsler-Bellevue Scale

11. In the years since the Supreme Court decision on school segregation, the extent of integration in schools in northern urban centers has

    (A) been slow, but is steadily increasing

(B) increased in recent years after a slow start

(C) not kept up with changing populations, so that there are more black children in segregated schools than before

(D) been relatively rapid where de facto segregation existed, in contrast to where segregation was enforced by law

(E) been accomplished more easily in the more northern centers

12. Which of the following is usually increased or strengthened by overlearning?

(A) gratification
(B) retention
(C) incentive
(D) assimilation
(E) patience

13. Classroom discipline should have as its major goal the promotion of

(A) self-direction on the part of the pupils
(B) good study conditions
(C) democratic processes
(D) rational relationships to authority
(E) higher academic achievement

14. A temporary inability to increase learning is referred to as a (n)

(A) learning disability
(B) deceleration
(C) forgetting curve
(D) holding curve
(E) plateau

15. It is probable that intelligence tests measure chiefly

(A) ability to adjust to life situations
(B) inborn cognitive ability
(C) general intellectual ability
(D) what children have learned
(E) ability to succeed in school

16. A male teacher is prohibited from teaching kindergarten by his local school board. He feels this decision is based on sexual discrimination. He may seek assistance from all but the

(A) Association of American School Boards
(B) Equal Employment Opportunity Commission
(C) Office of Federal Contract Compliance Programs of the Department of Labor
(D) Office of Civil Rights of the Department of Education
(E) local teacher association or professional organization

17. Learning theories are concerned chiefly with describing or explaining the

(A) dynamics of experimentally induced behavior
(B) manner in which stimuli are perceived and discriminated
(C) manner in which responses become stimuli to further behavior
(D) processes leading to changes in behavior
(E) unconscious memories

18. Which one of the following five comments made by teachers on pupils' records

best illustrates good anecdotal recording of pupil behavior?

(A) "Seems shiftless and lazy. Likes to read but otherwise inattentive."
(B) "Absentminded. Is not working to best of his ability."
(C) "Creative, intelligent, pleasant personality."
(D) "Is a good pupil. Gives no trouble. Very quiet."
(E) "Apologized for being late yesterday. Had to feed baby sister. Mother ill."

19. In a learning experiment involving a comparison of distributed and massed practice, one would expect that the average recall score would be

(A) about the same for both kinds of practice
(B) unpredictable
(C) higher for massed practice
(D) higher for distributed practice
(E) a function of the learning curve

20. Which of the following constitutes an *operational* definition of test anxiety?

(A) an unpleasant emotional response to an evaluative situation
(B) a physiological change resulting from an aversive stimulus, in this case, a test
(C) the appearance of behavior geared to reduce anxiety
(D) a score on the Sarason Test-Anxiety Scale
(E) the absence of behavior geared to reduce stress

21. As a teacher of eleventh grade English, you wish your students to read some contemporary literature containing "taboo" words. Your decision should be based on
 I. relevance and quality of the story
 II. opinions of other English teachers
 III. the maturity of your students
 IV. the effect on the class

(A) I only
(B) I and II only
(C) III only
(D) III and IV only
(E) all of the above

22. A student who has had a year of Spanish starts the study of French. He finds that his knowledge of French interferes with his recall of Spanish. This interference is called

(A) associative inhibition
(B) retroactive inhibition
(C) temporal extinction
(D) synaptical resistance
(E) proactive inhibition

23. The *chief* reason for including music and art materials in an elementary school social studies unit should be to

(A) provide for integration of different subject-matter fields
(B) add variety and interest to the basic materials of the unit
(C) give more status to cultural subjects so that they are not viewed as "frills"
(D) aid in the understanding and learning of the major problem of the unit
(E) break up the boredom with some "fun"

24. Based upon the current research on retention, it would be most reasonable to predict that students would most rapidly forget

    (A) general information
    (B) application of facts
    (C) technical information
    (D) broad principles
    (E) material they found "boring"

25. A character test was constructed that, after it had been given, was found to correlate +.92 with intelligence and +.20 with social behavior. From this evidence, it is most logical to conclude that the test was *not*

    (A) valid
    (B) reliable
    (C) objective
    (D) standardized
    (E) culture-fair

26. When John Dewey maintains that "there is nothing to which education is subordinate save more education," he means that

    (A) schooling must be regarded basically as preparation for the next stage of schooling
    (B) the primary function of formal education is to enable people to continue to educate themselves
    (C) genuine study and learning, regardless of subject or level, is its own justification (learning for learning's sake)
    (D) there is no necessary relationship between education and social goals
    (E) most practical endeavors are superior to "school learning"

27. Three terms used in discussing various stages of physiological development of the human organism are (1) embryo, (2) neonate, and (3) fetus. The correct *developmental* order for these terms is

    (A) 2, 1, 3
    (B) 1, 2, 3
    (C) 3, 1, 2
    (D) 1, 3, 2
    (E) 3, 2, 1

28. A review lesson on materials covered in a subject-matter unit, such as the causes of the American Revolution, should be viewed primarily as a

    (A) testing device to determine the success of the previous instruction
    (B) drill procedure to fix the major learnings of the unit clearly
    (C) resynthesis to develop deeper understanding of the relationships involved in the unit
    (D) means of providing an introduction or bridge to the next learning unit
    (E) means of teaching material slower learners couldn't absorb before

29. The chief observable difference between good and poor readers lies in the fact that

    (A) good readers make fewer pauses per line in their eye movement

(B) the eye movements of good readers are spaced regularly along the line of print

(C) the eye movements of good readers show that they frequently go back to check words and phrases as they read

(D) good readers use a larger number of small eye movements in a given passage

(E) good readers blink more frequently than poor ones

30. Given the following graph of test scores, which of the following is the most appropriate statement that can be made about the suitability of this test for the group?

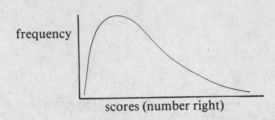

(A) the test is too easy

(B) the test is too difficult

(C) the test is just about at the right level of difficulty for the group

(D) no judgment regarding the difficulty of the test for this group can be made without additional information

(E) only the brightest students took the test

31. The pragmatic notion, "truth happens to an idea," means that

(A) you will always believe in the rightness of your ideas

(B) a real objective is clearly and distinctly perceived

(C) a belief is accepted by democratic consensus

(D) empirical evidence precedes the formulation of a hypothesis

(E) a belief is confirmed in experience

32. According to Piaget, rigid adherence to a rule ("moral realism") is *most* characteristic of

(A) girls and boys over ten years of age

(B) girls and boys between six and eight years of age

(C) boys between six and eight years

(D) girls over ten years of age

(E) boys and girls between three and five years of age

33. In which order below are the several kinds of treatment correctly arranged from *most* effective to *least* effective?

(A) praise, reproof, no attention

(B) praise, no attention, reproof

(C) reproof, no attention, praise

(D) reproof, praise, no attention

(E) no attention, reproof, praise

34. The concept of "developmental tasks" can be of *greatest* help to the teacher in

   (A) judging readiness
   (B) providing appropriate motivation
   (C) evaluating group projects
   (D) delegating classroom duties
   (E) determining class maturity

35. In a group of scores on a standardized test, the median would correspond to the

   (A) arithmetic average
   (B) 50th percentile
   (C) score with the highest frequency
   (D) quartile deviation
   (E) most reliable scores

36. The point of view that "the school must act as a spearhead of social progress" is an important tenet of the school of educational philosophy called

   (A) Essentialist
   (B) Idealist
   (C) Realist
   (D) Reconstructionist
   (E) Existentialist

37. The dominant characteristic of the child who has been maternally deprived since earliest infancy is his

   (A) preference for male adults over female adults
   (B) excessive guilt feelings
   (C) compensatory need to love and protect others
   (D) extreme acting out of aggressive tendencies
   (E) inability to form relationships

38. Which of the following activities would be the most likely to elicit "divergent thinking" as defined by Guilford?

   (A) working at the correct answers to a crossword puzzle
   (B) considering ways to improve a car seat for infants
   (C) proving a geometry theorem
   (D) playing in a school orchestra or band
   (E) learning to do classical calligraphy

39. Studies have been made of the operation of specific personality traits, such as honesty, in different situations. Of the following statements, which one is *false*?

   (A) There is a positive but low correlation between the expression of a specific trait in different situations.
   (B) Peer-group standards are often the determining factor in behavior.
   (C) There is generally a high degree of consistency in the expression of each trait.
   (D) Observed inconsistent behavior is often perceived as consistent by the subject according to his/her own code.
   (E) Within any one trait, an individual is generally consistent.

40. Two classes are given the same arithmetic computation test, and the mean score for both classes is 57. The standard deviation for Class A is 5.1, and the standard deviation for Class B is 10.3. On the basis of the above we may conclude that, with respect to arithmetic computation achievement,

    (A) Class A is more heterogeneous than Class B
    (B) the teaching of arithmetic is more effective in Class A
    (C) both classes have about the same range of accomplishment in this area
    (D) there is not sufficient data for making a comparison
    (E) Class B is more heterogeneous than Class A

41. The characteristic educational philosophy of the progressive movement held that schools should

    (A) interpret present-day social institutions and support their functioning
    (B) pass on the social and cultural heritage of our civilization to the present generation
    (C) equip youth to think critically about social issues to foster progress
    (D) provide a blueprint of a desirable society and prepare youth to bring about changes needed for the future
    (E) focus on the individual progress of each student

42. Psychoanalytic writers have labeled the middle-childhood years as the

    (A) phallic period
    (B) genital period
    (C) latency period
    (D) anal period
    (E) Oedipal period

43. The major reason for providing for supervision of teachers is to

    (A) improve the quality of instruction of pupils
    (B) obtain information on the teacher's performance legally required in matters of tenure and promotion
    (C) promote more effective staff utilization and coordination
    (D) help teachers improve their understanding of children
    (E) maintain records on the competency of their performance

44. The aspect of Freud's theory of most direct significance to the classroom teacher's work is Freud's analysis of the

    (A) use of defense mechanisms
    (B) Oedipal conflict
    (C) psychosexual stages of development
    (D) role of libido
    (E) various fixations

45. John's reading score is at the 65th percentile. This means that in comparison to the base population, his achievement is

    (A) superior to that of 35% of the students
    (B) superior to that of 65% of the students
    (C) equivalent to a passing mark of 65%
    (D) approximately 3.5 standard deviations above the mean
    (E) based on a criterion-referenced test

46. John Dewey's most significant work on education is entitled

    (A) *Democracy in America*
    (B) *Education and Liberty*
    (C) *Education in America*
    (D) *Education and Freedom*
    (E) *Democracy and Education*

47. According to Erikson, the major problem of adolescence is

    (A) sexual adjustment
    (B) establishing identity
    (C) meeting superego demands
    (D) competition with peers
    (E) making career decisions

48. A curriculum that revisits basic ideas repeatedly at different grade levels and builds upon them until the student has gained a deep, comprehensive, workable knowledge of them is known as the

    (A) core curriculum
    (B) progressive curriculum
    (C) basic curriculum
    (D) spiral curriculum
    (E) reinforced curriculum

49. In regard to promotion policies, experience has shown that regular retention of pupils whose work fails to reach a required standard

    (A) is necessary in order to motivate some children
    (B) does not reduce class variability in ability and achievement
    (C) results in more learning for the students retained
    (D) simplifies the problem of meeting the needs of individual pupils
    (E) rarely produces social or personality adjustment problems

50. One of the functions of an educational system is to reconcile what is good for the individual with what is good for the group (of which the individual is a part). Which statement below is consistent with this idea?

    (A) The individual functioning in a group does not necessarily lose his identity.
    (B) The educative process should encourage the "love thy neighbor" attitude.
    (C) The individual must submerge himself within the group.
    (D) Education is a collectivistic process.
    (E) Providing for individual differences is antithetical to genuine democratic society.

51. With regard to the construction of multiple-choice class tests, which one of the following procedures is *least* defensible? To

    (A) compose the individual test items on the basis of a previously prepared list of objectives
    (B) select test items covering a wide range of difficulty
    (C) avoid test items so phrased that the correct answer depends upon a single key word
    (D) place the easiest questions at the end of the test
    (E) include test items from previous homework assignments as well as from classwork

52. The derivation of concepts from abstract symbols is related to the theory of intellectual development propounded by

    (A) Gates
    (B) Cattell
    (C) Conant
    (D) Rafferty
    (E) Piaget

53. The utilization of realia, charts, models, tape recordings, and films on the same science subjects is likely to improve learning principally because of

    (A) a more intellectual atmosphere in the room
    (B) increased opportunities for student participation in hanging charts, operating equipment, etc.
    (C) the multiple-sensory appeal inherent in these items
    (D) the positive results of using these items to reward good effort and behavior
    (E) variety serving as the spice of learning

54. The trial-and-error method of learning is closely allied to which other learning procedure?

    (A) programmed
    (B) rote
    (C) lecture
    (D) discovery
    (E) core curriculum

55. Of the following, the *least* acceptable use of standardized tests is to

    (A) provide meaningful standards of comparison
    (B) diagnose pupils' strengths and weaknesses
    (C) provide a basis for assigning marks
    (D) establish a uniform basis for measuring individual growth and achievement
    (E) capitalize on more efficient measuring devices

56. Mrs. Brownstein, a homeroom teacher for tenth-grade students, is asked by one of her fifteen-year-olds to see his records. She must

    (A) refer him to the guidance office
    (B) demand written permission from his parents
    (C) show them to him
    (D) explain that he cannot have access to them until he is eighteen
    (E) be polite, but firmly refuse

57. Which of the statements below best applies to most young adolescents? They

    (A) struggle to establish themselves as important members of the family, but question family controls
    (B) struggle to establish themselves as important members of the family, and accept family controls without question
    (C) are content with secondary roles in the family, provided the family relinquishes all controls over them
    (D) prefer to be told what to do by parents in order to be relieved of all responsibility for making decisions
    (E) join radical organizations

58. Of the following possible justifications for surprise quizzes, the best one is that

   (A) they are periodically necessary to deflate the sense of superiority of the students who ordinarily get high marks
   (B) it is best to punish a class for poor discipline with these quizzes
   (C) they encourage the students to study regularly
   (D) they cause the students to have more respect for the teacher
   (E) they help to keep order in the class

59. Which of the following theories of learning have the most closely related underlying logic?
   I. Functionalism
   II. Organismic Theory
   III. Connectionism
   IV. Behaviorism

   (A) I, II, and III only
   (B) I, II, and IV only
   (C) I, III, and IV only
   (D) II, III, and IV only
   (E) II and IV only

60. Which one of the following is a correct statement concerning the administration of a pretest?

   (A) It unnecessarily consumes time to acquire information that the teacher can more readily discover by informal means.
   (B) It should be confined to the beginning of the school year, for the entire grade.
   (C) It dispenses with the need for review.
   (D) It serves in part as a survey of individual and class background and readiness.
   (E) It is the best motivation for introducing a new topic or unit.

61. "Certain basic ideas and skills essential to our culture should be taught to all alike by certain time-tested methods." This is

   (A) progressivism
   (B) existentialism
   (C) essentialism
   (D) pragmatism
   (E) scholasticism

62. All of the following principles of growth and development in young children are valid *except* that growth

   (A) is spontaneous and continuous
   (B) is irregular but orderly
   (C) and maturation are interrelated
   (D) is slow during the early years
   (E) rates vary between boys and girls

63. Summaries of learnings elicited during and at the end of a lesson are usually

   (A) a waste of time
   (B) useful only to slow learners

(C) important in focusing attention on the concepts developed

(D) not as good as summaries dictated by the teacher for copying into pupils' notebooks

(E) a quick check on the comprehension of new concepts

64. The gestalt theory is most closely associated with the concept that

(A) the general learnings acquired in one subject readily transfer in learning a second, independent subject

(B) improving the physical development of a pupil has a beneficial effect on intellectual growth

(C) total learning is the sum of the learnings in the individual subjects

(D) learning is accomplished through grasp of the meaning of a problem in terms of the total situation

(E) learning comprises a series of "educated" guesses

65. Of the following, the most useful for studying pupil-pupil relationships is the

(A) Rorschach Test

(B) Thematic Apperception Test

(C) Sociogram

(D) Anecdotal Record

(E) Personality Quotient

66. More than three centuries ago Comenius enunciated the principle of "Things—Ideas—Words." This principle is most clearly explained by the statement that

(A) essay themes should deal with concrete ideas

(B) the sequence of learning proceeds from experiencing to conceiving to defining

(C) all learning requires manipulation of things

(D) abstract ideas grow out of concrete concepts

(E) all concepts must be expressible in writing

67. Of the following, the one most characteristic of the normally developing adolescent is

(A) continuous need for parental support

(B) development of emotional maturity

(C) desire for constant domination by siblings

(D) freedom from peer-group identification

(E) increased dependence upon teachers

68. Of the following statements about memorization of selected prose and poetry by children, the one with which most educators would agree is that

(A) memorization no longer has a place in the language arts area

(B) work on memorization should be postponed until grade four

(C) memorization should be tested periodically through the use of written tests

(D) the child should be led to see that a major value of memorization is that it trains the mind

(E) even when pupils have learned a selection, they should continue studying it, because "overlearning" increases retention

69. Which of the following is *least* likely to be an example of secondary reinforcement?

(A) parental praise
(B) a candy bar
(C) a one-dollar bill
(D) a gold medal
(E) an ice-cream cone

70. Assuming that there are three marking periods per term, which one of the following is the best approach in arriving at a grade for a student for the second marking period? To

(A) average all test marks of the student for that marking period and assign the multiple of five closest to this average as his grade
(B) average all test marks for each student and assign a grade to a particular student that will indicate his relative standing in the class according to these averages
(C) using test marks, class work, and homework as a guide, assign as his grade your estimate of the percentage of the work that has been presented that the student has mastered to date
(D) average all test marks of the student since the beginning of the term and assign the multiple of five closest to his average as his grade
(E) using test marks, behavior, and attitude as a guide, assign as his grade your estimate of the percentage of the work that has been presented that the student has mastered to date

71. Which of the following statements is *not* consistent with the educational philosophy of John Dewey?

(A) Education must be conceived as a continuing reconstruction of experience.
(B) The process and the goal of education are one and the same thing.
(C) Moral discipline should be a part and outcome of school life, not something proceeding from the teacher.
(D) Man is an organism in an environment, remaking as well as made.
(E) The acquisition of subject matter by children remains the basic task of the school.

72. Team teaching is a clear indication of

(A) the proliferation of "frills" in education
(B) the deprofessionalization of the certified teacher
(C) the use of psychological principles in education
(D) the tendency to avoid wherever possible the waste of money in educational administration
(E) how new teachers may be trained in a practical and speedy manner

73. Independent study is a prime aspect of which teaching method?

(A) trial-and-error
(B) practice-makes-perfect
(C) discovery
(D) role-playing
(E) programmed learning

74. Thorndike's association theory of learning

(A) is closely related to the theory of the nineteenth-century "Atomists"

(B) had Freudian implications

(C) had little influence upon later educators

(D) was the basis of B. F. Skinner's programmed learning research

(E) has no connection with behavioristic psychology

75. All of the following are basic to the teaching of English as a second language *except* that

(A) instruction should be systematic

(B) where possible, instruction should be based on direct experience

(C) the teacher must be aware of pupil needs

(D) the conversational approach should be used

(E) instruction need not differentiate between English and other language patterns

76. A child who looks blank and bites his nails when he is reprimanded by the teacher is probably demonstrating a pattern of behavior termed

(A) introversion

(B) repression

(C) egocentrism

(D) regression

(E) autism

77. In the contemporary elementary school the greatest proportion of instructional time is devoted to

(A) moral and ethical values

(B) mathematics and science

(C) reading and language arts

(D) social studies and humanities

(E) health and physical education

78. Which one of the following educators has stressed that intellectual improvement and development ought to be the primary function of our educational institutions?

(A) Theodore Brameld

(B) Jerome Bruner

(C) Horace Mann

(D) George Counts

(E) Arthur Bestor

79. Carmela just didn't like her biology teacher. As a result, she often wanted to cut the class but feared that her parents would punish her if they discovered she was cutting. She barely passed the course. Her grade advisor compelled her to take chemistry the following year. The first day that she attended the chemistry class, she experienced a tense emotional state of fear and apprehension. The psychological term for this feeling is

(A) displaced aggression

(B) alienation

(C) repression

(D) inhibition

(E) extension

80. The procedure of addressing a question to the class before designating a pupil to respond is

(A) inadvisable, because the pupil designated may not have heard the question
(B) advisable, because it gives the teacher an opportunity to call upon volunteers
(C) inadvisable, because it tends to make the entire class apprehensive
(D) advisable, because it gives all pupils an opportunity to formulate a tentative answer
(E) advisable, because it permits the teacher to call upon someone who may not have been paying attention

The table below summarizes a dozen different investigations having to do with familial resemblances in mental abilities and physical characteristics. Questions 81, 82, and 83 are based on this table.

**CORRELATION FOUND BETWEEN RELATED PAIRS OF PERSONS.
NORTHERN EUROPEAN STOCK IN TWELVE DIFFERENT INVESTIGATIONS**

People Compared	Physical Measures	Mental Measures
(a) unrelated children	X	−.19 to .09
(b) parents	.00 to .15	.46 to .49
(c) parent-child	.42 to .53	.45 to .55
(d) siblings, same home	.42 to .53	.60
(e) identical twins	.91	.97

81. Based on the observed data only, which group seems to be *least* related in mental measures?

(A) unrelated children
(B) parents
(C) parent-child
(D) siblings, same home
(E) identical twins

82. The correlations for parents and children indicate

(A) heredity to some extent causes mental ability
(B) heredity is a more powerful causal factor in identical twins than in siblings
(C) you can accurately predict the intelligence of a child if you know the intelligence of the parents
(D) nothing at all about causes of mental ability
(E) heredity causes physical and mental ability to about the same extent

83. What is the meaning of the correlation of −.19 in the Mental Measures column?

(A) Mental measures are unrelated to each other.
(B) Among unrelated children, mental and physical measures are unrelated.
(C) Among unrelated children, those high on mental measures are low on physical measures.
(D) Among unrelated children, those high on one mental measure are low on a second mental measure.
(E) Children did poorly on mental measure tests.

84. Divergent thinking may best be encouraged by a school's providing the students with

    (A) a great variety of subjects for them to choose from
    (B) many occasions to socialize during school hours
    (C) frequent trips and excursions
    (D) opportunities for doing work independently
    (E) specialized activities for the gifted

85. Which one of the following statements about lesson plans is *least* acceptable?

    (A) They should be done anew each year even if the same subjects are to be taught.
    (B) They become less and less necessary as your years of experience increase.
    (C) They should include the actual phraseology of pivotal questions to be asked.
    (D) They should be prepared weekly but be flexible enough to permit daily additions and corrections.
    (E) They should include planning for individual pupils.

86. Of the following, the child most likely to be overlooked in "meeting the needs of all the children" is the

    (A) aggressive youngster
    (B) shy, quiet child
    (C) child who is frequently absent
    (D) slow learner
    (E) economically underprivileged child

87. State certification of teachers has as its main function

    (A) guarding of teacher applicants who have training in pedagogy against the competition of applicants who do not possess that training
    (B) provision for an index of public commitment to the support of education
    (C) exclusion of teaching candidates who would be harmful to, or ineffective with, children and youth from the school milieu
    (D) assurance of higher salaries and other conditions relevant to better service and higher professional status
    (E) arranging for competition between one state education department and another state education department

88. A major reason for the growth of community control of schools is

    (A) dissatisfaction of teachers with administrative procedures
    (B) dissatisfaction of parents unable to make changes in school procedures
    (C) the high costs of a centralized system of education
    (D) growing spirit of democracy in our country
    (E) loss of confidence in the political process

89. Robbie thinks that a rolling ball is alive, since it is moving. He is displaying the concept of

    (A) realism
    (B) animism
    (C) artificialism

(D) egocentrism
(E) conservation

90. Which one of the following procedures is *most* acceptable to use in class when several pupils make flagrant errors in grammar and usage? To

(A) suggest that the pupils concentrate more on their English notes
(B) take a few minutes to explain and then go on with the lesson
(C) ignore the errors, since such deviations are time-consuming and interfere with covering the required course of study
(D) write a note to each pupil's parents to inform them of the errors
(E) ask bright students to work with these students outside of class

Questions 91, 92, and 93 are based on the following table.

MEANS AND STANDARD DEVIATIONS FOR STUDENT TEACHERS AND COLLEGE WOMEN NORMATIVE GROUP ON SELECTED VARIABLES

| | Student Teachers N = 104 | | Other College Women N = 749 | |
Variable	Mean	Standard Deviation	Mean	Standard Deviation
Achievement	13.03	3.20	13.08	4.19
Deference	14.63	2.91	12.40	3.72
Order	5.11	1.74	10.24	4.37
Exhibition	4.65	1.45	14.00	3.00

Use the following code to answer questions 91 and 92 about the table above.

(A) achievement
(B) deference
(C) order
(D) exhibition
(E) cannot be determined from table

91. For which variable did student teachers score highest, on the basis of the *observed* data?

92. For which variable did student teachers vary least, on the basis of the *observed* data?

93. Assuming normality, between what two score-values do two-thirds (67%) of the other college women scores fall for exhibition?

(A) between 3 and 14
(B) between 11 and 17
(C) between 14 and 17
(D) between 4 and 14
(E) cannot be determined

94. The school counselor who wishes to overcome shyness or resistance should begin testing with a measure of

(A) intelligence
(B) personality

(C) interest

(D) achievement

(E) attitude

95. Educators generally would accept all of the following statements about the use of a motion picture as a teaching aid *except* that

(A) children should know what to look for before the picture is shown

(B) the teacher should know before the lesson that the equipment is in operating order

(C) while the class is watching the film, the teacher should take notes in order to question the class later

(D) the showing should be followed by some activity, such as discussion, evaluation, or question-and-answer period

(E) the teacher should learn what the film is about before using it

96. A teacher may be dismissed for conduct that is generally considered immoral. Critical aspects of such a charge include

   I. if the conduct was personal and private

  II. if a teacher's indiscretion made the behavior public

 III. if the behavior involved a student or students

(A) I only

(B) II only

(C) III only

(D) II and III only

(E) all of the above

97. The major significance to American education of the Tenth Amendment to the United States Constitution is that it

(A) guarantees the right of each citizen to equal opportunity for education

(B) assures equitable funding for education

(C) instructs the states to set up school systems for public education

(D) guarantees the right to establish religious and other private schools

(E) reserves to the states the powers not specifically granted to the Federal government, including education

98. Which of the following educational institutions can validly be called American in origin?

(A) vocational school

(B) comprehensive high school

(C) nursery school

(D) all of the above

(E) none of the above

99. A child who can discuss with you differences between cows and sheep but who, when asked by you how they are similar, is at a loss to answer has the concepts "cow" and "sheep"

(A) undifferentiated

(B) differentiated but not abstracted

(C) differentiated and abstracted, but not generalized

(D) differentiated and generalized, but not abstracted

(E) generalized

100. A newly arrived Puerto Rican child who speaks English haltingly enters a teacher's class. Of the following procedures the one *last* in order of priority is

   (A) to increase the child's English vocabulary so that he can function better
   (B) to provide useful experiences that will help the child to adjust more readily to mainland life
   (C) to determine the health and nutritional needs of the child
   (D) to eliminate the foreign accent from the child's speech so that he will bear no stigma in his relations with his peers
   (E) to provide the child with a classroom buddy who will help him in his adjustment

Questions 101 and 102 refer to the following table.

**PERCENTAGES OF THE POPULATION 60 YEARS OF AGE AND OVER
RESIDING IN DIFFERENT KINDS OF COMMUNITIES,
BY SEX, UNITED STATES**

Sex	Urban	Rural Non-Farm	Farm
Male	53.2	21.3	25.5
Female	60.6	20.6	18.8
Total	57.0	20.9	22.1

101. Select a pair of words that best completes this sentence about the table:
   A _____ proportion of older men than of older women live on farms, and a _____ proportion of the men than of the women in that age group live in urban communities.

   (A) similar, similar
   (B) higher, lower
   (C) lower, higher
   (D) similar, lower
   (E) higher, similar

102. The circled number under the heading "Urban," 60.6, is to be read as follows:

   (A) 60.6% of the population live in urban communities
   (B) 60.6% of the total female population live in urban communities
   (C) 60.6% of the female population over 60 years of age live in urban communities
   (D) 60.6% of the female population 60 years of age and over live in urban communities
   (E) 60.6% of urban population is female

103. If a survey were made of the elementary school population of the United States to compare the number of students having an IQ of 90 –100 with the number having an IQ of 100 –110, it would be found that

   (A) no definite statement can be made on the basis of the information given
   (B) there were more students with an IQ of 90 –100
   (C) there were more students with an IQ of 100 –110
   (D) the numbers would be the same for rural and urban schools
   (E) the two groups were approximately equal in number

104. A proposal for federal action made by Dr. Clark Kerr called for the founding of "urban grant" universities. The term "urban grant" was used to stress a parallel with

(A) grants made by private foundations
(B) science-grant legislation
(C) land-grant colleges
(D) urban renewal programs
(E) urban education programs

105. A workable and worthwhile activity program should

(A) include appropriate activities with a few that are not appropriate yet interesting
(B) keep the children interested at all times
(C) make sure that there is a logical and psychological tie-up of substantial learning experiences
(D) have available a goodly supply of materials and should be rich in facilities
(E) have the approval of the more conservative parents

106. Ms. Wilcox, who is a new teacher in the district, has been told that she is to be observed by the Principal. Under normal professional practice she has a right to expect
   I. the Principal will remain for at least one instructional period
  II. a written report on the observation within a week
 III. that she will be allowed to select the particular class to observe

(A) II only
(B) II and III only
(C) I and II only
(D) all of the above
(E) none of the above

107. The primary purpose of tenure is to

(A) provide a reasonable measure of security for the members of the teaching profession
(B) assure that all those who teach will have a proven measure of competence
(C) make it difficult for teachers to transfer from one system to another
(D) provide employing personnel with a greater degree of authority over the teaching personnel
(E) raise the standards of entrance to the teaching profession

108. During the first year of the Reagan Administration, the Department of Education proposed that bilingual education

(A) be implemented for all languages
(B) be implemented for the five most common languages
(C) while successful, be discontinued because it simply costs too much
(D) be abandoned excepted for supplementary instruction in English as a second language
(E) be implemented as each state chooses

109. Which of the following is *not* associated with the concept of the ungraded class?

(A) A student's progress may be uneven—faster in some years and slower in others.
(B) A student's progress is even and unified—one year is like the next.
(C) Learning is viewed vertically.
(D) Movement from one class to another is flexible.
(E) Children of different ages work together.

110. All of the following are desirable educational practices *except*

    (A) starting the lesson promptly at the beginning of the period
    (B) completing the lesson even if the class has to be detained a few minutes
    (C) planning a motivation for each lesson
    (D) eliciting the lesson aim from the pupils
    (E) permitting the students to help set up course objectives

111. In many parts of the country, students cannot be graduated until they demonstrate their ability to achieve on a given level. The purpose of these exit exams is to focus on

    (A) accountability
    (B) emotional maturity
    (C) validity of IQ scores
    (D) significance of the "3 R's"
    (E) none of the above

112. The legal basis of the principle that education is a state function is found in the

    (A) Declaration of Independence
    (B) Northwest Ordinance
    (C) Fifteenth Amendment to the Constitution
    (D) Articles of Confederation
    (E) Tenth Amendment to the Constitution

113. When an evaluation refers to norm-referenced tests, it is most likely reporting data from

    (A) teacher-made tests
    (B) local, city-wide tests
    (C) standardized achievement tests
    (D) criterion-referenced tests
    (E) projective tests

114. When we say that a child's cultural background is important to the teacher, we imply that

    (A) prestige and status depend mainly upon individual initiative and effort
    (B) a child's values and habits are an outgrowth of his family and group membership
    (C) the influence of a peer group tends to be minor
    (D) little can be done to counter-influence an ethnic background
    (E) all children in a classroom tend to be alike in their values and habit patterns

115. When a teacher is trying to encourage more outside reading by the pupils in his/her classes, which one of the following methods is most likely to be successful?

    (A) The teacher gives additional credit to the pupil who submits a written report on a book or magazine article that he/she has read.
    (B) Several books and magazines are brought to class, and the teacher takes part of the class period to comment on each of them.
    (C) A list of suggested books and magazine articles is put into the hands of each pupil, and the pupil is asked to make a selection from this list.

(D) The teacher takes the class to the school library.

(E) Time is set aside periodically for pupils to report to the class on the books or magazine articles that they have read, and for pupil discussion following this.

116. All of the following are commonly associated with a student-centered curriculum *except*

(A) having students participate in evaluating their work
(B) teaching subject matter that has immediate utility
(C) involving students in selecting the subject matter to be studied
(D) differentiating among experiences provided for students (as opposed to standard offerings for everyone)
(E) teaching subject matter to students (as opposed to working with students)

117. In introducing learning tasks, the most important element for success is that the

(A) goals be clearly identified for the class by the teacher
(B) new learning be paced to the learner's maturation and previous knowledge
(C) class be organized into homogeneous groups
(D) teacher provide suitable motivation for the children
(E) necessary materials be readily available

118. A test score is meaningless without

(A) an equal-unit scale
(B) an explicit statement of objectives
(C) a wide variety of content
(D) a basis for comparison
(E) knowing the child's birthplace

119. Which of the following is the best example of an instructional objective?

(A) Pupils will demonstrate skill in spelling.
(B) Pupils will develop an appreciation of poetry and music.
(C) Pupils will, from memory, identify five freedoms contained in the Bill of Rights.
(D) Pupils will develop an ability to think independently.
(E) The attitude of pupils toward school will improve.

120. Of the following, the most significant deficiency of the lecture method in secondary school is that it fails adequately to

(A) treat content
(B) develop concepts
(C) meet adolescents' social and personal needs
(D) develop self-discipline
(E) prepare the student for college-level instruction

121. "Compensatory education" describes

(A) courses about labor, salary, and wages
(B) public school programs in which students are paid to participate
(C) programs intended to offset social or cultural deficiencies among disadvantaged students

(D) remedial programs for students who fall behind in their studies

(E) programs in which cash rewards are used as incentives to learn

122. The extent to which a test reflects the content and instructional objectives of the unit for which it was written is an indication of the test's

(A) difficulty

(B) objectivity

(C) validity

(D) discriminating power

(E) reliability

123. The major objective of the reading program in the primary grades is development of

(A) good eye movements

(B) word-recognition skills

(C) dictionary skills

(D) independent study skills

(E) love for reading

124. In the broad sense of the term, which of the following would be considered an alternative school?

(A) a storefront school

(B) a military academy

(C) an independent private school

(D) a parochial school

(E) all of the above

125. A test used to assess interim achievement in a unit of instruction is called a

(A) formative test

(B) normative test

(C) placement test

(D) summative test

(E) pretest

126. You are using a criterion-referenced test in teaching mathematics. This means that a student's score will be compared with the

(A) mean score of all students who took the test

(B) student's scores on previous tests of the same type

(C) national norm for students in the same grade on similar tests

(D) the passing grade of 65%

(E) number of items you have set as the minimum acceptable score

127. The case of *Tinker* v. *Des Moines* involved

(A) busing

(B) teachers' rights

(C) students' rights

(D) bilingual education programs

(E) special education

128. Today "curriculum" is usually defined by more progressive educators as

     (A) a well-graded, continuous course of study
     (B) a series of well-organized, planned learning activities
     (C) the sum total of a child's experiences under the guidance of the school
     (D) a functional approach to many areas of learning
     (E) specific content areas covered in each grade

129. You are taking a true-false test in an ancient language you do not know at all. On a 20-item test you can expect to get a score of

     (A) 0
     (B) 1 or 2
     (C) 4
     (D) 5
     (E) 10

130. When discussing teachers' salaries, we can safely say all but which of the following?

     (A) They are determined by each independent school system.
     (B) They increase yearly until the teacher retires.
     (C) They are increased to reward teachers who receive advanced degrees.
     (D) They differ from school system to school system by locale.
     (E) They are lower than industry in the same locale.

Stop

End of section. If you have any time left, go over your work in this section only. Do not work in any other section of the test.

Answer Key
Section 1: Professional Knowledge

Use this Key to score your examination by circling the number of each item you answered correctly. To be certain you have scored your examination accurately, take an extra few minutes to rescore it, and so verify your first scoring.

1. E	27. D	53. C	79. E	105. C
2. D	28. C	54. D	80. D	106. C
3. D	29. A	55. C	81. A	107. A
4. B	30. A	56. C	82. D	108. E
5. E	31. E	57. A	83. D	109. B
6. D	32. B	58. C	84. A	110. B
7. C	33. B	59. C	85. B	111. E
8. D	34. A	60. D	86. B	112. E
9. A	35. B	61. C	87. C	113. C
10. D	36. D	62. D	88. B	114. B
11. C	37. E	63. C	89. B	115. E
12. B	38. B	64. D	90. B	116. E
13. A	39. C	65. C	91. B	117. B
14. E	40. E	66. B	92. D	118. D
15. E	41. C	67. B	93. B	119. C
16. A	42. C	68. E	94. C	120. B
17. D	43. A	69. D	95. C	121. C
18. E	44. C	70. C	96. E	122. C
19. D	45. B	71. B	97. E	123. B
20. D	46. E	72. E	98. B	124. E
21. E	47. B	73. E	99. C	125. D
22. B	48. D	74. D	100. D	126. E
23. D	49. B	75. E	101. B	127. C
24. C	50. A	76. D	102. D	128. C
25. A	51. D	77. C	103. E	129. E
26. B	52. E	78. B	104. C	130. B

Diagnostic Table for the
Professional Knowledge Examination

The table below is intended to provide you with a detailed insight into your performance on the Professional Knowledge Examination on the first Diagnostic Core Battery. The score sheet will provide you with separate scores in the thirteen different areas tested.

To use the table, first score your performance on the Professional Knowledge Examination. Then, circle the number of each item you answered correctly on score in any one area would be ten; therefore, any time you have achieved fewer than six correct, you have identified an area in need of further study. A score lower than four identifies an area needing major review.

Area Covered	Question Numbers	Number Correct
1. Historical, Philosophical Foundations	11, 26, 31, 36, 41, 46, 61, 66, 71, 98	
2. Social and Cultural Foundations	78, 88, 97, 104, 107, 108, 114, 121, 127, 130	
3. Child and Adolescent Development	3, 27, 32, 37, 42, 47, 52, 57, 62, 67	
4. Application of Child/Adolescent Development	29, 34, 39, 44, 49, 76, 79, 84, 89, 99	
5. Learning Theories and Principles	2, 7, 12, 17, 22, 54, 59, 64, 69, 74	
6. Application of Learning Theory, Principles	4, 9, 14, 19, 24, 53, 58, 63, 68, 73	
7. Test Development, Evaluation, and Assessment Principles	5, 10, 15, 20, 51, 55, 60, 65, 94, 103	
8. Understanding Test and Measurement Concepts, Grading	25, 30, 45, 70, 113, 118, 122, 125, 126, 129	
9. Research and Statistical Concepts	35, 40, 81, 82, 83, 91, 92, 93, 101, 102	
10. Teaching Principles, Practices	75, 80, 85, 90, 95, 100, 105, 110, 115, 120	
11. Classroom Management	8, 13, 18, 23, 28, 33, 38, 72, 77, 86	
12. Curriculum Development and Supervision	43, 48, 109, 111, 116, 117, 119, 123, 124, 128	
13. Professional Awareness	1, 6, 16, 21, 50, 56, 87, 96, 106, 112	

Answer Sheet
Section 2: General Knowledge

SOCIAL STUDIES

1 Ⓐ Ⓑ Ⓒ Ⓓ Ⓔ 6 Ⓐ Ⓑ Ⓒ Ⓓ Ⓔ 11 Ⓐ Ⓑ Ⓒ Ⓓ Ⓔ 16 Ⓐ Ⓑ Ⓒ Ⓓ Ⓔ 21 Ⓐ Ⓑ Ⓒ Ⓓ Ⓔ 26 Ⓐ Ⓑ Ⓒ Ⓓ Ⓔ 31 Ⓐ Ⓑ Ⓒ Ⓓ Ⓔ

2 Ⓐ Ⓑ Ⓒ Ⓓ Ⓔ 7 Ⓐ Ⓑ Ⓒ Ⓓ Ⓔ 12 Ⓐ Ⓑ Ⓒ Ⓓ Ⓔ 17 Ⓐ Ⓑ Ⓒ Ⓓ Ⓔ 22 Ⓐ Ⓑ Ⓒ Ⓓ Ⓔ 27 Ⓐ Ⓑ Ⓒ Ⓓ Ⓔ 32 Ⓐ Ⓑ Ⓒ Ⓓ Ⓔ

3 Ⓐ Ⓑ Ⓒ Ⓓ Ⓔ 8 Ⓐ Ⓑ Ⓒ Ⓓ Ⓔ 13 Ⓐ Ⓑ Ⓒ Ⓓ Ⓔ 18 Ⓐ Ⓑ Ⓒ Ⓓ Ⓔ 23 Ⓐ Ⓑ Ⓒ Ⓓ Ⓔ 28 Ⓐ Ⓑ Ⓒ Ⓓ Ⓔ 33 Ⓐ Ⓑ Ⓒ Ⓓ Ⓔ

4 Ⓐ Ⓑ Ⓒ Ⓓ Ⓔ 9 Ⓐ Ⓑ Ⓒ Ⓓ Ⓔ 14 Ⓐ Ⓑ Ⓒ Ⓓ Ⓔ 19 Ⓐ Ⓑ Ⓒ Ⓓ Ⓔ 24 Ⓐ Ⓑ Ⓒ Ⓓ Ⓔ 29 Ⓐ Ⓑ Ⓒ Ⓓ Ⓔ 34 Ⓐ Ⓑ Ⓒ Ⓓ Ⓔ

5 Ⓐ Ⓑ Ⓒ Ⓓ Ⓔ 10 Ⓐ Ⓑ Ⓒ Ⓓ Ⓔ 15 Ⓐ Ⓑ Ⓒ Ⓓ Ⓔ 20 Ⓐ Ⓑ Ⓒ Ⓓ Ⓔ 25 Ⓐ Ⓑ Ⓒ Ⓓ Ⓔ 30 Ⓐ Ⓑ Ⓒ Ⓓ Ⓔ 35 Ⓐ Ⓑ Ⓒ Ⓓ Ⓔ

LITERATURE

1 Ⓐ Ⓑ Ⓒ Ⓓ Ⓔ 6 Ⓐ Ⓑ Ⓒ Ⓓ Ⓔ 11 Ⓐ Ⓑ Ⓒ Ⓓ Ⓔ 16 Ⓐ Ⓑ Ⓒ Ⓓ Ⓔ 21 Ⓐ Ⓑ Ⓒ Ⓓ Ⓔ

2 Ⓐ Ⓑ Ⓒ Ⓓ Ⓔ 7 Ⓐ Ⓑ Ⓒ Ⓓ Ⓔ 12 Ⓐ Ⓑ Ⓒ Ⓓ Ⓔ 17 Ⓐ Ⓑ Ⓒ Ⓓ Ⓔ 22 Ⓐ Ⓑ Ⓒ Ⓓ Ⓔ

3 Ⓐ Ⓑ Ⓒ Ⓓ Ⓔ 8 Ⓐ Ⓑ Ⓒ Ⓓ Ⓔ 13 Ⓐ Ⓑ Ⓒ Ⓓ Ⓔ 18 Ⓐ Ⓑ Ⓒ Ⓓ Ⓔ 23 Ⓐ Ⓑ Ⓒ Ⓓ Ⓔ

4 Ⓐ Ⓑ Ⓒ Ⓓ Ⓔ 9 Ⓐ Ⓑ Ⓒ Ⓓ Ⓔ 14 Ⓐ Ⓑ Ⓒ Ⓓ Ⓔ 19 Ⓐ Ⓑ Ⓒ Ⓓ Ⓔ 24 Ⓐ Ⓑ Ⓒ Ⓓ Ⓔ

5 Ⓐ Ⓑ Ⓒ Ⓓ Ⓔ 10 Ⓐ Ⓑ Ⓒ Ⓓ Ⓔ 15 Ⓐ Ⓑ Ⓒ Ⓓ Ⓔ 20 Ⓐ Ⓑ Ⓒ Ⓓ Ⓔ 25 Ⓐ Ⓑ Ⓒ Ⓓ Ⓔ

FINE ARTS

1 Ⓐ Ⓑ Ⓒ Ⓓ Ⓔ 6 Ⓐ Ⓑ Ⓒ Ⓓ Ⓔ 11 Ⓐ Ⓑ Ⓒ Ⓓ Ⓔ 16 Ⓐ Ⓑ Ⓒ Ⓓ Ⓔ

2 Ⓐ Ⓑ Ⓒ Ⓓ Ⓔ 7 Ⓐ Ⓑ Ⓒ Ⓓ Ⓔ 12 Ⓐ Ⓑ Ⓒ Ⓓ Ⓔ 17 Ⓐ Ⓑ Ⓒ Ⓓ Ⓔ

3 Ⓐ Ⓑ Ⓒ Ⓓ Ⓔ 8 Ⓐ Ⓑ Ⓒ Ⓓ Ⓔ 13 Ⓐ Ⓑ Ⓒ Ⓓ Ⓔ 18 Ⓐ Ⓑ Ⓒ Ⓓ Ⓔ

4 Ⓐ Ⓑ Ⓒ Ⓓ Ⓕ 9 Ⓐ Ⓑ Ⓒ Ⓓ Ⓔ 14 Ⓐ Ⓑ Ⓒ Ⓓ Ⓔ 19 Ⓐ Ⓑ Ⓒ Ⓓ Ⓔ

5 Ⓐ Ⓑ Ⓒ Ⓓ Ⓔ 10 Ⓐ Ⓑ Ⓒ Ⓓ Ⓔ 15 Ⓐ Ⓑ Ⓒ Ⓓ Ⓔ 20 Ⓐ Ⓑ Ⓒ Ⓓ Ⓔ

SCIENCE

1 Ⓐ Ⓑ Ⓒ Ⓓ Ⓔ 6 Ⓐ Ⓑ Ⓒ Ⓓ Ⓔ 11 Ⓐ Ⓑ Ⓒ Ⓓ Ⓔ 16 Ⓐ Ⓑ Ⓒ Ⓓ Ⓔ 21 Ⓐ Ⓑ Ⓒ Ⓓ Ⓔ 26 Ⓐ Ⓑ Ⓒ Ⓓ Ⓔ 31 Ⓐ Ⓑ Ⓒ Ⓓ Ⓔ

2 Ⓐ Ⓑ Ⓒ Ⓓ Ⓔ 7 Ⓐ Ⓑ Ⓒ Ⓓ Ⓔ 12 Ⓐ Ⓑ Ⓒ Ⓓ Ⓔ 17 Ⓐ Ⓑ Ⓒ Ⓓ Ⓔ 22 Ⓐ Ⓑ Ⓒ Ⓓ Ⓔ 27 Ⓐ Ⓑ Ⓒ Ⓓ Ⓔ 32 Ⓐ Ⓑ Ⓒ Ⓓ Ⓔ

3 Ⓐ Ⓑ Ⓒ Ⓓ Ⓔ 8 Ⓐ Ⓑ Ⓒ Ⓓ Ⓔ 13 Ⓐ Ⓑ Ⓒ Ⓓ Ⓔ 18 Ⓐ Ⓑ Ⓒ Ⓓ Ⓔ 23 Ⓐ Ⓑ Ⓒ Ⓓ Ⓔ 28 Ⓐ Ⓑ Ⓒ Ⓓ Ⓔ

4 Ⓐ Ⓑ Ⓒ Ⓓ Ⓔ 9 Ⓐ Ⓑ Ⓒ Ⓓ Ⓔ 14 Ⓐ Ⓑ Ⓒ Ⓓ Ⓔ 19 Ⓐ Ⓑ Ⓒ Ⓓ Ⓔ 24 Ⓐ Ⓑ Ⓒ Ⓓ Ⓔ 29 Ⓐ Ⓑ Ⓒ Ⓓ Ⓔ

5 Ⓐ Ⓑ Ⓒ Ⓓ Ⓔ 10 Ⓐ Ⓑ Ⓒ Ⓓ Ⓔ 15 Ⓐ Ⓑ Ⓒ Ⓓ Ⓔ 20 Ⓐ Ⓑ Ⓒ Ⓓ Ⓔ 25 Ⓐ Ⓑ Ⓒ Ⓓ Ⓔ 30 Ⓐ Ⓑ Ⓒ Ⓓ Ⓔ

MATHEMATICS

1 ⒶⒷⒸⒹⒺ   6 ⒶⒷⒸⒹⒺ   11 ⒶⒷⒸⒹⒺ   16 ⒶⒷⒸⒹⒺ   21 ⒶⒷⒸⒹⒺ

2 ⒶⒷⒸⒹⒺ   7 ⒶⒷⒸⒹⒺ   12 ⒶⒷⒸⒹⒺ   17 ⒶⒷⒸⒹⒺ   22 ⒶⒷⒸⒹⒺ

3 ⒶⒷⒸⒹⒺ   8 ⒶⒷⒸⒹⒺ   13 ⒶⒷⒸⒹⒺ   18 ⒶⒷⒸⒹⒺ   23 ⒶⒷⒸⒹⒺ

4 ⒶⒷⒸⒹⒺ   9 ⒶⒷⒸⒹⒺ   14 ⒶⒷⒸⒹⒺ   19 ⒶⒷⒸⒹⒺ

5 ⒶⒷⒸⒹⒺ   10 ⒶⒷⒸⒹⒺ   15 ⒶⒷⒸⒹⒺ   20 ⒶⒷⒸⒹⒺ

Diagnostic Core Battery I
Section 2. General Knowledge

1 Hour 35 Minutes — 135 Questions

SOCIAL STUDIES

25 Minutes—35 Questions

Directions: Each question is followed by five choices.
Select the choice that is correct or most nearly correct.

1. Several men served the United States as both President and Vice-President. Of the following, who served the most years in these two offices?

   (A) John Adams
   (B) Richard Nixon
   (C) Andrew Johnson
   (D) Lyndon Johnson
   (E) Theodore Roosevelt

2. One reason for the importance of the Northwest Ordinance (1787) was that it provided for

   (A) the government of Texas
   (B) the sale of western lands
   (C) free navigation on the Great Lakes
   (D) the eventual admission of territories as equal states
   (E) the judicial system of the United States

3. Which one of the following statements is true of the Monroe Doctrine?

   (A) It was of long-range rather than immediate significance.
   (B) It forestalled a planned intervention by the Concert of Europe.
   (C) It received the formal assent of Congress.
   (D) It led to abandonment by the European powers of their colonies in the Western Hemisphere.
   (E) Its basic outlines had been opposed by the British, whom Monroe had consulted in 1823.

4. The Gentlemen's Agreement of 1907 between the United States and Japan provided for

   (A) mutual recognition of the Open Door policy in China
   (B) establishment of a specific quota for Japanese immigration to the United States
   (C) restrictions on the naval armaments of the two nations
   (D) United States restrictions on Japanese immigration
   (E) Japanese restriction of Japanese emigration to the United States

79

5. Microeconomics is concerned with

   (A) an overall view of the functioning of an economic system
   (B) determination of distribution of income
   (C) the aggregate levels of income, employment, and output
   (D) the prediction of specific demands in a sector of the economy
   (E) an examination of specific economic units that constitute an economic system

6. Some of the best arguments in support of the adoption of the United States Constitution are found in

   (A) *Common Sense*
   (B) the Articles of Confederation
   (C) the New Freedom
   (D) the Freeport Doctrine
   (E) *The Federalist Papers*

7. Which one of the following is generally characteristic of modern underdeveloped countries?

   (A) rising nationalism, population problems, middle-class philosophy
   (B) low savings rate, inequality of wealth, need for land reform
   (C) poor endowment of natural resources, failure of the wealthy to invest in manufacturing, security of foreign investments
   (D) desire for western material goods, large role of government investment, full utilization of manpower
   (E) overpopulation, full utilization of manpower, security of foreign investments

8. Which one of the following is *incorrect* with regard to congressional organization and procedure?

   (A) In each house, one-fifth of the members present are guaranteed the right to demand a record vote on any question.
   (B) The only congressional officers that are mentioned in the Constitution are the Speaker of the House of Representatives, the Vice-President, and the President Pro-Tempore of the Senate.
   (C) There is not a word in the Constitution about the committee structure of Congress.
   (D) The seniority system determines committee chairmanships.
   (E) Each house may punish its members for disorderly behavior or may, by a majority vote, expel a member.

9. Of the following, which one is *not* a characteristic of monopolistic competition?

   (A) standardized product
   (B) strong feeling of mutual interdependence
   (C) paucity of firms
   (D) comparatively easy entry
   (E) little price competition

10. Which of the following was a result of the others?

    (A) Alien and Sedition Acts
    (B) disappearance of the Federalist Party

(C) Hartford Convention

(D) increase in the democratic spirit of the United States

(E) none of these

11. The so-called "new right" in American politics of the 1980s had a political agenda which included which of the following:

    I. return of school prayer

    II. restriction of abortion rights

    III. restoration of full employment

(A) I, II, and III

(B) II only

(C) I and II only

(D) I only

(E) none of the above

12. Which one of the following is paired correctly with the work that he wrote?

(A) Galileo Galilei—*Principia*

(B) John Milton—*Areopagitica*

(C) Michel de Montaigne—*The Praise of Folly*

(D) Thomas More—*England's Treasure by Foreign Trade*

(E) John Locke—*On Liberty*

13. Of the following pairs, the one that *incorrectly* attributes a river system to a country is

(A) Yellow—China

(B) Vistula—Italy

(C) Murray Darling—Australia

(D) Loire—France

(E) Volga—Russia

14. The Treaty of 1795 with Spain was most popular with

(A) western farmers using the Mississippi River for shipping

(B) northern fur trappers seeking the removal of British troops from the Northwest Territory

(C) patriotic Americans attempting to stop the impressment of seamen

(D) New England merchants seeking to reopen triangular trade

(E) southerners seeking new markets for tobacco

15. Of the following, who was not a member of Ronald Reagan's original Cabinet?

(A) Alexander Haig

(B) Raymond Donovan

(C) George Schulz

(D) Drew Lewis

(E) Richard Schweiker

16. The Twenty-second Amendment

(A) limits the President's term of office to eight years

(B) limits the President to two terms plus any part of an unexpired term

(C) expressly exempted the incumbent President from its provisions

(D) designates the Speaker of the House as next to the Vice-President in the line

of presidential succession
(E) provides public funds to presidential candidates

17. Under the United States Constitution no state may, without the consent of Congress,

(A) tax business enterprise
(B) regulate public utilities
(C) enter into agreements or compacts with another state
(D) establish a militia
(E) determine administrative personnel for its educational system

18. Which statement best describes the reaction of many American colonists toward British colonial policy following the French and Indian War? They

(A) refused to accept the idea of Parliament's right to manage their internal affairs
(B) petitioned the British Parliament for immediate independence
(C) urged the colonial legislatures to enforce the taxation program of the British Parliament
(D) opposed the withdrawal of British troops from the Ohio Territory
(E) advocated higher taxes to cover the costs of the war

19. The Mesabi Range is famous for its rich deposits of

(A) coal
(B) copper
(C) iron
(D) uranium
(E) gold

20. Who of the following did *not* break with the Roman Catholic Church during the Protestant Reformation?

(A) John Calvin
(B) Desiderius Erasmus
(C) John Knox
(D) Huldreich Zwingli
(E) Henry Tudor

21. The friendship between the United States and France can be traced back to

(A) the Alliance of 1778
(B) the activities of Citizen Genet
(C) French aid during the War of 1812
(D) French support of the North during the Civil War
(E) the gift of the Statue of Liberty

22. Under existing budgetary procedures, the President of the United States of America

(A) may veto items in appropriation bills
(B) may reduce but not eliminate items from appropriation bills
(C) must accept or reject appropriation bills in their entirety
(D) may veto items in appropriation bills for expenditures other than military purposes
(E) may veto only congressional additions to his programs

23. With respect to the nomination and election of presidential candidates, the United States Constitution

    (A) directs that the convention system be used for nomination
    (B) provides for direct popular election of presidential electors
    (C) provides that nominations be made by either party conventions or primaries
    (D) makes no provision other than the electoral system
    (E) forbids popular election of the President

24. Which one of the following nineteenth-century scientists is paired correctly with the field in which he made his major contributions?

    (A) Agassiz—Chemistry
    (B) Dalton—Mathematics
    (C) Lamarck—Biology
    (D) Lyell—Zoology
    (E) Roentgen—Physics

25. Of the following, which is *not* one of the market models viewed from the seller's side of the market?

    (A) pure competition
    (B) monopoly
    (C) capitalism
    (D) monopolistic competition
    (E) oligopsony

26. Which one of the following statements does *not* apply to the Revolution of 1789 in France and to the Revolutions of 1848 in Europe? In both cases

    (A) serfdom was abolished
    (B) an immediate economic crisis helped to crystallize discontent into a revolution
    (C) a new industrial working class put forth an essentially identical social and economic program
    (D) constitutional monarchies were established
    (E) the revolution in France was a signal for a European tidal wave of disturbances

27. Of the following, the body of water that is completely land-locked is the

    (A) Black Sea
    (B) Tyrrhenian Sea
    (C) Ionian Sea
    (D) Caspian Sea
    (E) Baltic Sea

28. Which one of the following monarchs is *not* considered an enlightened or benevolent despot of the eighteenth century?

    (A) Catherine the Great of Russia
    (B) Frederick the Great of Prussia
    (C) Joseph II of Austria
    (D) Louis XV of France
    (E) Peter the Great of Russia

29. If we assume that price decreases as total expenditures increase, we may conclude that

    (A) elasticity of demand is greater than one
    (B) elasticity of demand is less than one
    (C) elasticity of demand is equal to one
    (D) all of the above are true
    (E) none of the above are true

30. Despite the fact that England is farther north than any point in the United States, its winters are generally warmer than those in the northern United States because

    (A) England has a Mediterranean climate
    (B) England's shores are warmed by the Gulf Stream
    (C) England is warmed by the breezes that blow from Africa
    (D) the winds that influence England's climate are the prevailing easterlies
    (E) the United States is cooled by Arctic air

31. Critics of the Beard Thesis maintain that at the Philadelphia Convention

    (A) the desire for a strong central government was in part an effort to obtain a favored position under the new government for the propertied classes
    (B) large numbers of adult males were unrepresented, because they did not own property
    (C) patriotic motivations of the delegates were not present to the degree cited by Beard
    (D) a number of delegates supported federalism because they expected that under a strong central government the depreciated Continental debt would be funded at par
    (E) there was no correlation between the delegates' property holdings and the position they took on constitutional issues

32. The city sometimes described as the "Pittsburgh of the South" because of its high production of steel is

    (A) Birmingham, Alabama
    (B) Nashville, Tennessee
    (C) Richmond, Virginia
    (D) Atlanta, Georgia
    (E) New Orleans, Louisiana

33. Which one of the following is *incorrectly* matched with a political principle he espoused?

    (A) Rousseau—Popular Sovereignty
    (B) Hegel—Totalitarianism
    (C) Hobbes—War of All vs. All
    (D) Nietzsche—Superiority of the Elite
    (E) Locke—Proletarianism

34. Which of the following decisions of the Supreme Court during the incumbency of Chief Justice John Marshall declared an Act of Congress to be unconstitutional?

    (A) *Fletcher* v. *Peek*
    (B) *McCulloch* v. *Maryland*

(C) *Dartmouth College* v. *Woodward*
(D) *Marbury* v. *Madison*
(E) *Gibbons* v. *Ogden*

35. Which one of the following was a cause of controversy between the United States and England in the period immediately preceding the War of 1812?

(A) debts owed to English merchants
(B) impressment of American seamen
(C) treatment of Loyalists
(D) presence of British garrisons on United States soil
(E) northern boundary of the new nation

Stop

End of section. If you have any time left, go over your work in this section only. Do not work in any other section of the test.

LITERATURE

15 Minutes—25 Questions

Directions: Each question is followed by five choices.
Select the choice that is correct or most nearly correct.

1. Which of the following novels is a polemic against slavery?

   (A) *The Nigger of the "Narcissus"*
   (B) *The Way of All Flesh*
   (C) *Of Human Bondage*
   (D) *Uncle Tom's Cabin*
   (E) *The Lord of the Rings*

2. Who among the following was a metaphysical poet?

   (A) Ezra Pound
   (B) H.D. (Hilda Doolittle)
   (C) John Donne
   (D) Alexander Pope
   (E) John Dryden

3. Jack Burden, a young intellectual, narrates the story of the rise and fall of Willie
   Stark, a Southern demagogue apparently modeled on Huey Long.
   The sentence above discusses

   (A) Osborne's *Look Back in Anger*
   (B) Miller's *Death of a Salesman*
   (C) Warren's *All the King's Men*
   (D) O'Neill's *The Great God Brown*
   (E) Williams' *The Glass Menagerie*

4. Which of the following novels was *not* written by Aldous Huxley?

   (A) *Eyeless in Gaza*
   (B) *Point Counter Point*
   (C) *Brave New World*
   (D) *Chrome Yellow*
   (E) *Animal Farm*

5. Which of the following novels is *not* by Henry James?

   (A) *The Wings of the Dove*
   (B) *The Princess Casamassima*
   (C) *The Ambassadors*
   (D) *The Pickwick Papers*
   (E) *Portrait of a Lady*

6. *Beowulf* is

   (A) an unfinished poetic work by Geoffrey Chaucer

(B) a narrative poem in blank verse

(C) an unfinished epic satire by Lord Byron

(D) a Middle English poem in alliterative verse

(E) an Old English (Anglo-Saxon) epic in alliterative verse

7. Which of the following is a famous series of essays by Joseph Addison and Richard Steele?

(A) *New Masses*

(B) *Broom*

(C) *The Spectator*

(D) *Transition*

(E) *The Rambler*

8. Which of the following novels takes place at sea?

(A) *The Mayor of Casterbridge*

(B) *Pamela*

(C) *The Grapes of Wrath*

(D) *Moby Dick*

(E) *Arrowsmith*

9. *The King and I* is based on

(A) *The Count of Monte Cristo*

(B) *Anna and the King of Siam*

(C) *The Royal Road to Romance*

(D) *If I Were King*

(E) "Gunga Din"

10. Which of the following Shakespearean characters is *incorrectly* paired with the play in which he appears?

(A) Prospero—*The Tempest*

(B) Shylock—*The Merchant of Venice*

(C) Christopher Sly—*The Taming of the Shrew*

(D) Dogberry—*The Comedy of Errors*

(E) Francis Flute—*A Midsummer Night's Dream*

11. Lytton Strachey, known for his work *Eminent Victorians*, was

(A) a poet

(B) an essayist

(C) a novelist

(D) a playwright

(E) a writer of children's stories

12. Which of the following is a play?

(A) *War and Peace*

(B) *Pygmalion*

(C) *Ulysses*

(D) *Beowulf*

(E) *The Canterbury Tales*

13. *Two Years Before the Mast* is based on

    (A) the author's actual experiences on a ship
    (B) Magellan's trip around the world
    (C) the adventures of pirates
    (D) the beginning of the United States Navy
    (E) a search for a white whale

14. Which of the following Shakespearean heroes is correctly matched with the heroine of the play in which he appears?

    (A) Malvolio—Juliet
    (B) Lear—Desdemona
    (C) Romeo—Olivia
    (D) Othello—Hermia
    (E) Prospero—Miranda

15. Which of the following characters is *incorrectly* paired with the novel in which he/she appears?

    (A) Mellors—*Lady Chatterley's Lover*
    (B) Eugene Gant—*Look Homeward, Angel*
    (C) Catherine Sloper—*Washington Square*
    (D) Raskolnikov—*War and Peace*
    (E) Antoine Roquentin—*Nausea*

16. *The Ugly American* is based on the success and failures of

    (A) American industrialists
    (B) United States citizens abroad
    (C) people in suburbia
    (D) a mythical United States dictator
    (E) the American occupation of Japan

17. Taking for his theme the arrest of time through memory, which of the following French novelists wrote *Remembrance of Things Past?*

    (A) Emile Zola
    (B) Victor Hugo
    (C) Marcel Proust
    (D) Andre Gide
    (E) Honore de Balzac

18. Which of the following characters does *not* appear in the *Odyssey?*

    (A) Circe
    (B) Calypso
    (C) Nestor
    (D) Andromache
    (E) Telemachus

19. *The Making of the President* is an account of the

    (A) political career of Franklin D. Roosevelt
    (B) elections of American presidents since the days of George Washington
    (C) election of John F. Kennedy as President
    (D) role of the presidency in American foreign affairs
    (E) shaping of the presidency by Washington and Jefferson

20. In which of the following works does the hero sell his soul to the devil for un-limited knowledge?

    (A) *Don Quixote*
    (B) *Faust*
    (C) *Don Juan*
    (D) *Tom Jones*
    (E) *Eugene Onegin*

21. In which of the following works does the poet John Milton attempt to "justify the ways of God to men"?

    (A) *Areopagitica*
    (B) *King Lear*
    (C) *Comus*
    (D) *Paradise Lost*
    (E) *The Faerie Queene*

22. The predominant mood of the author in "The Raven" is

    (A) angry
    (B) satirical
    (C) resigned
    (D) melancholy
    (E) joyful

23. The most expensive theater ticket in Broadway history was a ticket to *Nicholas Nickleby*, the dramatization of a novel by

    (A) William Shakespeare
    (B) Neil Simon
    (C) James Michener
    (D) Herman Wouk
    (E) Charles Dickens

24. All of the following poems are in rhyme except

    (A) "Little Boy Blue"—Eugene Field
    (B) "Paul Revere's Ride"—Henry Wadsworth Longfellow
    (C) "The Fog"—Carl Sandburg
    (D) "Stopping by Woods on a Snowy Evening"—Robert Frost
    (E) "Annabel Lee"—Edgar Allan Poe

25. All of the following literary characters are correctly identified *except*

    (A) Thunderhead—lighthouse
    (B) Little Toot—tugboat
    (C) Flag—fawn
    (D) Bambi—deer
    (E) Captain Hook—pirate

Stop

End of section. If you have any time left, go over your work in this section only. Do not work in any other section of the test.

FINE ARTS

10 Minutes—20 Questions

Directions: Each question is followed by five choices. Select the choice that is most correct or most nearly correct.

1. Which of the following sculptors was a Baroque master?

   (A) Donatello
   (B) Peter Flötner
   (C) Nikolaus Gerhaert
   (D) Gianlorenzo Bernini
   (E) Antonio Pollaiuolo

2. A term developed in the present century to describe the artistic manifestations, principally Italian, of the period c. 1520–1600 is

   (A) Rococo
   (B) Neoclassicism
   (C) Mannerism
   (D) Gothic
   (E) Baroque

3. Which of the following painters is *incorrectly* paired with the group or movement with which he was associated?

   (A) Bellows—Ashcan School
   (B) Miro—Impressionism
   (C) Millet—Barbizon School
   (D) Dali—Surrealism
   (E) Matisse—Fauvism

4. Which of the following is a method of painting in which the powdered pigment is mixed with hot glue-size?

   (A) gouache
   (B) acrylic
   (C) fresco
   (D) pastel
   (E) size color

5. "Her vaguely formed idea was that dance is the expression of an inner urge or impulse and that the source of this impulse comes, physically, from the solar plexus." The dancer referred to in the sentence above is

   (A) Martha Graham
   (B) Doris Humphrey
   (C) Isadora Duncan
   (D) Ruth St. Denis
   (E) Lois Fuller

6. Which of the following operas was composed by Puccini?

   (A) *Lucia di Lammermoor*
   (B) *Pagliacci*
   (C) *Don Giovanni*
   (D) *Fidelio*
   (E) *Tosca*

7. Which of the sculptures on the following page is by Alberto Giacometti?

   (A)
   (B)
   (C)
   (D)
   (E)

8. The Victory of Samothrace is a famous

   (A) bas-relief
   (B) cathedral
   (C) statue
   (D) mural
   (E) tapestry

9. Which of the works on the following page is by Marcel Duchamp?

   (A)
   (B)
   (C)
   (D)
   (E)

10. In a ballet, a beating step of elevation in which the dancer makes a weaving motion in the air is called

    (A) pirouette
    (B) an entrechat
    (C) an arabesque
    (D) a variation
    (E) a divertissement

11. An outstanding jazz pianist is

    (A) William "Count" Basie
    (B) Charlie Parker
    (C) Sonny Rollins
    (D) Scott Joplin
    (E) James Scott

12. Which of the following is an extended choral work with solo voices and usually with orchestral accompaniment?

    (A) cantata
    (B) sonata
    (C) symphony
    (D) opera
    (E) Gregorian chant

(A)

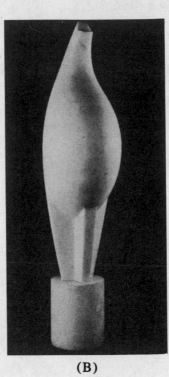

(B)

(C)

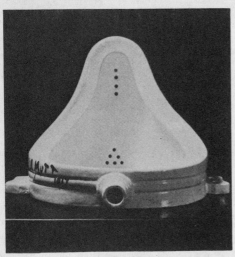

(D)

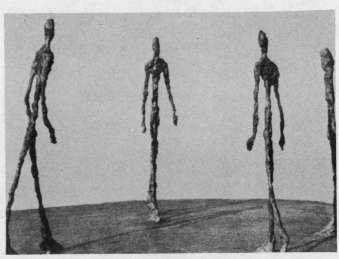

(E)

13. The sculpture above is

    (A) an Etruscan funerary figure
    (B) a symbol of a Polynesian fertility god
    (C) an artifact of Peking man
    (D) an artifact of Java man
    (E) a Venus figurine (from Willendorf, Austria)

14. *Messiah* is an oratorio composed by

    (A) Richard Strauss
    (B) Gustav Mahler
    (C) George Handel
    (D) (Franz) Joseph Haydn
    (E) Johann Sebastian Bach

15. Which of Beethoven's symphonies bears the title *Eroica,* the "Heroic Symphony"?

    (A) Ninth Symphony
    (B) Second Symphony
    (C) Fifth Symphony
    (D) Sixth Symphony
    (E) Third Symphony

16. In a normal twentieth-century orchestra, a tuba would be located in which of the following sections?

    (A) woodwind
    (B) strings
    (C) percussion
    (D) unclassified
    (E) brass

17. The main *decorative* features of the Gothic cathedral are

   (A) pointed arch and lancet windows
   (B) flying buttresses and groined vaults
   (C) tapestries and wall hangings
   (D) icons and marble tombs
   (E) sculpture and stained glass windows

18. Peasants singing, working, dancing, and feasting are shown vividly in the paintings of

   (A) Vermeer
   (B) Rubens
   (C) Brueghel
   (D) Ingres
   (E) Rembrandt

19. A vocal arrangement in which the same melody is sung by several voices starting one after the other at regular intervals to produce pleasant harmony and rhythm is called a(n)

   (A) art song
   (B) concerto
   (C) descant
   (D) a cappella
   (E) round

20. Gilbert and Sullivan composed all of the following *except*

   (A) *Princess Ida*
   (B) *Ruddigore*
   (C) *Pirates of Penzance*
   (D) *Patience*
   (E) *The Red Mill*

Stop

End of section. If you have any time left, go over your work in this section only. Do not work in any other section of the test.

SCIENCE

25 Minutes—32 Questions

Directions: Each question is followed by five choices.
Select the choice that is correct or most nearly correct.

1. A sphere and a cylinder start from rest at the same position and roll down the same incline.

   (A) The cylinder will reach the bottom first, independent of the mass and radius of the two objects.
   (B) Which one reaches the bottom first will depend on the volume of the object.
   (C) They will reach the bottom at the same time, independent of the mass and radius of the two objects.
   (D) Which one reaches the bottom first will depend upon the radius of the object.
   (E) The sphere will reach the bottom first, independent of the mass and radius of the two objects.

2. How many degrees does the earth rotate in four hours?

   (A) 20
   (B) 40
   (C) 60
   (D) 120
   (E) 360

3. The process of adding a basic solution to an acidic solution until the resulting solution is neither basic nor acidic is called

   (A) oxidation
   (B) reduction
   (C) nucleation
   (D) neutralization
   (E) precipitation

4. Which of the following statements characterize(s) the field of biology?
    I. Biology relates organic structures and activity to underlying chemical and physical activities.
   II. Biology relates organic structure and activity to their functions in and for organisms.
   III. Biology relates organic structure and activity to their evolutionary origin.

   (A) I only
   (B) II only
   (C) I and II only
   (D) II and III only
   (E) I, II, and III

5. The cyclotron is used to

   (A) measure radioactivity
   (B) measure the speed of the earth's rotation
   (C) split atoms
   (D) store radioactive energy
   (E) generate nuclear power

6. Fossils are *least* often found in

   (A) sedimentary rock
   (B) limestone
   (C) metamorphic rock
   (D) volcanic rock
   (E) sandstone

7. When small particles are added to a liquid, they can often be seen to be undergoing very rapid motion on the surface of the liquid. The explanation for this motion is best described as the

   (A) electrical interactions between the liquid and the suspended particles
   (B) molecular vibrations of the liquid causing collisions with the suspended particles
   (C) low density of the particles causing them to try to rise above the surface of the liquid
   (D) air currents above the liquid moving the particles
   (E) heat rising, causing the particles to move

8. Lamarck's ideas on evolution included which of the following?
   I. Organs which were not used, weakened and ultimately disappeared.
   II. Environment played no role in evolution.
   III. Acquired characteristics could be passed on to offspring.

   (A) All of the above
   (B) III only
   (C) II and III only
   (D) I and III only
   (E) I only

9. The most efficient absorber of rays given off by radioactive substances is

   (A) carbon 14
   (B) the Geiger counter
   (C) steel
   (D) uranium
   (E) lead

10. A person is more buoyant when swimming in salt water than in fresh water because

   (A) one keeps one's head out of salt water
   (B) salt coats the body with a floating membrane
   (C) salt water has greater tensile strength
   (D) salt water weighs more than an equal volume of fresh water
   (E) the body absorbs salt

11. Final cellular differentiation within a developing embryo is

    (A) determined by the physical and chemical environment surrounding the cell
    (B) not dependent upon the germ-layer
    (C) dependent upon the specific chromosomes the cell receives
    (D) controlled by the cytoplasm of the unfertilized egg
    (E) determined before gastrulation of the embryo

12. Of the following, the gas needed for burning is

    (A) carbon dioxide
    (B) oxygen
    (C) nitrogen
    (D) argon
    (E) hydrogen

13. Which of the following statements best describes the action of catalysts?

    (A) They alter the ratio of products.
    (B) They change the rate of reactions.
    (C) They change the ratio of products and the rate of reaction.
    (D) They change the products.
    (E) They change neither the products nor the rate of reaction.

14. Of the following, the most common metal found in the earth's crust is

    (A) iron
    (B) copper
    (C) silver
    (D) tin
    (E) aluminum

15. The air around us is composed mostly of

    (A) carbon
    (B) hydrogen
    (C) nitrogen
    (D) oxygen
    (E) ozone

16. Animals pass on traits to their offspring through which of the following units?

    (A) genes
    (B) proteins
    (C) plasmas
    (D) polysaccharides
    (E) corpuscles

17. One is most likely to feel the effects of static electricity on a

    (A) cold, damp day
    (B) cold, dry day
    (C) warm, humid day
    (D) warm, dry day
    (E) warm, damp day

18. An organism lacking chlorophyll but nevertheless able to manufacture food has been found among which of the following?

   (A) bacteria
   (B) viruses
   (C) phaeophytes
   (D) zoophytes
   (E) protozoa

19. Ferns, conifers, and flowering plants are classified as

   (A) bryophyta
   (B) spermatophyta
   (C) psilophyta
   (D) chlorophyta
   (E) tracheophyta

20. The number of degrees on the Fahrenheit thermometer between the freezing point and the boiling point of water is

   (A) 100
   (B) 180
   (C) 212
   (D) 273
   (E) 32

21. If other factors are compatible, a person who can most safely receive blood from any donor belongs to the basic blood type

   (A) O
   (B) A
   (C) B
   (D) AB
   (E) Rh

22. Of the following substances, the one that is non-magnetic is

   (A) iron
   (B) nickel
   (C) aluminum
   (D) cobalt
   (E) steel

23. The normal height of a mercury barometer at sea level is

   (A) 15 inches
   (B) 30 inches
   (C) 32 feet
   (D) 34 feet
   (E) 0 inches

24. Of the following phases of the moon, the invisible one is called

   (A) crescent
   (B) full moon
   (C) new moon

(D) waxing and waning
(E) dark side

25. The vitamin that helps coagulation of the blood is

(A) C
(B) D
(C) E
(D) K
(E) B₁

26. A tree common in parts of New York State that is native to Japan and *not* to the United States is the

(A) silver maple
(B) chestnut
(C) gingko
(D) tulip tree
(E) oak

27. One-celled animals belong to the group of living things known as

(A) protozoa
(B) porifera
(C) annelida
(D) arthropoda
(E) coelenterates

28. It is believed by scientists that worker bees indicate to their hive-mates the direction and distance of a supply of food by

(A) strokes of their antennae
(B) buzzing sounds
(C) an oriented dance in front of the hive
(D) all of the above
(E) none of the above

29. On the film in a camera, the lens forms an image that, by comparison with the original subject, is

(A) right-side up and reversed from left to right
(B) upside down and reversed from left to right
(C) right-side up and not reversed from left to right
(D) upside down and not reversed from left to right
(E) unchanged

30. The halving of the chromosome complement during meiotic division of the sex cells lends credence to the Darwinian theory of evolution because

(A) it prevents doubling the chromosome complement during fertilization
(B) it separates like chromosomes
(C) it provides a means of genetic variation
(D) sex cells differ
(E) mutations may be lost

31. Which of the following rocks can be dissolved with a weak acid?

    (A) sandstone
    (B) granite
    (C) gneiss
    (D) limestone
    (E) uranium

32. A circuit-breaker is used in many homes instead of a

    (A) switch
    (B) antenna
    (C) fire extinguisher
    (D) meter box
    (E) fuse

Stop

End of section. If you have any time left, go over your work in this section only. Do not work in any other section of the test.

MATHEMATICS

20 Minutes — 23 Questions

Directions: Select the correct answer to each of the following questions.

1. Which one of these quantities is the smallest?

    (A) $\frac{4}{5}$

    (B) $\frac{7}{9}$

    (C) .76

    (D) $\frac{5}{7}$

    (E) $\frac{9}{11}$

2. A typist uses lengthwise a sheet of paper 9 inches by 12 inches. She leaves a 1-inch margin on each side and a $1\frac{1}{2}$-inch margin on top and bottom. What fractional part of the page is used for typing?

    (A) $\frac{21}{22}$

    (B) $\frac{7}{12}$

    (C) $\frac{5}{9}$

    (D) $\frac{3}{4}$

    (E) $\frac{5}{12}$

3. If $820 + R + S - 610 = 342$, and if $R = 2S$, then $S =$

    (A) 44
    (B) 48
    (C) 132
    (D) 184
    (E) 192

4. An equilateral triangle 3 inches on a side is cut up into smaller equilateral triangles one inch on a side. What is the greatest number of such triangles that can be formed?

    (A) 3
    (B) 6
    (C) 9
    (D) 12
    (E) 15

5. What is the cost, in dollars, to carpet a room x yards long and y yards wide, if the carpet costs ten dollars per square foot?

   (A) xy
   (B) 5xy
   (C) 15xy
   (D) 30xy
   (E) 90xy

6. On a certain army post, 30% of the recruits are from New York State, and 10% of these are from New York City. What percentage of the recruits on the post are from New York City?

   (A) 3
   (B) .3
   (C) .03
   (D) 13
   (E) 20

7. $\frac{1}{6}$ of an audience consisted of boys and $\frac{1}{3}$ consisted of girls. What percentage of the audience consisted of children?

   (A) $66\frac{2}{3}$

   (B) 50

   (C) $37\frac{1}{2}$

   (D) 40

   (E) $33\frac{1}{3}$

8. There are just two ways in which 5 may be expressed as the sum of two different positive (non-zero) integers; namely 4 + 1 and 3 + 2. In how many ways may 9 be expressed as the sum of two different positive (non-zero) integers?

   (A) 3
   (B) 4
   (C) 5
   (D) 6
   (E) 7

9. A board 7 feet 9 inches long is divided into three equal parts. What is the length of each part?

   (A) 2 ft. 7 in.

   (B) 2 ft. $6\frac{1}{3}$ in.

   (C) 2 ft. $8\frac{1}{3}$ in.

   (D) 2 ft. 8 in.

   (E) 2 ft. 9 in.

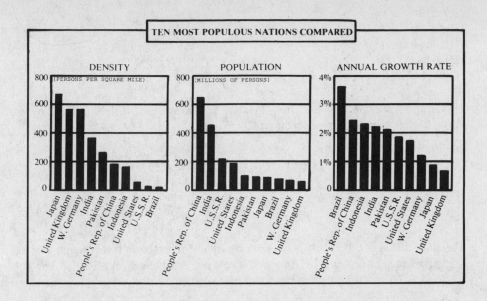

10. According to the graphs above, a comparison between the United States and the U.S.S.R. reveals that

(A) the United States will soon have the larger population
(B) the U.S.S.R.'s growth rate is lower
(C) the U.S.S.R. is more densely populated but has a smaller total population
(D) if both countries maintain the present rate of growth, the proportionate difference in population will remain about the same
(E) the majority of people in the United States live in cities, while most people in the U.S.S.R. live on farms.

11. A man drives 60 miles by car to his destination at an average speed of 40 miles per hour and makes the return trip at an average rate of 30 miles per hour. His average speed for the entire trip is

(A) 35 miles per hour
(B) 34 $^2/_7$ miles per hour
(C) 43⅓ miles per hour
(D) 20 miles per hour
(E) none of these

12. By the distributive property of multiplication over addition, which of the following is equivalent to 8×47?

(A) $8 \times 40 + 7$
(B) $8 \times 4 + 8 \times 7$
(C) $(8 \times 40) + (8 \times 7)$
(D) $8 + 40 \times 7$
(E) $(8 \times 40) \times 7$

13. Which of the following is equal to 3.14×10^6 ?

    (A) 314
    (B) 3,140
    (C) 31,400
    (D) 314,000
    (E) 3,140,000

14. If 2 and 54 are the first and fourth terms respectively of a geometric progression, the *second* and *third* terms are

    (A) 6, 18
    (B) 6, 8
    (C) 8, 24
    (D) 12, 36
    (E) 4, 16

15. The time difference between New York and San Francisco is three hours. For example, when it is 6 p.m. in California, it is 9 p.m. in New York. Thus, when it is 12 noon in New York, the time in San Francisco is

    (A) 8 A.M.
    (B) 9 A.M.
    (C) 2 P.M.
    (D) 3 P.M.
    (E) 5 P.M.

16. An illustration in a dictionary is labeled "Scale $\frac{1}{8}$." A measure of $1\frac{1}{2}$ inches in the illustration corresponds to a real measure of

    (A) $\frac{3}{16}$ inches

    (B) $\frac{3}{8}$ inches

    (C) $\frac{3}{8}$ foot

    (D) 2 feet

    (E) 1 foot

17. The sum of the first *ten* terms of the series 1, 3, 5 . . . is

    (A) 240
    (B) 19
    (C) 81
    (D) 100
    (E) 98

18. What is the area of a right triangle of which the hypotenuse is 5 inches and one of the legs is 3 inches?

    (A) 4 square inches

    (B) $7\frac{1}{2}$ square inches

    (C) 15 square inches

(D) 12 square inches

(E) 6 square inches

19. Four men working together full-time can dig a ditch in 42 days. They begin, but one man works only half-days. How long will it take to complete the job?

(A) 48 days
(B) 45 days
(C) 43 days
(D) 44 days
(E) 84 days

20. Barbara invests $2,400 in the Security National Bank at 5%. How much additional money must she invest at 8% so that the total annual income will be equal to 6% of her entire investment?

(A) $2,400
(B) $3,600
(C) $1,000
(D) $3,000
(E) $1,200

21. What is the numerical equivalent of the Roman number MDCCLXXVI?

(A) 15,276
(B) 4,274
(C) 1,226
(D) 1,346
(E) 1,776

Questions 22 and 23 refer to the graph below which depicts the precipitation and evaporation for City Λ.

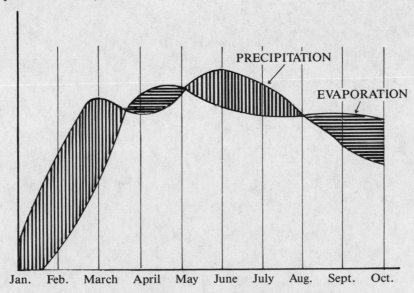

Legend: Water Surplus   Water Deficit

22. For how many months of the year did City A have a water surplus?

   (A) 4
   (B) 6
   (C) 8
   (D) 10
   (E) 5

23. During which of the following months were precipitation and evaporation in equilibrium?

   (A) January
   (B) April
   (C) August
   (D) September
   (E) December

Stop

End of section. If you have any time left, go over your work in this section only. Do not work in any other section of the test.

Answer Key
Section 2: General Knowledge

SOCIAL STUDIES

1. B	8. E	15. C	22. C	29. A
2. D	9. D	16. C	23. D	30. B
3. A	10. B	17. C	24. A	31. E
4. E	11. C	18. A	25. E	32. A
5. E	12. B	19. C	26. C	33. E
6. E	13. B	20. B	27. D	34. D
7. B	14. A	21. A	28. D	35. B

LITERATURE

1. D	6. E	11. B	16. B	21. D
2. C	7. C	12. B	17. C	22. D
3. C	8. D	13. A	18. D	23. E
4. E	9. E	14. E	19. C	24. C
5. D	10. D	15. D	20. B	25. A

FINE ARTS

1. D	5. C	9. D	13. E	17. E
2. C	6. E	10. B	14. C	18. C
3. B	7. E	11. A	15. E	19. E
4. B	8. C	12. A	16. E	20. E

SCIENCE

1. E	8. D	15. C	22. C	29. B
2. C	9. E	16. A	23. B	30. C
3. D	10. D	17. B	24. C	31. D
4. E	11. A	18. A	25. D	32. E
5. C	12. B	19. E	26. C	
6. C	13. B	20. B	27. A	
7. B	14. E	21. D	28. D	

MATHEMATICS

1. D	6. A	11. B	16. E	21. E
2. B	7. B	12. C	17. D	22. E
3. A	8. B	13. E	18. E	23. C
4. C	9. A	14. A	19. A	
5. E	10. D	15. B	20. E	

Answer Sheet
Listening Ability

Tear out this sheet. Have it ready to use with the Answer Options on page 115.

1. LISTENING TO SINGLE SENTENCES

1 Ⓐ Ⓑ Ⓒ Ⓓ   6 Ⓐ Ⓑ Ⓒ Ⓓ   11 Ⓐ Ⓑ Ⓒ Ⓓ

2 Ⓐ Ⓑ Ⓒ Ⓓ   7 Ⓐ Ⓑ Ⓒ Ⓓ   12 Ⓐ Ⓑ Ⓒ Ⓓ

3 Ⓐ Ⓑ Ⓒ Ⓓ   8 Ⓐ Ⓑ Ⓒ Ⓓ   13 Ⓐ Ⓑ Ⓒ Ⓓ

4 Ⓐ Ⓑ Ⓒ Ⓓ   9 Ⓐ Ⓑ Ⓒ Ⓓ   14 Ⓐ Ⓑ Ⓒ Ⓓ

5 Ⓐ Ⓑ Ⓒ Ⓓ   10 Ⓐ Ⓑ Ⓒ Ⓓ   15 Ⓐ Ⓑ Ⓒ Ⓓ

2. LISTENING TO CONVERSATIONS

Conversation 1

1 Ⓐ Ⓑ Ⓒ Ⓓ   2 Ⓐ Ⓑ Ⓒ Ⓓ

Conversation 2

1 Ⓐ Ⓑ Ⓒ Ⓓ   2 Ⓐ Ⓑ Ⓒ Ⓓ

Conversation 3

1 Ⓐ Ⓑ Ⓒ Ⓓ

2 Ⓐ Ⓑ Ⓒ Ⓓ

3 Ⓐ Ⓑ Ⓒ Ⓓ

3. LISTENING TO BRIEF PASSAGES

Passage 1

1 Ⓐ Ⓑ Ⓒ Ⓓ   2 Ⓐ Ⓑ Ⓒ Ⓓ

Passage 2

1 Ⓐ Ⓑ Ⓒ Ⓓ   2 Ⓐ Ⓑ Ⓒ Ⓓ

Diagnostic Core Battery I
Section 3: Communication Skills

1 Hour 50 Minutes — 95 Questions

Listening Ability

20 Minutes — 26 Questions

Script (Detach for Speaker)
Directions: To simulate the actual NTE Listening Ability test, you need a second person (the speaker) to assist you. Detach the pages of this script for the speaker and have the speaker read you the stimulus material (the entire script). When the conversations are read, the speaker should indicate to you which person is speaking.

You should have both Question and Answer Sheets in front of you. Go through the entire Listening Ability test without repeating anything and without pausing. Answer options begin on page 115.

1. LISTENING TO SINGLE SENTENCES

(Speaker should read and pause as noted in script.)

1. *Read*
   Is that porcelain lamp imported?
   > *Pause for answer*

2. *Read*
   Did he tell you about Mary's operation?
   > *Pause for answer*

3. *Read*
   Because of Henry's careful planning, everything was done on time.
   > *Pause for answer*

4. *Read*
   What was the source of the President's information on the economy?
   > *Pause for answer*

5. *Read*

   There was no vaccine available, and the entire population was wiped out by the disease.

   Pause for answer

6. *Read*

   The portion of the budget set aside for research should be even more generous than last year's.

   Pause for answer

7. *Read*

   There's to be greater emphasis on field work this semester, which will be reflected in the way grades are calculated.

   Pause for answer

8. *Read*

   No one expected the public to respond so generously with offers of help for the victims.

   Pause for answer

9. *Read*

   Has your family always been interested in the Orient?

   Pause for answer

10. *Read*

    Cooking has become my only enjoyable hobby.

    Pause for answer

11. *Read*

    Have you made your vacation plans yet?

    Pause for answer

12. *Read*

    Most of the people at the meeting disagreed with the proposal.

    Pause for answer

13. *Read*

    The number of students in science subjects increased this year by 25%, putting an unanticipated strain on classroom and laboratory space.

    Pause for answer

14. *Read*

    Did you do the interior decoration yourself?

    Pause for answer

15. *Read*

    Teachers' strikes in recent years have turned some people against them.

    Pause for answer

2. LISTENING TO CONVERSATIONS

(Speaker should read each entire conversation and indicate who is speaking. Pause and ask questions as indicated in script.)

Conversation 1
Read
Woman: I'm afraid we're going to have to call in outside help on the matter.
Man: Has anyone on the staff had legal experience?
Woman: Mr. Anthony has worked with Legal Aid, but since he's on the faculty he would be accused of prejudice.
Man: You're right. We need an independent adviser to make sure that students' rights are seen to be protected.
Pause 5 seconds, then ask
1. Help from outside the school is needed because
Pause for answer, then ask
2. The man feels that, in a conflict involving students,

Conversation 2
Read
Man: The weather forecast is for scattered showers. I wonder if we should cancel the game?
Woman: Moving it up one or two days would be almost impossible. Only the small gym is ready for use, and that would only hold half the number who have already bought tickets.
Man: But if we postpone it for a couple of weeks, the other gym will be ready if we need it—and the weather is sure to improve!
Pause 5 seconds, then ask
1. When is the sports match scheduled for?
Pause for answer, then ask
2. The man favors which plan?

Conversation 3
Read
Woman: Can you tell me which subway line goes to the Opera House?
Man: From here, you'll have to take the RR, and change to the number 3 at Times Square.
Woman: Will I have to pay an extra fare?
Man: No, a single token entitles you to unlimited transfers.
Pause 5 seconds, then ask
1. Which subway line actually goes to the Opera House?
Pause for answer, then ask
2. Where will the woman have to change trains?
Pause for answer, then ask
3. Will the woman be paying more than one fare?

3. LISTENING TO BRIEF PASSAGES

(Speaker should read each passage. Pause and ask questions as indicated.)

Passage 1
Read

The notion that children have rights, particularly the right to happiness, is fairly recent, in part because the concept of childhood itself is so recent. In medieval society, there was no childhood. The concept of childhood as a separate stage of life, as a psychological and social as well as biological phenomenon, simply did not exist. Children moved directly from infancy into adulthood.

Pause 5 seconds, then ask

1. According to the speaker, how did medieval society regard the process of human development?

Pause for answer, then ask

2. How does the speaker describe children's rights?

Passage 2
Read

Twenty years ago the corporate community's interest in women — expressed in their philanthropic programs — derived from a humane concern for women who had remained at home to raise their children and wanted a useful role in society in the second half of their lives. During the past ten years, there has been a growing recognition — expressed in the form of corporate social responsibility — of the need to provide career opportunities for women in business. Today many companies have taken a further step; they have begun to realize that it is in their self-interest — that it will increase their profits — to assimilate women at all levels.

Pause 5 seconds, and then ask

1. According to the speaker, how could most women working in corporate positions be described twenty years ago?

Pause for answer, then ask

2. According to the speaker, why are companies today interested in hiring women?

Answer Options for Listening Ability Questions

These are the answer options for the Listening Ability test. On the NTE they will be printed in your question booklet. Keep them in front of you as you listen, and when you hear a basis for selecting an answer, fill in the answer blank corresponding to that answer on your Answer Sheet. Be certain you fill in the answer space corresponding to the question number you are answering.

1. LISTENING TO SINGLE SENTENCES

Select the option most consistent with the statement read by the speaker.

1. (A) My father gave it to me.
   (B) It's a copy of a Japanese original, but made in this country.
   (C) It's my favorite color—dark red.
   (D) I have another just like it.

2. (A) She's one of my closest friends.
   (B) I heard about it from her sister.
   (C) I hate going to hospitals.
   (D) Henry had a similar problem.

3. (A) Henry's scheduling proved both realistic and efficient.
   (B) A few important things had to be left undone, however.
   (C) Knowledge of the territory was vital.
   (D) People were upset at his constant nagging.

4. (A) He's always had a keen interest in domestic affairs.
   (B) His Cabinet ministers prepare lengthy reports as well as statistical abstracts for him.
   (C) With the economy like it is now, something must be done soon.
   (D) Many experts are questioning his accuracy.

5. (A) Specialists knew how to combat the disease, but supplies were unavailable.
   (B) They faced the disaster with unusual courage.
   (C) In modern times, such disasters are rare.
   (D) We have become overly dependent on medical technology.

6. (A) Research is not one of the firm's top priorities.
   (B) Every department must be prepared to make cuts.
   (C) Recent support for research has been encouraging.

(D) There's no way to justify expenditures on the basis of quick returns.

7. (A) In the past, students have shown little interest in field work.
    (B) Theoretical work should always be supplemented by applications.
    (C) Response to such programs in the past has been encouraging.
    (D) Excellent field work should have the effect of raising the grades.

8. (A) Many had been injured in the disaster.
    (B) In times of economic hardship, it had been thought that few people would be willing to offer assistance.
    (C) Human nature seems to have a basic need to help those less fortunate.
    (D) Help from other sources proved substantial as well.

9. (A) My brother had a wonderful time in Japan.
    (B) We ought to know more about that part of the world.
    (C) Because of the difficult languages involved, few of us read Asian newspapers.
    (D) A grandfather's visit to Bangkok at the turn of the century started it all.

10. (A) Everyone should have a hobby involving practical skills.
    (B) Other hobbies have lost their interest for me.
    (C) I have learned to enjoy making things for other people.
    (D) Eating a properly balanced diet is most important.

11. (A) It's becoming too expensive to travel.
    (B) There's no way of knowing what the weather will be like.
    (C) I'm waiting to find out the exact dates I have free before planning.
    (D) Last year we went to the mountains north of here.

12. (A) The committee had worked long and hard on their recommendations.
    (B) People are often reluctant to accept change, even when needed.
    (C) Possibly they felt the proposal was based on insufficient data.
    (D) Everything else on the agenda was approved.

13. (A) This is in line with increases across the country.
    (B) Other departments are experiencing similar jumps.
    (C) The faculty are concerned about this sudden increase.
    (D) The rise was not expected.

14. (A) My wife has a real flair for decorating, and she did all the work.
    (B) The color scheme was taken from an antique tapestry.
    (C) The whole job was done in a few days.

(D) When we moved in, the apartment had been vacant for years.

15. (A) They were all resolved satisfactorily, however.
    (B) Teachers are entitled to the same rights as other employees.
    (C) Some members of the general population feel that teachers have a soft enough life as it is.
    (D) Established complaint procedures proved inadequate.

2. LISTENING TO CONVERSATIONS

Conversation 1

1. (A) Someone already on the staff would seem to be biased.
   (B) The case is attracting public attention.
   (C) It's too delicate a matter for an amateur to tackle.
   (D) Rules prevent staff from taking on additional paid services.

2. (A) Matters are best handled by teachers who know the parties well.
   (B) Matters should be handled confidentially, to prevent embarrassment.
   (C) An outside professional would prove that the authorities are acting fairly.
   (D) Faculty members should only play a behind-the-scenes role.

Conversation 2

1. (A) One or two days from now.
   (B) The same day.
   (C) A month away.
   (D) In a nearby school district.

2. (A) Going ahead with the game as scheduled.
   (B) Cancelling the game and refunding the ticket money.
   (C) Moving the game into the small gym.
   (D) Postponing it for at least two weeks.

Conversation 3

1. (A) The RR
   (B) The number 3
   (C) There is no line which goes directly to the Opera House.
   (D) Can't tell from the conversation.

2. (A) Union Square
   (B) Times Square
   (C) At the Opera House
   (D) Grand Central Station

3. (A) She will if she transfers more than once.
   (B) No, since unlimited transfers are allowed.
   (C) Each separate trip will require an additional fare.
   (D) Extra fares will be collected at Times Square.

3. LISTENING TO BRIEF PASSAGES

Passage 1

1. (A) It classified childhood as a separate biological stage.
   (B) Children and infants were kept separate until adolescence.
   (C) Adults looked upon children as psychologically immature.
   (D) It provided no transition between infancy and adulthood.

2. (A) It is a social concept with a long history.
   (B) It is fairly recent.
   (C) It was common in medieval society and universally accepted
   (D) It is dependent on psychological and biological processes
       that are even now incompletely understood.

Passage 2

1. (A) They were lacking in aggressiveness and ambition.
   (B) They were working against their wills to support families.
   (C) They were mothers who had raised thier children and wanted to spend the rest
       of their life usefully.
   (D) They were taking advantage of charity programs reluctantly offered by the
       companies.

2. (A) Women have broken down sexual discrimination by twenty years of crusading.
   (B) They realize that it is in their interest financially to hire women at all levels.
   (C) The role of philanthropic programs has grown enormously over the last twenty
       years.
   (D) Women already working in the companies are now in a position to hire other
       women.

Stop

End of section. If you have any time left, go over your work in this section only. Do
not work in any other section of the test.

Answer Key
Listening Ability

1. LISTENING TO SINGLE SENTENCES

1. B	6. C	11. C
2. B	7. D	12. C
3. A	8. C	13. D
4. B	9. D	14. A
5. A	10. B	15. C

2. LISTENING TO CONVERSATIONS

Conversation 1:
1. A
2. C

Conversation 2:
1. B
2. D

Conversation 3:
1. B
2. B
3. B

3. LISTENING TO BRIEF PASSAGES

Passage 1
1. D
2. B

Passage 2
1. C
2. B

Answer Sheet
READING ABILITY

1 Ⓐ Ⓑ Ⓒ Ⓓ Ⓔ   6 Ⓐ Ⓑ Ⓒ Ⓓ Ⓔ   11 Ⓐ Ⓑ Ⓒ Ⓓ Ⓔ   16 Ⓐ Ⓑ Ⓒ Ⓓ Ⓔ   21 Ⓐ Ⓑ Ⓒ Ⓓ Ⓔ

2 Ⓐ Ⓑ Ⓒ Ⓓ Ⓔ   7 Ⓐ Ⓑ Ⓒ Ⓓ Ⓔ   12 Ⓐ Ⓑ Ⓒ Ⓓ Ⓔ   17 Ⓐ Ⓑ Ⓒ Ⓓ Ⓔ   22 Ⓐ Ⓑ Ⓒ Ⓓ Ⓔ

3 Ⓐ Ⓑ Ⓒ Ⓓ Ⓔ   8 Ⓐ Ⓑ Ⓒ Ⓓ Ⓔ   13 Ⓐ Ⓑ Ⓒ Ⓓ Ⓔ   18 Ⓐ Ⓑ Ⓒ Ⓓ Ⓔ   23 Ⓐ Ⓑ Ⓒ Ⓓ Ⓔ

4 Ⓐ Ⓑ Ⓒ Ⓓ Ⓔ   9 Ⓐ Ⓑ Ⓒ Ⓓ Ⓔ   14 Ⓐ Ⓑ Ⓒ Ⓓ Ⓔ   19 Ⓐ Ⓑ Ⓒ Ⓓ Ⓔ

5 Ⓐ Ⓑ Ⓒ Ⓓ Ⓔ   10 Ⓐ Ⓑ Ⓒ Ⓓ Ⓔ   15 Ⓐ Ⓑ Ⓒ Ⓓ Ⓔ   20 Ⓐ Ⓑ Ⓒ Ⓓ Ⓔ

Diagnostic Core Battery I
Section 3: Communication Skills

Reading Ability

50 Minutes — 23 Questions

Directions: Each of the following passages is followed by one or more questions. The questions following each passage refer to that passage only, and are to be answered using only the information presented in the passage. If you prefer, you may read the questions before reading the passage, or you may read the passage, read the questions, re-read the passage, and then answer the questions. Use these practice passages to decide on the style which is most efficient for you.

There is only one answer to each question. In some instances more than one answer may seem to be reasonable; thus, you should select the answer which is most consistent with the material presented in the passage.

Questions 1 and 2 refer to the following passage.

While Alexander Graham Bell was trying to develop the telephone during the 1860's, a newspaper editor wrote that "Well-informed people know that it is impossible to transmit the voice over wires and that, were it possible to do so, the thing would be of no practical value." Within ten years after this statement was printed, Bell had developed and marketed the telephone, and the nature of communication had changed dramatically.

1. The main idea expressed in this statement is that
   (A) newspaper editors typically have little understanding of electronics
   (B) the telephone has greatly influenced the way we live
   (C) people have a tendency to deny the novel possibilities of the future
   (D) technological advances generally have widespread practical application
   (E) educated people of the nineteenth century were narrow-minded

2. The author of this passage would be most likely to agree with which of the following statements?

   (A) We need to re-examine the role of the press in keeping the public well-informed.
   (B) Change is a dynamic and inevitable force which shapes the future.
   (C) Research in communications should be supported by public funds.
   (D) The most important technological developments affecting our lives today took place in the nineteenth century.

(E) People are generally only interested in those scientific discoveries that help them directly.

Questions 3 and 4 refer to the following passage.

As societies become literate, both precedent and the opinions of authority begin to be written down. This has the advantage for posterity of more permanently, and hopefully more accurately, preserving the actions taken and their consequence. It also makes the record available on a far wider scale than before. With a written record, a person interested in a problem can now call on all of the authorities of the past, and all of the precedents of the past which have been recorded, before acting in his own situation.

3. The author suggests that an important step in understanding what happens when an action is taken, came when

(A) precedent was understood
(B) written records became available
(C) it became possible to talk to famous authorities
(D) posterity became interested in literacy rates
(E) people understood that actions have consequences

4. Which of the following statements is consistent with the view expressed in this passage?

(A) Precedent is the most important way to solve problems.
(B) Literate societies solve problems the same way as preliterate societies.
(C) Authority is more important than precedent in solving problems.
(D) Preliterate societies don't understand the consequences of actions.
(E) Writing down a precedent converts it to an authority.

Questions 5 and 6 refer to the following passage.

Rivalry gives zest to work that is otherwise uninteresting. If we were to spend the day stamping cards as rapidly as possible, we would undoubtedly find that the introduction of some scheme of rivalry relieves some of the boredom. There would be satisfaction on those occasions when we won the contest, and a minor emotional thrill when we lost. In school, rivalry may be used to enliven the more routine activities. Drill periods in arithmetic, which easily sink to the level of drudgery, may be enlivened by the introduction of individual or group rivalry.

5. If people are involved in a dull task, the author believes that they would

(A) be satisfied if rewarded
(B) find it emotionally difficult
(C) use competition to add interest
(D) use arithmetic to liven up the task
(E) end the day as rapidly as possible

6. What would the author advise the teacher who is planning to use drill to increase vocabulary?

(A) Don't spend the entire day doing it.
(B) Alternate it with drill in arithmetic.
(C) Be certain the children understand the routine.
(D) Divide the children into teams.
(E) Correct errors, but don't count scores.

Questions 7 and 8 refer to the following passage.

Britain had not fought a war of consequence in several decades, since the war in Suez, when they decided to contest the Argentinean occupation of the Falkland Islands. They were successful in this war, beating the Argentinean army and navy in less than a month. The price Britain paid was enormous, with more than 250 dead, nearly 1,000 more wounded, and nearly $1.5 billion dollars' worth of materials and warships lost in combat.

7. How could the writer's attitude toward Britain's action be summed up?

(A) The victory was won at a considerable expense of life and supplies.
(B) Britain's involvement was justified and long overdue.
(C) In their first military confrontation since Suez, the British showed themselves to be still a strong power.
(D) Britain should have relied on diplomacy to resolve the problem.
(E) Britain should have fought more wars since Suez.

8. Where would the passage be *least* likely to appear?

(A) a history of military confrontations in 1982
(B) a history of the Falkland Islands
(C) a history of the Suez
(D) a pacifist pamphlet
(E) a history of British military actions

Questions 9 and 10 refer to the following passage.

American law, descending from the English common law, continued the basic orientation to male power and male control until the nineteenth century. Then, within the framework of other social movements, the law was modified to permit married women the same property rights as those extended to single women in eighteenth-century England. The first American state to institute the reform was Mississippi, in 1839, followed by Maine, in 1844. Once begun, a series of legal reforms gradually took effect, giving a married woman the right to enter into contracts, to control the expenditure of her own earnings, to bring suit in her own name, to establish a separate domicile (whether or not her husband agreed), and to make her own will.

9. From the passage, one can assume that in 1790 a woman living in London, and her cousin living in New York,

(A) had full equality with men under the law
(B) had different rights, with the New Yorker enjoying more rights
(C) had few property rights

    (D) had different rights, with the woman in London able to hold property
    (E) had both signed marriage contracts giving their husbands control

10. In the United States, Mississippi innovated the notion that

    (A) married women should have property rights
    (B) a woman had the right to freely choose a husband
    (C) single women could hold jobs and sign contracts
    (D) women could live alone
    (E) single women had property rights similar to those of married women

Questions 11 and 12 refer to the following passage.

Students who now reside in New York State, but who have had an address out of the state, must submit proof of New York State residence to the Registrar's Office. Proof can be processed only by mail. If, at the time of registration, proof of New York State residence has not been approved, students must pay the out-of-state rates; a refund application may be made to the Bursar's Office if acceptable proof is submitted and is subsequently approved during the term by the Registrar's Office.

11. A student only obtains proof of New York State residence after having registered and paid the out-of-state fee. If he wishes a refund, he should

    (A) go in person to the Registrar's Office, bringing his proof
    (B) bring his proof of residence to the Bursar's Office
    (C) mail his proof of residence to the Registrar's Office
    (D) ask the registrar to provide him with proof of registration
    (E) mail in his transcript

12. The implication in this passage is that, compared to residents, those from out of the state

    (A) are not welcome at this college
    (B) are given a discount if they can prove residence
    (C) must prove where they live with the Registrar's Office
    (D) are asked to pay higher rates
    (E) cannot take a full program load

Questions 13 and 14 refer to the following passage.

In describing the nature of learning experiences, it is difficult to choose terminology that is not subject to misuse in interpreting learning activities. Such is the case in using the terms direct and vicarious to designate types of learning activity. The term direct experience refers to learning activity that involves first-hand experience with the elements concerned in the learning product or outcome to be acquired. It includes what is commonly referred to as perceptual learning, but it is broader than that, since it includes experience with other relationships as well as with concrete things. Vicarious experience is experience through which we acquire the learning product or outcome without first-hand or direct experience with the relationships involved.

13. A child who learns that her teacher teases children who give the wrong answer, by watching what happens when her classmates volunteer in class, has learned through what this author calls

(A) direct experience
(B) vicarious experience
(C) perceptual experience
(D) first-hand experience
(E) concrete experience

14. The author of this statement would probably agree that

(A) there is some confusion between direct and vicarious learning
(B) learning is an area with clear distinctions in terminology
(C) while terms may vary, outcomes are clearly predictable
(D) perceptual learning includes both direct and vicarious elements
(E) concrete learning is the most general term available to teachers

Questions 15 and 16 refer to the following passage.

Mental hygienists approve of punishment only when it is used as one means of removing a tendency to unsocial behavior. Punishment must be seen not as a separate entity, but as part of the educative process. The specific offense becomes secondary as the teacher adjusts the nature and the degree of the punishment to the child. Considerations of retribution are, of course, irrelevant. Viewing punishment as a corrective measure reveals the weakness of those class codes which define in advance the penalty for such breaches as doing homework carelessly, coming in late, or being insolent. Even in punishment, the teacher is primarily a teacher and a leader, not a policeman and a magistrate. To make the punishment fit the crime may be satisfactory for Gilbert and Sullivan; the school, however, should make the punishment fit the "criminal" so well that he ceases to be a "criminal."

15. With which of the following statements would the author of this passage most likely agree?

(A) Schools should teach Gilbert and Sullivan.
(B) In considering punishment, teachers must primarily consider what the child did wrong.
(C) The teacher is not a policeman, and punishment is not education.
(D) Appropriate punishment seeks to relate the child, the deed, and the future.
(E) Every teacher should make clear the punishment for the common offenses.

16. If two children came to class without their homework, what advice would this author give to the teacher in terms of "punishing" the children?

(A) Treat them both the same, no matter what you do.
(B) Follow the class code as to what the punishment is for not having homework.
(C) Consider each case separately, depending on the child's past record.
(D) First analyze your own feelings, so you can decide how severe the punishment should be.
(E) Refer the children to the Principal, who should serve as school "magistrate."

Questions 17, 18, and 19 refer to the passage below.

Parental participation, and close and continuing interactions between parent and child, remain important when the process of the child's formal education begins, particularly because now, for the first time, the child will undergo formative experiences outside the family circle and thus, beyond parental supervision and control. The present-day trend toward greater parental and community involvement in the administration and operation of the public schools is long overdue—and even in those cases where parents band together to oppose an educational innovation, it is an indication that the classroom can neither be isolated from nor irrelevant to wider social concerns. Parents should, of course, know who is teaching their child, and how and what he is being taught; and by keeping the lines of communication open with the child and with his teacher, parents can and should keep a close watch on the child's progress throughout his school years. But apart from these broad and commonsense concerns, parents should be no less insistent that the school complement and reinforce—not contradict—the free and full development of the child as a unique and individual human being, whatever his shape, color, or size, and whatever his sex.

17. Which of the following educational practices would this author urge parents to oppose?

   I. Separate physical education classes for girls and boys
  II. Individualized reading programs
 III. Banning books which are considered racist or sexist in content.

  (A) I, II, and III
  (B) II and III
  (C) I and III
  (D) I only
  (E) III only

18. Which of the following implications follows from this passage?

  (A) The school has the responsibility to determine what takes place in the classroom.
  (B) Parent and community involvement has set back the advance of educational innovation.
  (C) Parents should participate in recruiting and hiring teachers.
  (D) Every child is entitled to the same educational program as every other child.
  (E) The school can make childrearing difficult when it teaches values which differ from those taught in the family.

19. What is the author's view of parent participation in education?

   I. It is a long-standing American tradition.
  II. The schools would be better had it increased many years ago.
 III. It is positive, but can be dangerous if uncontrolled.

  (A) I only
  (B) II only
  (C) III only
  (D) I and II
  (E) I and III

Questions 20, 21, 22, and 23 refer to the following passage.

If experimentation is defined as involving some new and untried element, or condition, then experimentation involves the evaluation of the effects of this condition or element. The condition or element being evaluated is referred to as the independent variable in the experiment, while the criteria by which it is to be evaluated are referred to as the dependent variables. Ideally, an experiment is so designed that there is a direct relationship between the independent and dependent variables—direct in the sense that it is reasonable to believe that whatever differences exist on the dependent variables after the experiment can be attributed to the independent variable. In most educational research this ideal design is not realizable, for other variables come between the independent and dependent variables. These other variables, referred to as intervening variables, can, in the simplest sense, be defined as all conditions which impede, attributing all differences in dependent variables to the independent variable. Note that this definition does not require that the independent variables necessarily precede the intervening variables in time. A difference in intelligence between two groups being compared in a learning experiment would make intelligence an intervening variable, as it is defined here. Why? Because that initial difference in intelligence would impede attributing final differences on the dependent measures to the different learning processes studied.

20. In an experiment to determine if different class sizes will have an impact of reading scores, the variable "class size" is

    (A) the ideal design
    (B) the intervening variable
    (C) the dependent variable
    (D) the independent variable
    (E) not determinable from the information given

21. If, after an experiment, the researcher discovers that there are no differences on the dependent variable, he or she can conclude that

    (A) differences on the independent variable were not significant
    (B) the intervening variables were extremely powerful
    (C) differences in intelligence must have existed
    (D) the independent variables did not precede the dependent variables in time
    (E) the wrong criteria were chosen

22. With which of the following statements would this author probably agree?

    (A) Sound experimentation requires a clear identification of the possible intervening variables.
    (B) Good educational experiments follow the ideal design.
    (C) All groups must be equated for differences in intelligence.
    (D) Learning processes are the most important area for educational experimentation.
    (E) In sensible experiments there is a sequence in time of independent variables, intervening variables, and dependent variables.

23. According to this author, when an experimenter uses the variable "intelligence" in an educational experiment, that variable

    (A) is an intervening variable
    (B) is too vague and ambiguous to be useful
    (C) could be any of the three kinds of variable
    (D) should be an independent variable in an ideal design
    (E) will impede understanding the results

Answer Key
Reading Ability

1.	C	13.	B
2.	B	14.	A
3.	B	15.	D
4.	A	16.	C
5.	C	17.	C
6.	D	18.	E
7.	A	19.	B
8.	C	20.	D
9.	C	21.	A
10.	A	22.	A
11.	B	23.	C
12.	D		

Answer Sheet
Writing Ability

ENGLISH USAGE

1 Ⓐ Ⓑ Ⓒ Ⓓ Ⓔ   5 Ⓐ Ⓑ Ⓒ Ⓓ Ⓔ   9 Ⓐ Ⓑ Ⓒ Ⓓ Ⓔ   13 Ⓐ Ⓑ Ⓒ Ⓓ Ⓔ   17 Ⓐ Ⓑ Ⓒ Ⓓ Ⓔ

2 Ⓐ Ⓑ Ⓒ Ⓓ Ⓔ   6 Ⓐ Ⓑ Ⓒ Ⓓ Ⓔ   10 Ⓐ Ⓑ Ⓒ Ⓓ Ⓔ   14 Ⓐ Ⓑ Ⓒ Ⓓ Ⓔ   18 Ⓐ Ⓑ Ⓒ Ⓓ Ⓔ

3 Ⓐ Ⓑ Ⓒ Ⓓ Ⓔ   7 Ⓐ Ⓑ Ⓒ Ⓓ Ⓔ   11 Ⓐ Ⓑ Ⓒ Ⓓ Ⓔ   15 Ⓐ Ⓑ Ⓒ Ⓓ Ⓔ   19 Ⓐ Ⓑ Ⓒ Ⓓ Ⓔ

4 Ⓐ Ⓑ Ⓒ Ⓓ Ⓔ   8 Ⓐ Ⓑ Ⓒ Ⓓ Ⓔ   12 Ⓐ Ⓑ Ⓒ Ⓓ Ⓔ   16 Ⓐ Ⓑ Ⓒ Ⓓ Ⓔ   20 Ⓐ Ⓑ Ⓒ Ⓓ Ⓔ

SENTENCE CORRECTION

1 Ⓐ Ⓑ Ⓒ Ⓓ Ⓔ   6 Ⓐ Ⓑ Ⓒ Ⓓ Ⓔ   11 Ⓐ Ⓑ Ⓒ Ⓓ Ⓔ   16 Ⓐ Ⓑ Ⓒ Ⓓ Ⓔ   21 Ⓐ Ⓑ Ⓒ Ⓓ Ⓔ

2 Ⓐ Ⓑ Ⓒ Ⓓ Ⓔ   7 Ⓐ Ⓑ Ⓒ Ⓓ Ⓔ   12 Ⓐ Ⓑ Ⓒ Ⓓ Ⓔ   17 Ⓐ Ⓑ Ⓒ Ⓓ Ⓔ   22 Ⓐ Ⓑ Ⓒ Ⓓ Ⓔ

3 Ⓐ Ⓑ Ⓒ Ⓓ Ⓔ   8 Ⓐ Ⓑ Ⓒ Ⓓ Ⓔ   13 Ⓐ Ⓑ Ⓒ Ⓓ Ⓔ   18 Ⓐ Ⓑ Ⓒ Ⓓ Ⓔ   23 Ⓐ Ⓑ Ⓒ Ⓓ Ⓔ

4 Ⓐ Ⓑ Ⓒ Ⓓ Ⓔ   9 Ⓐ Ⓑ Ⓒ Ⓓ Ⓔ   14 Ⓐ Ⓑ Ⓒ Ⓓ Ⓔ   19 Ⓐ Ⓑ Ⓒ Ⓓ Ⓔ   24 Ⓐ Ⓑ Ⓒ Ⓓ Ⓔ

5 Ⓐ Ⓑ Ⓒ Ⓓ Ⓔ   10 Ⓐ Ⓑ Ⓒ Ⓓ Ⓔ   15 Ⓐ Ⓑ Ⓒ Ⓓ Ⓔ   20 Ⓐ Ⓑ Ⓒ Ⓓ Ⓔ   25 Ⓐ Ⓑ Ⓒ Ⓓ Ⓔ

Diagnostic Core Battery I
Section 3: Comunication Skills
Writing Ability

40 Minutes — 45 Questions

ENGLISH USAGE

20 Minutes — 20 Questions

Directions: The sentences below contain errors in grammar, usage, word choice, and idiom. Parts of each sentence are underlined and lettered. Decide which underlined part contains the error and mark its letter on your answer sheet. If the sentence is correct as it stands, mark (E) on your answer sheet. No sentence contains more than one error.

1. Many themes considered sacrilegious in the nineteenth century are treated
   A   B
   casually on today's stage. No error.
   C   D   E

2. The color of his eyes are brown. No error.
   A   B   C   D   E

3. All of my experience as a reporter of sports events indicate that the
                                                        A
   San Francisco Giants cannot possibly lose the pennant. No error.
   B   C   D   E

4. We need further information before we can accede to your request. No error.
       A   B   C   D   E

5. Just between you and I, these theories won't work. No error.
   A   B   C   D   E

6. If you would have gone into the hall, you would have met your friends.
   A   B   C   D
   No error.
   E

7. The Confederate Army retreated during the winter in order to conserve their
       A   B   C   D
   strength. No error.
            E

133

8. Let's keep this strictly between you and me. No error.
      A   B   C   D   E

9. In this type of problem, the total of all the items are always a positive
        A   B   C D
   number. No error.
            E

10. I abhor their tactics while applauding their goals. No error.
      A   B   C   D   E

11. His clothing laid on the floor until his mother picked it up. No error.
         A   B   C   D   E

12. When the coach makes the decision as to which of the two boys will play,
           A   B
    you may be sure that he will choose the best one. No error.
                      C   D   E

13. He would have been more successful if he would have had the training all of
          A   B   C
    us received. No error.
      D   E

14. Mr. Martin, together with all the members of his family, are having a
       A   B
    good time in Europe. No error.
     C   D   E

15. This technique may be usable in your business if you can adopt it to your
         A   B   C
    particular situation. No error.
      D   E

16. He had a chance to invest wisely, establish his position, and displaying his
                   A   B   C
    ability as an executive. No error.
       D   E

17. Inspecting Robert's report card, his mother noted that he had received high
      A   B   C
    ratings in Latin and history. No error.
            D   E

18. When one buys tickets in advance, there is no guarantee that you will be free
                  A   B
    to attend the play on the night of the performance. No error.
     C   D   E

19. His brother, the captain of the squad scored many points. No error.
      A   B   C   D   E

20. People who are too credulous are likely to be deceived by unscrupulous
                 A   B   C   D

individuals. No error.
           E

Stop

End of section. If you have any time left, go over your work in this section only. Do not work in any other section of the test.

SENTENCE CORRECTION

20 Minutes—25 Questions

Directions: The sentences below contain problems in grammar, sentence construction, word choice, and punctuation. Part or all of each sentence is underlined. Select the lettered answer that contains the best version of the underlined section. Answer (A) always repeats the original underlined section exactly. If the sentence is correct as it stands, select (A).

1. Crossing the bridge, a glimpse of the islands was caught.

   (A) a glimpse of the islands was caught.
   (B) a glimpse of the islands were caught.
   (C) we caught a glimpse of the islands.
   (D) the islands were caught a glimpse of.
   (E) we caught a glimpse of the islands' view.

2. This book has been laying here for weeks.

   (A) laying here for weeks.
   (B) laying here weeks.
   (C) laying down here weeks.
   (D) lieing here for weeks.
   (E) lying here for weeks.

3. When my brother will come home, I'll tell him you called.

   (A) will come home,
   (B) will come home
   (C) will have come home,
   (D) comes home,
   (E) has come home,

4. After he graduated school, he entered the army,

   (A) After he graduated school,
   (B) After he was graduated from school,
   (C) When he graduated school,
   (D) After he graduated from school
   (E) As he was graduated from school,

5. I think they, as a rule, are much more conniving than us.

   (A) as a rule, are much more conniving than us.
   (B) as a rule are much more conniving than us.
   (C) as a rule, are much more conniving than we.
   (D) as a rule; are much more conniving than us.
   (E) are, as a rule, much more conniving than us.

6. Sitting around the fire, <u>mystery stories were told by each of us.</u>

   (A) mystery stories were told by each of us.
   (B) mystery stories were told by all of us.
   (C) each of us told mystery stories.
   (D) stories of mystery were told by each of us.
   (E) there were told mystery stories by each of us.

7. The loud noise of the subway trains and the trolley cars <u>frighten people from the country.</u>

   (A) frighten people from the country.
   (B) frighten country people.
   (C) frighten persons from the country.
   (D) frightens country people.
   (E) frighten people who come from the country.

8. Inspecting Robert's report card, <u>his mother noted</u> that he had received high ratings in Latin and history.

   (A) his mother noted
   (B) it was noted by his mother
   (C) his mother had noted
   (D) a notation was made by his mother
   (E) Robert's mother noted

9. The old man told <u>Mary and I</u> many stories about Europe.

   (A) Mary and I
   (B) Mary and me
   (C) me and Mary
   (D) I and Mary
   (E) Mary together with me

10. The wild-game hunter stalked the tiger slowly, cautiously, <u>and in a silent manner.</u>

    (A) and in a silent manner.
    (B) and silently.
    (C) and by acting silent.
    (D) and also used silence.
    (E) and in silence.

11. European film distributors originated the art of "dubbing"<u>—the substitution of lip-synchronized translations</u> in foreign languages for the original soundtrack voices.

    (A) —the substitution of lip-synchronized translations
    (B) ; the substitution of lip-synchronized translations
    (C) —the substitutions of translations synchronized by the lips
    (D) ; the lip-synchronized substitution of translations
    (E) . The substitution of lip-synchronized translations

12. Every pupil understood the assignment <u>except I.</u>

    (A) except I.
    (B) excepting I.

(C) outside of me.

(D) excepting me.

(E) except me.

13. Of the two candidates, I think <u>he is the best suited</u>.

(A) he is the best suited.

(B) that he is the best suited.

(C) he is suited best.

(D) he is the better suited.

(E) he's the best suited.

14. <u>You need not go unless you want to.</u>

(A) You need not go unless you want to.

(B) You don't need to go not unless you want to.

(C) You need go not unless you want to.

(D) You need not go in case unless you want to.

(E) You can go not unless you want to.

15. There is <u>no man but would give</u> ten years of his life to accomplish that deed.

(A) no man but would give

(B) no man but who would give

(C) not no man who would not give

(D) no man who would but give

(E) not any man would give

16. I feel <u>as though I was being borne</u> bodily through the air.

(A) as though I was being born

(B) as though I were being born

(C) like I was being borne

(D) like as though I was being borne

(E) as though I were being borne

17. <u>Honor as well as profit are to be gained by this work.</u>

(A) Honor as well as profit are to be gained by this work.

(B) Honor as well as profit is to be gained by this work.

(C) Honor in addition to profit are to be gained by this work.

(D) Honor, as well as profit, are to be gained by this work.

(E) Honor also profit is to be gained by this work.

18. He was <u>neither in favor of or opposed to the plan.</u>

(A) He was neither in favor of or opposed to the plan.

(B) He was not in favor of or opposed to the plan.

(C) He was neither in favor of the plan or opposed to it.

(D) He was neither in favor of the plan or opposed to the plan.

(E) He was neither in favor of nor opposed to the plan.

19. <u>I don't do well in those kinds of tests.</u>

(A) I don't do well in those kinds of tests.

(B) I don't do well in those kind of tests.

(C) I don't do good in those kinds of tests.

(D) I don't do good in those kind of tests.

(E) I don't do good in tests like those.

20. We were amazed to see the <u>amount of people waiting in line at Macy's.</u>

   (A) amount of people waiting in line at Macy's.
   (B) number of people waiting in line at Macy's.
   (C) amount of persons waiting in line at Macy's.
   (D) amount of people waiting in line at Macys.
   (E) amount of people waiting at Macy's in line.

21. <u>Although it is contrary</u> to popular belief, no dialect of English is inherently superior to any other.

   (A) Although it is contrary
   (B) Contrarily
   (C) Contrary
   (D) Although contrary
   (E) Although it is being contrary

22. Do you think that Alice has shown <u>more progress than any girl in the class?</u>

   (A) more progress than any girl in the class?
   (B) greater progress than any girl in the class?
   (C) more progress than any girl in the class has shown?
   (D) more progress than any other girl in the class?
   (E) more progress from that shown by any girl in the class?

23. She insisted <u>on me going.</u>

   (A) on me going.
   (B) on I going.
   (C) for me to go.
   (D) upon me going.
   (E) on my going.

24. <u>Everyone, including Anne and Helen, was there.</u>

   (A) Everyone, including Anne and Helen, was there.
   (B) Everyone including Anne and Helen, was there.
   (C) Everyone, including Anne and Helen, were there.
   (D) Everyone including Anne, and Helen, was there.
   (E) Everyone including Anne and Helen was there.

25. The reason I plan to go is <u>because she will be disappointed</u> if I don't.

   (A) because she will be disappointed
   (B) that she will be disappointed
   (C) because she will have a disappointment
   (D) on account of she will be disappointed
   (E) because she shall be disappointed

Stop

End of section. If you have any time left, go over your work in this section only. Do not work in any other section of the test.

Answer Key
Writing Ability

ENGLISH USAGE

1. E	5. C	9. D	13. B	17. E
2. C	6. B	10. D	14. B	18. B
3. A	7. D	11. B	15. C	19. C
4. E	8. E	12. D	16. C	20. E

SENTENCE CORRECTION

1. C	6. C	11. A	16. E	21. C
2. E	7. D	12. E	17. B	22. D
3. D	8. A	13. D	18. E	23. E
4. B	9. B	14. A	19. A	24. A
5. C	10. B	15. A	20. B	25. B

Part Six

REVIEW EXAMINATION IN PROFESSIONAL KNOWLEDGE

REVIEW EXAMINATION IN PROFESSIONAL KNOWLEDGE

After you have completed the Professional Knowledge Subtest of Diagnostic Core Battery I and studied those areas where you need review, you should attempt the Review Examination. This examination tests the same concepts as the First Diagnostic Professional Knowledge Examination, but in a completion format, so that the problem posed for you is a bit more difficult.

The completion format forces you to provide the answer rather than recognize it, and thus it gives you good insight into the effectiveness of your additional study and review. The concepts involved in the questions have been kept the same so that you have a direct measure of whether your study plans are effectively providing you with more information and understanding than you had when you attempted Diagnostic Core Battery I. In the Review Examination the questions are grouped by area, so that you can easily review those specific areas in which you wish to verify improvement.

Directions: Select the areas you want to review and fill in the answers to the questions in the spaces provided. Allow ten minutes for each area. Score your answers with the Answer Key following the review. You should answer at least six items in each area correctly to be ready to move on to Diagnostic Core Battery II without additional study in the area.

Area 1: Historical, Philosophical Foundations

1. In the years since the Supreme Court decision on school desegregation, the proportion of black children attending integrated schools in northern urban centers has _____.

2. One example of a kind of school or educational institution that can validly be called American in origin is the _____.

3. When John Dewey maintains that "there is nothing to which education is subordinate save more education," he means that _____
_____
_____.

4. The pragmatic notion that "truth happens to an idea" means that a belief is confirmed in _____.

5. The point of view that "the school must act as a spearhead of social progress" is an important tenet of the school of educational philosophy called _____
_____.

6. The characteristic educational philosophy of the progressive movement held that the schools should equip youth to think critically about _____ issues in order to foster _____.

7. John Dewey's most significant work on education is entitled _____
_____.

8. "Certain basic ideas and skills essential to our culture should be taught to all alike by certain time-tested methods." This is part of the philosophy of _____
_____.

9. More than three centuries ago, Comenius enunciated the principle of "Things-Ideas-Words." This principle is most clearly explained by the statement that the sequence of learning proceeds from experiencing to conceiving to _____
_____.

10. Notions such as "Education must be conceived as a continuing reconstruction of

experience," and "Moral discipline should be a part and outcome of school life, not something proceeding from the teacher," and "Man is an organism in an environment, remaking as well as made," all stem from the educational philosophy of _____.

Area 2: Social and Cultural Foundations

1. An educator who has stressed that intellectual improvement and development ought to be the primary function of our educational institutions is _____

2. The dissatisfaction of parents unable to make changes in school procedures led to social pressure for _____.

3. The major significance of the Tenth Amendment to the United States Constitution to American education is that it reserves powers not specifically granted to the federal government (including education) to the_____.

4. A proposal for federal action made by Dr. Clark Kerr called for the founding of "urban grant" universities. The term "urban grant" was used to stress a parallel with _____ colleges.

5. During its first year, the Reagan Administration's Department of Education suggested a change in federal policy on bilingual education by proposing that bilingual education be _____.

6. The primary purpose of tenure is to provide a reasonable measure of _____ to the members of the teaching profession.

7. When we say that a child's cultural background is important to the teacher, we imply that a child's values and habits are an outgrowth of his/her _____ membership.

8. Programs intended to offset social or cultural deficiencies among disadvantaged students have usually been referred to as _____ programs.

9. The case of *Tinker* v. *Des Moines* involved _____.

10. Teachers' salary scales do not provide yearly increases in salary until retirement: True or false? _____.

Area 3: Child and Adolescent Development

1. It has been found that intellectually gifted children tend to surpass average children in several areas. Among these are _____, _____, and _____.

2. Three terms used in discussing various stages of the physiological development

of the human organism are (1) embryo, (2) neonate, and (3) fetus. The correct *developmental* order for these terms is _____, _____, and _____.

3. According to Piaget, rigid adherence to a rule ("moral realism") is *most* characteristic of children between the ages of _____ and _____.

4. The dominant characteristic of the child who has been maternally deprived since earliest infancy is his/her inability to _____ _____.

5. Psychoanalytic writers have labeled the middle-childhood years as the _____ period.

6. According to Erikson, the major problem of adolescence is _____ _____.

7. The derivation of concepts from abstract symbols is related to the theory of intellectual development propounded by _____.

8. "They struggle to establish themselves as important members of the family, but question family controls." The speaker is talking about the developmental period known as _____.

9. Growth and development in young children takes place in the early years at a rate considered _____.

10. One characteristic of the normally developing adolescent is that the need for parental support is _____.

Area 4: Application of Child/Adolescent Development

1. When the eye movements of good and poor readers are compared, the chief observable difference is that on each line good readers make _____ pauses.

2. The concept of "developmental tasks" can be of *greatest* help to the teacher in judging a child's _____.

3. Studies have been made of the operation of specific personality traits, such as honesty, in different situations. When one considers the results to estimate the consistency of expression of each trait, one finds that the trait is expressed _____.

4. The aspect of Freud's theory of most direct significance to the classroom teacher's work is Freud's analysis of the _____.

5. Experience with varied promotion policies has shown that regular retention

of pupils whose work fails to reach a required standard does little to reduce
_____ in ability or achievement.

6. A child who looks blank and bites his nails when he is reprimanded by the teacher is probably demonstrating a pattern of behavior termed _____.

7. Erica just didn't like her biology teacher. As a result, she often wanted to cut the class but feared that her parents would punish her if they discovered that she was cutting. She barely passed the course. Her grade adviser compelled her to take chemistry the following year. The first day that she attended the chemistry class, she experienced a tense emotional state of fear and apprehension. The psychological term for this feeling is _____.

8. If a school provides many and varied subjects in a relatively unstructured way, it is trying to encourage the kind of thinking referred to as _____.

9. Amy thinks that a rolling ball is alive since it is moving. She is displaying the concept of _____.

10. A child who can discuss with you differences between cows and sheep, but who is at a loss to answer when you ask how they are similar, has the concepts "cow" and "sheep" differentiated and abstracted, but not _____.

Area 5: Learning Theories and Principles

1. Mara, a very young child, learns that the small, furry, purring object in her house is a "kitty." When visiting another house, Mara points to a small dog there and says, "Kitty." This illustrates the learning principle called
_____.

2. The typical pattern of a generalized learning curve would show a _____ rise followed by a(n)_____.

3. Heather has done a household chore very well. Give an example of how her parents could respond using the principle of secondary reinforcement. _____
_____

4. Learning theories are concerned chiefly with describing or explaining the
_____.

5. A student has had a year of Spanish and starts the study of French. He finds that his knowledge of French interferes with his recall of Spanish. This interference is called _____.

6. The trial-and-error method of learning is closely allied to another learning procedure, called _____ learning.

7. Among Functionalism, Organismic Theory, Connectionism, and Behaviorism, the least closely related to the other three is _____.

8. The theory most closely associated with the concept that learning is accomplished through grasp of the meaning of a problem in terms of the total situation is known as the _____ theory.

9. "Overlearning" will usually increase or strengthen _____.

10. The basis of B.F. Skinner's programmed learning research was the association theory of learning developed by _____.

Area 6: Application of Learning Theory, Principles

1. The recommendation that a poem be read over in its entirety before memorizing individual lines illustrates an awareness of the principles of _____ _____.

2. Within learning theorists' frame of reference, probably the best way of approaching the organization of subject matter is to move from the _____ to the _____.

3. A temporary inability to increase learning is referred to as a(n) _____.

4. In a learning experiment involving a comparison of distributed and massed practice, one would expect that the average recall score for distributed practice would be _____ compared to the score for massed practice.

5. Based upon the current research on retention, the kind of information we would predict that students would most rapidly forget is _____.

6. The utilization of realia, charts, models, tape recordings, and films on the same science subjects is likely to improve learning principally because of the multiple _____ inherent in these terms.

7. The best justification for surprise quizzes is that they encourage the students to _____.

8. Summaries of learnings elicited during and at the end of a lesson are usually important in focusing attention on the _____developed.

9. In discussing how "overlearning" relates to memorization of selected prose and poetry by children, most educators would agree that when pupils have learned a selection, they should _____ studying it.

10. Independent study is a prime aspect of the teaching method known as _____.

Area 7: Test Development, Evaluation, and Assessment Principles

1. An author made the following statement:
   "Objective tests in history are superior to essay tests because they test understanding of history rather than ability in English composition."
   In this quotation, the author is indicating his belief that, in comparison to essay tests, short-answer history tests are more _____.

2. Which standardized test would be most desirable for testing the general mental ability of a second-grade pupil, aged seven years, three months? _____.

3. It is probable that intelligence tests measure chiefly the ability to _____ _____.

4. A score on the Sarason Test-Anxiety Scale constitutes a(n) _____ definition of test-anxiety.

5. Placing the easiest questions at the end of the test is a(n) _____ procedure in constructing multiple-choice tests.

6. Using standardized test results as a basis for assigning grades to pupils is a(n) _____ assessment practice.

7. A pretest is useful in determining individual and class background as well as _____ to study a new unit.

8. The most useful device for studying pupil-pupil relationships is the _____.

9. The school counselor who wishes to overcome shyness or resistance should begin testing with a measure of _____.

10. If a survey were made of the elementary school population of the United States to compare the number of students having an IQ of 90–100 with the number having an IQ of 100–110, it would be found that the numbers were _____.

Area 8: Understanding Test and Measurement Concepts, Grading

1. A character test was constructed, and after it had been given once, it was given again to the same children after a two-week interval. The correlation between the two sets of scores was .51. From this evidence, it is most logical to conclude that the test was *not* _____.

2. Given the following graph of test scores, we would conclude that the difficulty of this test for the group was _____.

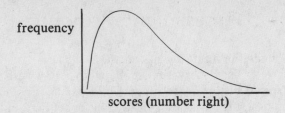

frequency

scores (number right)

3. John's reading score is at the 65th percentile. This means that in comparison to the base population, his achievement is superior to that of _____ percent of the students.

4. Assuming that there are three marking periods per term, which of the following items would you take into account in assigning a grade for the third marking period: grades of the first marking period, grades of the second marking period, attitude, interests, class work. I would consider _____.

5. When an evaluation refers to norm-referenced tests, it is most likely reporting data from _____ tests.

6. A test score is meaningless without some basis for _____.

7. The extent to which a test reflects the content and instructional objectives of the unit for which it was written indicates the test's _____.

8. A test used to assess interim achievement in a unit of instruction is called a _____ test.

9. If you are testing to evaluate progress in teaching mathematics, and you compare a student's score to the number of items you have set as the minimum acceptable score, the test is called a(n) _____ test.

10. You are taking a true-false test in an ancient language you do not know at all. On a 20-item test you can expect to get a score of _____ correct.

Area 9: Research and Statistical Concepts

1. In a group of scores on a standardized test the median would correspond to the _____ percentile.

2. Two classes are given the same arithmetic computation test, and the mean score for both classes is 57. The standard deviation for Class A is 5.1 and the standard deviation for Class B is 10.3. On the basis of the above we may conclude that with respect to arithmetic computation achievement Class B is more _____ than Class A.

The table below summarizes a dozen different investigations having to do with familiar resemblances in mental abilities and physical characteristics. Questions 3, 4, and 5 are based on this table.

CORRELATION FOUND BETWEEN RELATED PAIRS OF PERSONS. NORTHERN EUROPEAN STOCK IN TWELVE DIFFERENT INVESTIGATIONS

People Compared	Physical Measures	Mental Measures
a. Unrelated children	X	−.19 to .09
b. Parents	.00 to .15	.46 to .49
c. Parent-Child	.42 to .53	.45 to .55
d. Siblings, same home	.42 to .53	.60
e. Identical twins	.91	.97

3. Based on the observed data only, which group seems to be *least* related in mental measures? _____.

4. The correlations for parents and children indicate _____ about the causes of mental ability.

5. The correlation of −.19 in the Mental Measures column indicates that among unrelated children, those high on one mental measure are _____ on a second mental measure.

Questions 6, 7, and 8 are based on the following tables.

MEANS AND STANDARD DEVIATIONS FOR STUDENT TEACHERS AND COLLEGE WOMEN NORMATIVE GROUP ON SELECTED VARIABLES

Variable	Student Teachers N = 104		Other College Women N = 749	
	Mean	Standard Deviation	Mean	Standard Deviation
Achievement	13.03	3.20	13.08	4.19
Deference	14.63	2.91	12.40	3.72
Order	5.11	1.74	10.24	4.37
Exhibition	4.65	1.45	14.00	3.00

6. The variable on which student teachers scored highest, on the basis of the *observed* data, was _____.

7. The variable on which student teachers varied least, on the basis of the *observed* data, was _____.

8. Assuming normality, two-thirds (67%) of the scores in exhibition for other college women fall between _____ and _____.

Questions 9 and 10 refer to the following table.

**PERCENTAGES OF THE POPULATION 60 YEARS OF AGE AND OVER
RESIDING IN DIFFERENT KINDS OF COMMUNITIES, BY SEX, UNITED STATES**

Sex	Urban	Rural Non-Farm	Farm
Male	53.2	21.3	25.5
Female	60.6	20.6	18.8
Total	57.0	20.9	22.1

9. Complete this sentence about the table: "A _____ proportion of older men than of older women live on farms, and a _____ proportion of the men than of the women in that age group live in urban communities."

10. The circled number under the heading "Urban," 60.6, is to be read as follows: 60.6% of the _____ population 60 years of age and over live in _____ communities.

Area 10: Teaching Principles, Practices

1. Basic to the effective teaching of English as a second language is that, where possible, instruction should be based on direct _____.

2. The procedure of addressing a question to the class before designating a pupil to respond is considered _____ as a questioning technique.

3. Lesson plans should be prepared weekly but be _____ enough to permit daily additions and corrections.

4. In the seventh grade of School X Ms. Johnson teaches English, Mr. Carter teaches Social Studies and Ms. Santiago teaches Science. In Tuesday's lesson, Mr. Carter notes that several of his pupils make flagrant errors in grammar and English usage. The responsibility for explaining those errors is _____.

5. For the effective use of a motion picture as a teaching aid, the showing should be followed by _____.

6. Eliminating a foreign accent from the child's speech so that he/she will bear no stigma in relations with peers is a(n) _____ aspect of the instructional process for a newly arrived Puerto Rican child who speaks English haltingly.

7. A worthwhile activity program will make certain that there is a logical and substantial tieup among all of its _____.

8. Completing the lesson even if the class has to be detained a few minutes is considered a(n) _____ educational practice.

9. A teacher who periodically sets aside time for pupils to report to the class on the books or magazine articles that they have read, and for pupil discussion following this, is trying to encourage _____ reading.

10. The most significant deficiency of the lecture method in secondary school is the fact that it fails to develop _____ adequately.

Area 11: Classroom Management

1. A report of a classroom observation in a sixth grade class noted that there was a "high degree of disorganization, boredom, quarrelsomeness, and inefficiency." If one had to assess the teacher's style of leadership in the class from this evidence, it would seem most likely that control is _____.

2. Classroom discipline should have as its major goal the promotion of _____ on the part of the pupils.

3. A good anecdotal recording of pupil behavior is _____, and has no _____ by the teacher.

4. The *chief* reason for including music and art materials in an elementary school social studies unit should be to improve _____.

5. A review lesson on materials covered in a subject-matter unit, such as the causes of the American Revolution, should be viewed primarily as an effort to improve _____.

6. If you were considering the use of praise, reproof, and no attention, the order of arrangement from *most* effective to *least* effective would be: _____, _____, and _____.

7. Considering ways to improve a car seat for infants is an example of an activity Guilford calls _____ thinking.

8. One advantage of team teaching is that it is a practical and speedy way to _____.

9. In contemporary elementary schools, the largest proportion of instructional time is devoted to which subject area? _____.

10. The personality type most likely to be overlooked in "meeting the needs of all the children" is the child who is _____ and/or _____.

Area 12: Curriculum Development and Supervision

1. The major reason for providing supervision of teachers is to improve the quality of _____.

2. A curriculum that revisits basic ideas repeatedly at different grade levels and builds upon them until the student has gained a deep, comprehensive, workable knowledge of them is known as the _____ curriculum.

3. In a broad sense, a storefront school, a military academy, an independent private school, and a parochial school would be considered examples of _____ schools.

4. If children of different ages work together, and movement from one class to another is flexible, the classes are probably _____.

5. In many parts of the country, students cannot be graduated until they demonstrate their ability to achieve on a given level. The purpose of these exit exams is to focus on _____.

6. If you observe a class and notice that students participate in evaluating their work as well as in selecting the subject matter to be studied, you would conclude that the teacher is using a(n) _____ curriculum.

7. In introducing learning tasks, the most important element for success is that the new learning be paced to the learner's _____ and _____.

8. The statement that "the pupil will, from memory, identify the five freedoms contained in the Bill of Rights" is an example of how to state a(n) _____ objective.

9. The major objective of the reading program in the primary grades is the development of _____ skills.

10. When educators talk about the sum total of a child's experiences under the guidance of the school, the term they use is _____.

Area 13: Professional Awareness

1. Of the fifty United States, the proportion that have tenure laws which cover all the public schools in the state is _____.

2. A student who does not wish to participate in the daily salute to the flag has the right to _____.

3. If a male teacher believes that he has been subjected to sex discrimination in hiring, among the organizations he can ask for help are _____, _____, _____, and _____.

4. A teacher of the eleventh grade, who wishes her contemporary literature class to read material which contains "taboo" words, should decide, based upon criteria such as: _____, _____ and _____.

5. One of the functions of an educational system is to reconcile what is good for the

individual with what is good for the group (of which the individual is a part). This statement means that the individual functioning in a group does not necessarily lose his/her _____.

6. If a 15-year-old child asked to see his or her records, the teacher must _____ _____.

7. Excluding teaching candidates who would be harmful to, or ineffective with, children and youth from the school milieu is a primary reason we have teacher _____.

8. If a Board of Education wishes to dismiss a teacher for immoral conduct, they must consider criteria such as _____, _____, or _____.

9. A teacher, who has been told that she is to be observed by her Principal, has asked if she can select the period in which to be observed, how long the Principal will remain, and how she will find out the results. The Principal, if he or she follows normal professional practice, will respond that she _____ select the period, that the observation will last at least _____, and that she will find out the results within _____ through a _____.

10. The legal basis of the principle that education is a state function is found in the _____.

Answer Key

Review Examination

Listed below are the correct answers to the questions in the thirteen areas of the Review Examination. In some cases, the correct answer must be stated exactly as listed in the Key. These items are indicated with an asterisk (*). For the other questions, consider your answer correct if you stated the same idea but used different words or phrases. Some alternatives are given in parentheses.

If you did not achieve a score of six correct in the area reviewed, some additional review is suggested.

AREA 1: HISTORICAL AND PHILOSOPHICAL FOUNDATIONS

   1. decreased
* 2. comprehensive high school
   3. No purpose is more important than preparing people to educate themselves throughout life.
   4. experience
* 5. Reconstructionist
* 6. (a) social (b) progress
* 7. *Democracy and Education*
* 8. essentialism
* 9. defining
*10. John Dewey

AREA 2: SOCIAL AND CULTURAL FOUNDATIONS

* 1. Jerome Bruner
* 2. community control of schools
* 3. states
* 4. land grant
   5. implemented as each state chooses
   6. security (job security, stability)
   7. family (group or social class)
* 8. compensatory
* 9. children's rights
*10. true

AREA 3: CHILD AND ADOLESCENT DEVELOPMENT

   1. personal and social adjustment, physical size, health, social maturity, and poise

* 2. embryo, fetus, neonate
* 3. six and eight
  4. form relationships
* 5. latency
  6. establishing identity (a sense of self)
* 7. Piaget
* 8. adolescence
  9. spontaneous (continuous, irregular but orderly)
  10. diminished

AREA 4: APPLICATION OF CHILD AND ADOLESCENT DEVELOPMENT

* 1. fewer
* 2. readiness
* 3. consistently
* 4. psychosexual stages of development
  5. variability, range, spread
* 6. regression
* 7. extension
* 8. divergent
* 9. animism
*10. generalized

AREA 5: LEARNING THEORIES AND PRINCIPLES

* 1. primary stimulus generalization
  2. (a) rapid initial   (b) plateau (leveling off)
  3. giving her a candy bar (or any other pleasant food)
  4. processes leading to changes in behavior
* 5. retroactive inhibition
* 6. discovery
* 7. Organismic Theory
* 8. gestalt
  9. retention
*10. Thorndike

AREA 6: APPLICATION OF LEARNING THEORY PRINCIPLES

* 1. gestalt organization
  2. (a) familiar   (b) general
* 3. plateau
  4. higher (better)
  5. facts
* 6. stimuli
  7. study regularly
  8. concepts

9. continue (keep on)
*10. programmed learning

AREA 7: TEST DEVELOPMENT, EVALUATION, AND ASSESSMENT PRINCIPLES

* 1. valid
* 2. Wechsler Intelligence Scale for Children (WISC)
  3. do well in school (succeed in school)
* 4. operational
  5. unsound (unwise)
  6. bad (inadvisable)
  7. readiness (preparation)
* 8. sociogram
* 9. interest
 10. similar (comparable, about the same)

AREA 8: UNDERSTANDING TEST AND MEASUREMENT CONCEPTS, GRADING

* 1. reliable
  2. too low (not appropriate)
* 3. 65
  4. all of them
* 5. standardized
  6. comparison (evaluation)
* 7. validity
* 8. summative
* 9. criterion-referenced
*10. ten

AREA 9: RESEARCH AND STATISTICAL CONCEPTS

* 1. 50th
  2. heterogeneous (mixed in ability or levels)
  3. unrelated children
* 4. nothing
* 5. low
* 6. deference
* 7. exhibition
* 8. 11 and 17
  9. (a) higher (larger)   (b) lower (smaller)
*10. (a) female   (b) urban

AREA 10: TEACHING PRINCIPLES AND PRACTICES

* 1. experience

2. sensible (sound, desirable)
* 3. flexible
4. Mr. Carter's (his, the Social Studies teacher's)
5. a related activity (questioning, discussion)
6. unnecessary (unimportant, low-priority)
7. learning experiences (activities)
8. unsound (unwise)
9. outside (individual)
10. concepts (ideas)

AREA 11:   CLASSROOM MANAGEMENT

1. laissez-faire (loose)
2. self-direction (independence)
* 3. (a) objective   (b) judgments (personal opinions)
* 4. learning
5. understanding (comprehension)
* 6. praise, no attention, reproof
* 7. divergent
8. train new teachers
9. language arts (reading)
10. (a) quiet (shy)   (b) withdrawn   [can be in either order]

AREA 12:   CURRICULUM DEVELOPMENT AND SUPERVISION

1. instruction
* 2. spiral
* 3. alternative
* 4. ungraded
5. competency (minimum basic skills, math, and language literacy)
* 6. student-centered
7. (a) maturation (readiness)   (b) previous knowledge
* 8. behavioral
* 9. word-recognition
*10. curriculum

AREA 13:   PROFESSIONAL AWARENESS

1. about three-fourths
2. refuse, stay seated and silent
3. local teacher organization, Equal Opportunity Commission, Office of Civil Rights, Office of Federal Contract Compliance.
4. relevance and quality of story, opinions of other English teachers, maturity of the students, the effect on the class.
5. identity, individuality
6. show them to him
7. certification
8. if the conduct was personal and private; if students were involved; and if the behavior at issue was public
9. may not; one class period; a week, in a written report
10. the Tenth Amendment, the Constitution

Part Seven

DIAGNOSTIC CORE BATTERY II

DIAGNOSTIC CORE BATTERY II

This second Diagnostic Core Battery consists of three sections. The first, Professional Knowledge, involves questions about Professional Education, including questions on the psychological and social foundations of education and the application of these principles in the classroom, as well as general teaching principles and practices. The second section, General Knowledge, includes questions on the Humanities (Social Studies, Literature, and the Fine Arts), and on Science and Mathematics. The third section, Communication Skills, includes practice items in Listening and in Reading, as well as questions applying the rules of standard written English.

On the Diagnostic Core Battery, each question is followed by four or five answers. You are to consider the answers and choose the one answer that is correct or most nearly correct, and then blacken the answer space for that question-number on the Answer Sheet. Be certain to blacken only one space for each question. If you want to change an answer, carefully and thoroughly erase your first answer before entering your new answer. On the actual NTE you will have to follow this procedure if you want to change an answer. Also, adhere to the time restrictions allowed for each section of the Diagnostic Core Battery. This will also prepare you for actual NTE procedures.

Answer Sheet
Section 1. Professional Knowledge

1 Ⓐ Ⓑ Ⓒ Ⓓ Ⓔ	27 Ⓐ Ⓑ Ⓒ Ⓓ Ⓔ	53 Ⓐ Ⓑ Ⓒ Ⓓ Ⓔ	79 Ⓐ Ⓑ Ⓒ Ⓓ Ⓔ	105 Ⓐ Ⓑ Ⓒ Ⓓ Ⓔ
2 Ⓐ Ⓑ Ⓒ Ⓓ Ⓔ	28 Ⓐ Ⓑ Ⓒ Ⓓ Ⓔ	54 Ⓐ Ⓑ Ⓒ Ⓓ Ⓔ	80 Ⓐ Ⓑ Ⓒ Ⓓ Ⓔ	106 Ⓐ Ⓑ Ⓒ Ⓓ Ⓔ
3 Ⓐ Ⓑ Ⓒ Ⓓ Ⓔ	29 Ⓐ Ⓑ Ⓒ Ⓓ Ⓔ	55 Ⓐ Ⓑ Ⓒ Ⓓ Ⓔ	81 Ⓐ Ⓑ Ⓒ Ⓓ Ⓔ	107 Ⓐ Ⓑ Ⓒ Ⓓ Ⓔ
4 Ⓐ Ⓑ Ⓒ Ⓓ Ⓔ	30 Ⓐ Ⓑ Ⓒ Ⓓ Ⓔ	56 Ⓐ Ⓑ Ⓒ Ⓓ Ⓔ	82 Ⓐ Ⓑ Ⓒ Ⓓ Ⓔ	108 Ⓐ Ⓑ Ⓒ Ⓓ Ⓔ
5 Ⓐ Ⓑ Ⓒ Ⓓ Ⓔ	31 Ⓐ Ⓑ Ⓒ Ⓓ Ⓔ	57 Ⓐ Ⓑ Ⓒ Ⓓ Ⓔ	83 Ⓐ Ⓑ Ⓒ Ⓓ Ⓔ	109 Ⓐ Ⓑ Ⓒ Ⓓ Ⓔ
6 Ⓐ Ⓑ Ⓒ Ⓓ Ⓔ	32 Ⓐ Ⓑ Ⓒ Ⓓ Ⓔ	58 Ⓐ Ⓑ Ⓒ Ⓓ Ⓔ	84 Ⓐ Ⓑ Ⓒ Ⓓ Ⓔ	110 Ⓐ Ⓑ Ⓒ Ⓓ Ⓔ
7 Ⓐ Ⓑ Ⓒ Ⓓ Ⓔ	33 Ⓐ Ⓑ Ⓒ Ⓓ Ⓔ	59 Ⓐ Ⓑ Ⓒ Ⓓ Ⓔ	85 Ⓐ Ⓑ Ⓒ Ⓓ Ⓔ	111 Ⓐ Ⓑ Ⓒ Ⓓ Ⓔ
8 Ⓐ Ⓑ Ⓒ Ⓓ Ⓔ	34 Ⓐ Ⓑ Ⓒ Ⓓ Ⓔ	60 Ⓐ Ⓑ Ⓒ Ⓓ Ⓔ	86 Ⓐ Ⓑ Ⓒ Ⓓ Ⓔ	112 Ⓐ Ⓑ Ⓒ Ⓓ Ⓔ
9 Ⓐ Ⓑ Ⓒ Ⓓ Ⓔ	35 Ⓐ Ⓑ Ⓒ Ⓓ Ⓔ	61 Ⓐ Ⓑ Ⓒ Ⓓ Ⓔ	87 Ⓐ Ⓑ Ⓒ Ⓓ Ⓔ	113 Ⓐ Ⓑ Ⓒ Ⓓ Ⓔ
10 Ⓐ Ⓑ Ⓒ Ⓓ Ⓔ	36 Ⓐ Ⓑ Ⓒ Ⓓ Ⓔ	62 Ⓐ Ⓑ Ⓒ Ⓓ Ⓔ	88 Ⓐ Ⓑ Ⓒ Ⓓ Ⓔ	114 Ⓐ Ⓑ Ⓒ Ⓓ Ⓔ
11 Ⓐ Ⓑ Ⓒ Ⓓ Ⓔ	37 Ⓐ Ⓑ Ⓒ Ⓓ Ⓔ	63 Ⓐ Ⓑ Ⓒ Ⓓ Ⓔ	89 Ⓐ Ⓑ Ⓒ Ⓓ Ⓔ	115 Ⓐ Ⓑ Ⓒ Ⓓ Ⓔ
12 Ⓐ Ⓑ Ⓒ Ⓓ Ⓔ	38 Ⓐ Ⓑ Ⓒ Ⓓ Ⓔ	64 Ⓐ Ⓑ Ⓒ Ⓓ Ⓔ	90 Ⓐ Ⓑ Ⓒ Ⓓ Ⓔ	116 Ⓐ Ⓑ Ⓒ Ⓓ Ⓔ
13 Ⓐ Ⓑ Ⓒ Ⓓ Ⓔ	39 Ⓐ Ⓑ Ⓒ Ⓓ Ⓔ	65 Ⓐ Ⓑ Ⓒ Ⓓ Ⓔ	91 Ⓐ Ⓑ Ⓒ Ⓓ Ⓔ	117 Ⓐ Ⓑ Ⓒ Ⓓ Ⓔ
14 Ⓐ Ⓑ Ⓒ Ⓓ Ⓔ	40 Ⓐ Ⓑ Ⓒ Ⓓ Ⓔ	66 Ⓐ Ⓑ Ⓒ Ⓓ Ⓔ	92 Ⓐ Ⓑ Ⓒ Ⓓ Ⓔ	118 Ⓐ Ⓑ Ⓒ Ⓓ Ⓔ
15 Ⓐ Ⓑ Ⓒ Ⓓ Ⓔ	41 Ⓐ Ⓑ Ⓒ Ⓓ Ⓔ	67 Ⓐ Ⓑ Ⓒ Ⓓ Ⓔ	93 Ⓐ Ⓑ Ⓒ Ⓓ Ⓔ	119 Ⓐ Ⓑ Ⓒ Ⓓ Ⓔ
16 Ⓐ Ⓑ Ⓒ Ⓓ Ⓔ	42 Ⓐ Ⓑ Ⓒ Ⓓ Ⓔ	68 Ⓐ Ⓑ Ⓒ Ⓓ Ⓔ	94 Ⓐ Ⓑ Ⓒ Ⓓ Ⓔ	120 Ⓐ Ⓑ Ⓒ Ⓓ Ⓔ
17 Ⓐ Ⓑ Ⓒ Ⓓ Ⓔ	43 Ⓐ Ⓑ Ⓒ Ⓓ Ⓔ	69 Ⓐ Ⓑ Ⓒ Ⓓ Ⓔ	95 Ⓐ Ⓑ Ⓒ Ⓓ Ⓔ	121 Ⓐ Ⓑ Ⓒ Ⓓ Ⓔ
18 Ⓐ Ⓑ Ⓒ Ⓓ Ⓔ	44 Ⓐ Ⓑ Ⓒ Ⓓ Ⓕ	70 Ⓐ Ⓑ Ⓒ Ⓓ Ⓔ	96 Ⓐ Ⓑ Ⓒ Ⓓ Ⓔ	122 Ⓐ Ⓑ Ⓒ Ⓓ Ⓔ
19 Ⓐ Ⓑ Ⓒ Ⓓ Ⓔ	45 Ⓐ Ⓑ Ⓒ Ⓓ Ⓔ	71 Ⓐ Ⓑ Ⓒ Ⓓ Ⓔ	97 Ⓐ Ⓑ Ⓒ Ⓓ Ⓔ	123 Ⓐ Ⓑ Ⓒ Ⓓ Ⓔ
20 Ⓐ Ⓑ Ⓒ Ⓓ Ⓔ	46 Ⓐ Ⓑ Ⓒ Ⓓ Ⓔ	72 Ⓐ Ⓑ Ⓒ Ⓓ Ⓔ	98 Ⓐ Ⓑ Ⓒ Ⓓ Ⓔ	124 Ⓐ Ⓑ Ⓒ Ⓓ Ⓔ
21 Ⓐ Ⓑ Ⓒ Ⓓ Ⓔ	47 Ⓐ Ⓑ Ⓒ Ⓓ Ⓔ	73 Ⓐ Ⓑ Ⓒ Ⓓ Ⓔ	99 Ⓐ Ⓑ Ⓒ Ⓓ Ⓔ	125 Ⓐ Ⓑ Ⓒ Ⓓ Ⓔ
22 Ⓐ Ⓑ Ⓒ Ⓓ Ⓔ	48 Ⓐ Ⓑ Ⓒ Ⓓ Ⓔ	74 Ⓐ Ⓑ Ⓒ Ⓓ Ⓔ	100 Ⓐ Ⓑ Ⓒ Ⓓ Ⓔ	126 Ⓐ Ⓑ Ⓒ Ⓓ Ⓔ
23 Ⓐ Ⓑ Ⓒ Ⓓ Ⓔ	49 Ⓐ Ⓑ Ⓒ Ⓓ Ⓔ	75 Ⓐ Ⓑ Ⓒ Ⓓ Ⓔ	101 Ⓐ Ⓑ Ⓒ Ⓓ Ⓔ	127 Ⓐ Ⓑ Ⓒ Ⓓ Ⓔ
24 Ⓐ Ⓑ Ⓒ Ⓓ Ⓔ	50 Ⓐ Ⓑ Ⓒ Ⓓ Ⓔ	76 Ⓐ Ⓑ Ⓒ Ⓓ Ⓔ	102 Ⓐ Ⓑ Ⓒ Ⓓ Ⓔ	128 Ⓐ Ⓑ Ⓒ Ⓓ Ⓔ
25 Ⓐ Ⓑ Ⓒ Ⓓ Ⓔ	51 Ⓐ Ⓑ Ⓒ Ⓓ Ⓔ	77 Ⓐ Ⓑ Ⓒ Ⓓ Ⓔ	103 Ⓐ Ⓑ Ⓒ Ⓓ Ⓔ	129 Ⓐ Ⓑ Ⓒ Ⓓ Ⓔ
26 Ⓐ Ⓑ Ⓒ Ⓓ Ⓔ	52 Ⓐ Ⓑ Ⓒ Ⓓ Ⓔ	78 Ⓐ Ⓑ Ⓒ Ⓓ Ⓔ	104 Ⓐ Ⓑ Ⓒ Ⓓ Ⓔ	130 Ⓐ Ⓑ Ⓒ Ⓓ Ⓔ

Diagnostic Core Battery II
Section 1: Professional Knowledge

100 Minutes—130 Questions

Directions: For each of the following questions, select the choice that best answers the question or completes the statement.

1. Operation Head Start is:

   (A) the federally funded preschool program launched in the mid-1960s by the Office of Economic Opportunity
   (B) a program initiated in 1972 to move early childhood education into the home
   (C) the first infant program to be launched by a public school system
   (D) the federally funded elementary-school program developed by the Office of Child Development
   (E) a program for teaching foreign languages in early elementary grades

2. The theory that behavior is determined by reinforcements and rewards was promulgated by

   (A) Freud   (D) Skinner
   (B) Thoreau   (E) Piaget
   (C) Dewey

3. Which of the following is the best description of the relationship between a mother and her unborn child?

   (A) The child receives nutrition and oxygen from the mother, but otherwise their body systems are completely separate.
   (B) The mother and child have separate circulatory systems, but nutrition, chemicals, and hormones of many kinds are constantly exchanged between the two.
   (C) The child passively absorbs materials of all kinds from the mother; the child's body will not manufacture materials of any kind until after birth.
   (D) The child's and mother's bodies have one common circulatory system, so all substances are common to both.
   (E) The child and mother have the same Rh factor.

4. The most basic recommendation concerning frustration and the school is

   (A) eliminate frustration wherever possible
   (B) reduce irrelevant frustration to a minimum
   (C) reduce frustration tolerance
   (D) increase skipping to accommodate advanced students
   (E) provide psychological services whenever children become frustrated

5. Standardized achievement tests are characterized by all of the following principles *except*

(A) they often show differing results, depending upon the particular form of the test used

(B) they are administered in accordance with uniform procedures indicated in the manual of instructions

(C) they have norms for grade or age

(D) they are scored in accordance with standard procedures indicated in the manual of instructions

(E) their norms reflect a variety of educational settings

6. In which of the following situations may a teacher legally use force?

   I. to discipline students
  II. to quell a disturbance
 III. in self-defense
  IV. to obtain a weapon the student has

   (A) II, III, and IV only
   (B) I only
   (C) III only
   (D) III and IV only
   (E) all four

7. Skinner's view of human behavior corresponds best to which of the following statements?

   (A) Behavior is determined by a combination of genetic influences and free will.
   (B) Behavior is determined to a significant degree by inherited predispositions.
   (C) Behavior is under the control of the physical and social environment.
   (D) Behavior is unpredictable.
   (E) Behavior is a function of previously rewarded activities.

8. Of the following, which one represents the *least* effective disciplinary technique?

   (A) compelling pupils under threat of punishment to observe class rules
   (B) helping pupils to enjoy classwork through the use of meaningful activities
   (C) providing wide participation for all pupils in the work and administration of the class
   (D) discouraging lateness to class by starting each period with an interesting activity
   (E) helping pupils develop and participate in enforcing the rules of the classroom

9. If you want your students to work on an assignment at a steady rate, the best thing for you to do would be to

   (A) reward them as soon as they finish
   (B) let students reward themselves with a break after completing ten problems
   (C) check every ten minutes on how many problems they have completed
   (D) circulate around the room and praise students at unpredictable intervals
   (E) ignore them as they work

10. Intelligence tests call on which of the following ways of thinking?

   (A) divergent
   (B) convergent

(C) creative
(D) spontaneous
(E) dissonant

11. According to the Family Educational Rights and Privacy Act, parents may

    I. photocopy records
    II. request changes or the addition of an explanation to a child's records
    III. have access to records even if the child is not in his/her custody

    (A) I only
    (B) II only
    (C) III only
    (D) I and II only
    (E) I, II, and III

12. A man stopped petting his dog upon arriving home each day. Soon his dog stopped greeting him at the door. Which of the following has occurred?

    (A) discrimination
    (B) extinction
    (C) generalization
    (D) reinforcement
    (E) repression

13. Which one of the following is the best approach for an eighth-grade teacher to take in helping pupils who have difficulty in reading verbal problems in the available textbooks?

    (A) Stop teaching content and teach reading.
    (B) Avoid giving verbal problems on homework assignments.
    (C) Postpone problem-solving until later in the school year.
    (D) Omit verbal problems from this class's work.
    (E) Duplicate work sheets containing verbal problems constructed by teacher and pupils.

14. If a teacher decided to promote greater participation in class discussion by first praising students who were merely looking at each other, then by praising any verbal exchange, the teacher would be

    (A) shaping behavior
    (B) employing intrinsic rewards
    (C) practicing Pavlovian conditioning
    (D) attempting a class sociogram
    (E) implementing Maslow's theory of self-actualization

15. The primary function of testing is to help people

    (A) understand one another
    (B) make decisions
    (C) measure basic abilities
    (D) learn more efficiently
    (E) graduate

16. A colleague requests that you sign a letter being sent to the local newspaper, criticizing the amount of money spent on athletic activities rather than on improving teachers' salaries. You agree, and as a non-tenured teacher, you should

    (A) realize that, if you sign, you are providing the Board with grounds for non-reappointment

(B) sign it only if your immediate supervisor gives permission
(C) politely refuse to sign it
(D) sign it, if you agree strongly enough
(E) sign it only if the union representative agrees

17. Negative transfer is most likely to occur in which of the following situations?

(A) An American boy who played varsity football moves to Canada and tries out for a team that plays by slightly different Canadian rules.
(B) A girl who skies every weekend decides to take up skydiving.
(C) A boy used to riding a bicycle begins to take driver education.
(D) A woman who has been a housewife begins a job in an office.
(E) A former teacher becomes a consumer advocate.

18. Which one of the following statements is true with regard to the "activity program"?

(A) The child is displaced as the center of the educative process.
(B) Maximum preparation for effective group-living is considered essential.
(C) The learning of a definite body of factual material is stressed.
(D) Distinct effort is made to keep children "up to standard" in drill subjects.
(E) Physical education is the basis of all units.

19. If you wanted to teach for *transfer*, you would try to teach in such a way that

(A) one subject or topic would be related to another.
(B) your students would be prepared for the next highest grade or an advanced course
(C) what is learned would be likely to be applied to out-of-school situations
(D) what your students learned would be consistent with what students in other schools learn
(E) children with high mobility could easily move from one school to another

20. Evaluation goes beyond testing in that evaluation also involves

(A) systematic procedures
(B) levels of measurement
(C) value judgments
(D) behavioral objectives
(E) statistical analysis

21. A pregnant woman applies for a teaching position. Under current legal regulations,

(A) the local Board of Education need not consider her application
(B) must consider her application along with any other
(C) must hire her, in order to not violate her Civil Rights
(D) cannot assign her below grade three
(E) need not be informed by her that she is pregnant

22. If you were teaching tennis and knew that the student learning would be consistent with typical learning curves, you would expect your students to

(A) do very well at first, then backslide when the novelty wore off, then progress steadily
(B) be enthusiastic at first but gradually lose interest
(C) be awkward at first, then increase noticeably in skill, then seem to reach a stage of no apparent improvement

(D) do poorly at first, then progress steadily until the end of the year
(E) learn consistently and steadily

23. When a child asks a question the answer to which you, the teacher, do not know, the best of the following actions for you to take is to

(A) say, "Look up the answer and make a report to the class."
(B) say, "I don't know; let's both try to find out."
(C) say, "Let's not worry about it now," and then look it up yourself
(D) give the child three or four references and say, "See whether you can find it out for yourself."
(E) keep going with the lesson as if nothing happened

24. Your students genuinely understood the meaning of the concept of social class after you defined it if they could

(A) give the same definition without adding any extraneous meaning
(B) write the definition three months later, retaining each element in your definition
(C) give the definition at any time
(D) explain the term in their own words, retaining the meaning of your definition
(E) write an essay elaborating on the long-range implications of social class differences

25. Which one of the following objectives points to behavior that can be observed and counted? To

(A) acquire an appreciation for laws and regulations
(B) understand the application of algebra to everyday mathematics
(C) demonstrate ability to add two-digit numbers with and without carrying
(D) acquire an appreciation for classical music
(E) have a good attitude towards mathematics

26. The Essentialist Movement in education was mainly

(A) a condemnation of the extremes of the Progressive Movement
(B) a plea to reduce social education to the barest essentials
(C) a call for indoctrination for a new collectivist society
(D) based on the teachings of William H. Kilpatrick and John Dewey
(E) an attempt to stress science education as necessary for a growing technological society

27. Social class influences are likely to be greatest in relation to

(A) physical development
(B) the development of verbal skills
(C) primary drives
(D) sex differences in development
(E) frequency of dreaming

28. Of the following, the most important element in a problem situation in terms of the pupil's learning is that

(A) the pupil feels a need or desire to find a solution
(B) the problem situation comes from the experiences of the pupil
(C) the teacher considers the problem important
(D) the problem be clear-cut and solvable in only one way
(E) there be no barrier between the pupil and the solution

29. An enlightened approach to discipline would stress the

    (A) complete freedom of the child
    (B) necessity for limits
    (C) presence of prompt punishment
    (D) proverb, "spare the rod; spoil the child"
    (E) power of the teacher

30. Which statement is amenable to scientific inquiry?

    (A) All schools should teach driver education.
    (B) Driver education is an important part of the curriculum.
    (C) Driver education is more important than drug abuse education.
    (D) Driver education graduates have fewer accidents than drivers without driver education.
    (E) Driver education teachers have good attitudes towards children.

31. John Dewey's philosophy
    I. makes the aim of education acceptance of our social institutions
    II. views the school as a place to prepare pupils for the future
    III. views education as a continuous process of revising or reorganizing experience

    (A) I only is correct
    (B) II only is correct
    (C) III only is correct
    (D) I and III are correct
    (E) I, II, and III are correct

32. The term that describes the infant's unique perspective and self-interest is

    (A) ethnocentrism
    (B) egocentrism
    (C) geocentrism
    (D) altruism
    (E) socialization

33. A project in a dressmaking class requires a quick and simple pattern layout, very little cutting, but a considerable amount of sewing. As a class to be evaluated by teacher observation, this project

    (A) emphasizes the basic skill, sewing, and is therefore a good one
    (B) should be rated on only one skill, not on all three
    (C) should include additional samples of each skill
    (D) samples too little of some skills and too much sewing
    (E) will provide a good overall estimate of the students' dressmaking ability

34. Jodie can string beads and draw designs quite well with either a pencil or crayon. She is probably how many years old?

    (A) two
    (B) three
    (C) four
    (D) five
    (E) six

35. Which of the following correlation coefficients would yield the strongest basis for prediction?

    (A) .05
    (B) .40
    (C) − .50
    (D) 1.20
    (E) − .70

36. Which of the following are reasons that teacher professional organizations give for the need for tenure?

    I. Tenure provides for faculty stability
    II. Tenure protects innovative teachers from attack
    III. Tenure provides job security for the teacher of average ability
    IV. Tenure gives freedom to teach in the face of special interest groups

    (A) all of the above
    (B) I and II only
    (C) I, II, and IV only
    (D) II, III, and IV only
    (E) III and IV only

37. Two 3-year-olds who are strangers to one another meet in a yard without other persons present. After they stare at each other, John hits Bob and stands back to watch while Bob cries. Bob stops crying. This sequence is repeated. What is the most likely motive for the hitting? John is

    (A) trying to establish social dominance
    (B) releasing hostility
    (C) exploring
    (D) probably unloved and punished too much at home
    (E) seeking attention

38. "Creative writing," as understood by most teachers, can be achieved by

    (A) all children on their own level
    (B) only very bright children
    (C) only talented children
    (D) only those children who have developed an appreciation for literature
    (E) only children reading above grade level

39. Rose, age three, sees her mother applying makeup. When she goes to nursery school, she goes to the housekeeping corner and begins to apply lipstick and powder to her face. Rose is displaying

    (A) symbolic play
    (B) centration
    (C) deferred imitation
    (D) egocentrism
    (E) conservation

40. A researcher reports that a sample of 100 children on the average (the mean) first spoke a meaningful word at age 8 months with a standard deviation of 2

months. This means that two-thirds of the children first spoke meaningful words between the ages of

(A) birth and eight months
(B) eight and twelve months
(C) eight and ten months
(D) six and ten months
(E) four and twelve months

41. Those whose educational philosophy is rooted in pragmatism

(A) reject the scientific method of experimentation
(B) maintain that complete objectivity is possible
(C) accept the stimulus-response learning theory
(D) consider that IQ is innate and constant
(E) claim that knowledge is tentative and truth is relative

42. Past research suggests that four- and five-year-old children differentiate the sexes on the basis of

(A) anatomical differences
(B) clothing and hairdo
(C) psychological dimensions
(D) facial characteristics
(E) voice quality

43. The American version of the British Infant Schools is the

(A) laissez-faire policy
(B) "room without teachers" program
(C) open classroom
(D) token reward system
(E) Head Start program

44. An understanding of Piaget's work helps teachers

(A) teach language
(B) reduce cognitive dissonance
(C) create discipline in the classroom
(D) to be warm and understanding
(E) decide when and how to present various concepts to children

45. The median, mean, and mode are identical

(A) in a positively skewed distribution
(B) in a negatively skewed distribution
(C) in a normal distribution
(D) under no circumstances
(E) in all distributions

46. A child who exhibits a level of retardation that is characterized by intellectual capacity as measured on a standardized test of intelligence which falls within a range from one-and-one-half to three standard deviations below the mean is considered

(A) neurologically impaired

(B) learning disabled
(C) educable
(D) trainable
(E) disadvantaged

47. Children usually perceive all kinds of things as possessing life, feelings, and purposes. This tendency is known as

(A) animism
(B) vitalism
(C) teleology
(D) ontology
(E) centration

48. One of the chief aims of the junior high school that differentiates it from the senior high school is that the junior high school

(A) makes provision for prevocational training
(B) seeks to meet individual differences through individual pupil programs
(C) has a wider variety of course offerings
(D) has a larger number of extracurricular activities
(E) emphasizes an exploratory program through curricular and extracurricular activities

49. Women teachers typically mishandle boys (from a mental hygiene point of view) by

(A) attempting to repress outward displays of aggression
(B) giving them more responsibility than they can handle
(C) subjecting them to curricular content which is unduly "feminine" in its orientation (for example, literature)
(D) making academic demands that are inappropriate
(E) being unconsciously seductive

50. The cross-sectional approach in child study is one by which the investigator

(A) compares children of the same age from different subcultures
(B) studies different children of different ages
(C) studies only one aspect of a child, such as personality
(D) uses stratified samples from the same populations
(E) studies children as they grow over several years

51. Which of the following statements about sex typing is *not* true?

(A) Different cultures regard different behaviors as sex-appropriate.
(B) Male or female behavior is probably determined by a combination of hormonal and environmental influences.
(C) Male or female behavior is unalterably established biologically.
(D) United States society is less rigid in its sex-role definitions than many others.
(E) Cultures have clearer views of male than female roles.

52. In our society, sex-role continuity is greatest for

    (A) middle-class children
    (B) boys
    (C) girls
    (D) middle-years children
    (E) adolescent girls

53. A Board of Education debating the use of performance contracting is

    (A) using a system of merit pay
    (B) about to increase teachers' salaries indirectly
    (C) spending money on private firms
    (D) purchasing computers to replace teachers
    (E) disappointed by the results of recent testing

54. Teachers can help adolescents into maturity by

    (A) forcing them to carry out adult responsibilities in a mature manner
    (B) leaving them alone and letting maturity appear automatically
    (C) giving them adult responsibilities that are not overwhelming
    (D) having them associate with other adolescents who have reached maturity
    (E) carefully giving reading assignments about good role models

55. To evaluate an innovative education program properly, which of the following is (are) necessary?

     I. behavioral objectives
    II. reliable and valid measures
    III. children of average or above ability

    (A) I only
    (B) II only
    (C) III only
    (D) I, II, and III
    (E) I and II only

56. In primitive societies the individual moves from childhood into adulthood via

    (A) a self-derived interpretation of adult functions
    (B) rites of passage
    (C) adolescence
    (D) marriage
    (E) education

57. "Homeostasis" refers to

    (A) cultural change in the direction of homogeneity
    (B) the consistency of behavior across different cultures
    (C) a process by which children are able to resolve emotional conflicts
    (D) mechanisms that keep the organism's physiology in balance
    (E) sexual identification of human males

58. A test measures what it is supposed to measure as judged by how well it correlates with other measures. The test is

    (A) valid
    (B) standardized
    (C) reliable
    (D) normed
    (E) objective

59. A child is asked how a cow and horse are similar. Which of the responses below is *least* mature?

    (A) They are both animals.
    (B) They are both bigger than people.
    (C) The dog chases the cat, the horse runs fast.
    (D) They are both farm animals.
    (E) They both have tails.

60. You have a set of ten scores. Eight of the scores range from 16 to 20 and the other two scores are 28 and 30. These two extreme scores would have the greatest effect on the

    (A) mode
    (B) mean
    (C) median
    (D) quartile deviation
    (E) low point of the range

61. In adolescence a conspicuous social-class difference is that

    (A) working-class girls have greater freedom than middle-class girls
    (B) working-class youths assume adult roles with less strain than middle-class youths
    (C) middle-class boys have greater sexual freedom than working-class boys
    (D) masturbation is more acceptable for working-class boys than for middle-class boys
    (E) working-class youths place greater value on education as a means of upward mobility

62. When a child begins behaving more childishly than in recent months, this behavior is called

    (A) regression
    (B) fixation
    (C) growth reverberations
    (D) anaclitic depression
    (E) sublimation

63. In using the *contract* approach, you

    (A) devise a series of learning contracts and help students
    (B) meet with students and come to mutual agreement about work to be completed
    (C) meet with students individually and go over exams
    (D) tell students the grade they could earn if they complete a given number of contracts (or assigned learning units)

(E) avoid tenure by placing all your staff on annual contracts

64. If you want to put into practice the suggestions of Kohlberg, the best way to encourage the development of moral reasoning would be to

(A) confront students with moral dilemmas and lead open-ended discussions on these dilemmas
(B) encourage the study of classic moral works such as the Bible
(C) provide readings and curricular materials with "moral" lessons
(D) show the relevancy of proper obedience to authority and be consistent and firm in enforcing rules
(E) arrange debates and reward the team with the greatest number of right arguments

65. In scientific inquiry the term *theory* is best defined as

(A) an untested speculation
(B) a generalization induced from observation
(C) a generalization deduced from experimentation
(D) a generalization which is both deduced from observation and induced from experimentation
(E) the researcher's hunch or best guess about the results

66. School busing is associated with the Coleman report because school busing was

(A) evaluated by researchers who wrote the Coleman Report
(B) based on findings of the Coleman Report
(C) reaffirmed by the Coleman Report
(D) developed from misinterpretations of the Coleman Report
(E) based on a brief Coleman wrote to the Supreme Court

67. According to Erikson's stage theory of man,

(A) a person's behavior and his understanding of himself are partly determined by social-role expectations
(B) a person's personality and his social self undergo different lines of development
(C) basic mistrust is a necessary first step in the development of personality
(D) a person who conforms to social expectations is unable to actualize his potential
(E) sexual fantasies dominate development until adolescence

68. On the Spring reading achievement test, Julie achieved a score that placed her at the 82nd percentile. This means that

(A) she did better than 82% of the children who took the test
(B) she scored 82 out of the 100 items correct
(C) 82% of those who took the test did better than Julie
(D) she scored at a level that is average for the eighth grade, second month
(E) she answered 82% of the items correctly, but we don't know how long the test was

69. Pupils who don't chew gum in class because they fear the punishment they might receive if caught may be classified as

(A) at the formal operations stage of Piaget's scale
(B) emotionally unstable
(C) at the lowest stage of Kohlberg's scale of moral development
(D) students who understand the reason for the rules
(E) all of the above

70. The following is an excerpt from a research report:
"The question then arises whether learning under such conditions transfers. It is to the clarification of the latter problem that the present research is directed."
The excerpt is most properly called the

(A) hypothesis
(B) introduction
(C) statement of the problem
(D) operational hypothesis
(E) definition

71. The unit of government in the United States generally responsible for the safe-guarding of educational standards is the

(A) federal government
(B) township
(C) state government
(D) municipal government
(E) local school board

72. A fully developed program for bilingual-bicultural children in a school system would include which of the following:
  I. classes with instruction in the content areas in the child's native language
  II. classes in English as a second language
  III. transition classes for children developing fluency

(A) I only
(B) I and II only
(C) I, II, and III
(D) II and III only
(E) I and III only

73. Which of the following is *not* a characteristic of the educational theory and practice of Maria Montessori?

(A) Sense training is strongly emphasized.
(B) Work began with mentally deficient children.
(C) It resembles the "Summerhill" system of England's A.S. Neill.
(D) Stress is laid on involvement of the child with self-teaching materials.
(E) The teacher remains somewhat in the background.

74. Which of the following groups is excluded from being considered as learning-disabled under P.L. 94–142?

(A) visually impaired
(B) hearing impaired
(C) mentally retarded

    (D) economically disadvantaged
    (E) neurologically impaired

75. When a research report calls a finding "statistically significant," this means that

    (A) it is likely to have occurred by chance
    (B) the professional implications are critical
    (C) findings such as this never occur by chance alone
    (D) findings such as this can occur only by chance
    (E) findings such as this occur very rarely by chance

76. A student misbehaved badly enough for a school to consider a five-day suspension. Place the following steps in their proper sequence according to recent court decisions on student rights:

    I. suspension
    II. oral or written notice of charges
    III. a hearing on charges

    (A) I, II, III
    (B) I, III, II
    (C) II, III, I
    (D) II, I, III
    (E) III, II, I

77. Our society's high rate of child abuse is most probably an outgrowth of

    (A) our overly large percentage of poor
    (B) our high level of education
    (C) the great popularity of TV shows and films that show violence
    (D) our general acceptance of physical force in child rearing
    (E) lack of legal penalties

78. Criterion-referenced testing is based on the notion that

    (A) you can establish passing scores for any educational experience
    (B) behavioral objectives need criteria for teaching
    (C) norms provide the best insight into achievement
    (D) grade equivalents are more reliable than percentiles
    (E) a child's performance on a few properly chosen items can tell you if he knows a concept

79. A critical piece of legislation in establishing public support for education in the United States was the

    (A) Missouri Compromise
    (B) Declaration of Independence
    (C) Plymouth Compact
    (D) Virginia Resolution
    (E) Northwest Ordinance

80. A primary purpose for developing a table of specifications showing the relationship of content to objectives in a test is to

(A) insure appropriate representation of each objective and content category
(B) show the pupils the kind of questions to be included in the test
(C) translate statements of ultimate goals to immediate goals that can be measured
(D) include items over the range of difficulty levels
(E) make for objective scoring

81. Research on reinforcement suggests that

(A) intermittent reinforcement leads to more rapid and more efficient learning
(B) intermittent reinforcement leads to learning highly resistant to extinction
(C) delayed reinforcement leads to effective long-term retention
(D) delay in reinforcement has no effect on rote learning or its retention
(E) immediate reinforcement leads to maximal forgetting

82. The controversy over alleged cultural bias in current intelligence tests revolves around

(A) confusion as to the purpose of the IQ
(B) the use of "achievement-type" items as indexes of innate intellectual ability
(C) the isolation of the lower classes, with no benefit to them
(D) the unreliability of all testing
(E) the use of the IQ for the grade placement

83. The difficulty of a test item can be expressed in terms of the

(A) mean score on the test for the group tested
(B) percentage of all pupils who answer it correctly
(C) percentage of lower-scoring pupils who answer it correctly
(D) discrimination index between high and low scorers on the test
(E) number of pupils who omit it

84. Of the following statements, which states most accurately what we mean by an "instructional objective"? At the end of this unit, the student will

(A) have read two chapters in the textbook
(B) fully understand *Hamlet*
(C) appreciate the poetry of Shelley
(D) be able to multiply a two-digit number by a two-digit number
(E) be more highly motivated to learn

85. Objective-type test items are *least* adequate in assessing ability to

(A) select correct alternatives
(B) apply a general principle to a situation
(C) recognize an error in given material
(D) organize thoughts about a situation
(E) recall names, dates, and events

86. When Locke spoke of a "tabula rasa," he referred to his belief that the

(A) doctrine of innate ideas was essentially correct
(B) organism reacts as a whole to a stimulus
(C) mind "starts from scratch" in gathering sense data
(D) mind is composed of "faculties" to be exercised

(E) mind itself is a result of the process of evolution

87. The simplest kind of learning is represented by

   (A) the conditioned response
   (B) rote learning
   (C) skill development
   (D) concept formation
   (E) moral development

Use the code below to answer questions 88, 89, and 90

   (A) completion items
   (B) matching items
   (C) multiple-choice item
   (D) true-false items
   (E) no differences in item types

88. Which is the most flexible kind of objective item?

89. For which kind of item does guessing have the most effect on test scores?

90. In an Industrial Arts class the teacher wants to know how well the students can relate tools to their functions. Which is the most efficient kind of objective item to use?

91. Which of the following is most likely *not* a learned behavior?

   (A) saying, "Excuse me" when bumping into someone
   (B) crying when slicing an onion
   (C) preferring watermelon to oatmeal
   (D) scrambling an egg
   (E) spelling "achieve" as "acheive"

92. The teacher's greatest ally in the maintenance of classroom discipline is a

   (A) clear understanding on the part of the students that nonsense will not be tolerated
   (B) constructive program of classroom activities
   (C) firm hand
   (D) system of rewards for good behavior
   (E) strong detention system

93. Some examinations permit students to answer a given number of items from a larger set of items. Such use of optional items is

   (A) not recommended, because students may not have time to decide which items to answer
   (B) not recommended, because all students do not take the same test

    (C) recommended, because students may be knowledgeable in most topics, but not all

    (D) recommended, because it encourages weak students to answer questions

    (E) essential in criterion-referenced testing

94. In learning motor skills, one often sees a leveling off of performance that is called

    (A) resistance

    (B) a learning block

    (C) minimum proficiency

    (D) a plateau

    (E) extinction

95. To use classical conditioning in a classroom, a teacher would attempt to

    (A) condition students to appreciate the classics in all fields

    (B) get students to imitate the behavior of the best students in the class

    (C) associate school with pleasure in students' minds

    (D) ignore behavior she did not wish to condition

    (E) help a child who did not raise her hand

96. The theory of the five steps in teaching (preparation, presentation, association, generalization, and application) is most closely associated with

    (A) Herbart

    (B) Pestalozzi

    (C) Froebel

    (D) Comenius

    (E) Kilpatrick

97. According to Skinner, the greatest single cause of inefficiency in the classroom is the

    (A) failure to coordinate its efforts with the child's developmental stages

    (B) inappropriateness of its curriculum

    (C) infrequency of its reinforcements

    (D) overemphasis on expository teaching

    (E) size of classes

98. A researcher decides to use height as a measure of intelligence. He will measure children and add 31 to their height to reach an IQ so that a child 61 inches tall will have an IQ of 92. This measure of IQ is

    (A) reliable but not valid

    (B) valid but not reliable

    (C) neither reliable nor valid

    (D) both reliable and valid

    (E) useful for children under six feet

99. Which of the following curricular dimensions is most closely associated with the selection of topics to be included in a curriculum?

    (A) scope

    (B) sequence

    (C) articulation

    (D) evaluation

    (E) none of the above

100. A teacher notices that Linda, first violinist in the school band, has quickly learned the cello. This is an example of

    (A) high motivation

    (B) reinforcement

    (C) learning by doing

    (D) proactive inhibition

    (E) positive transfer of training

101. Tom, who is in the fourth grade, took a standardized reading test and achieved a grade equivalent of 4.3. This means that Tom

    (A) reads and understands an average of 4.3 of every ten words he reads

    (B) reads at the 43rd percentile for fourth graders

    (C) reads better than most fifth graders

    (D) reads at the level of the average fourth-grade student in the third month of the fourth grade

    (E) is an average fourth grader

102. Bloom's *Taxonomy* is a guide to

    (A) educational outcomes

    (B) statistical techniques

    (C) rules for writing objective items

    (D) school subjects suitable for testing

    (E) body types

103. In recording anecdotes, which of the following procedures would *not* be advisable?

    (A) separating observer opinion from the objective behavior observed

    (B) writing anecdotes at the end of each week

    (C) recording both positive and negative incidents of the relevant behaviors

    (D) limiting anecdotes to single events

    (E) including as much specific detail as possible

104. When we speak of the *affective* aspect of curriculum, we are referring to the learning of

    (A) skills to alter the environment

    (B) better ways to retain facts

    (C) attitudes and values

    (D) habits and reflexes

    (E) high performance levels

105. If memorizing in school is justified today, it is because

    (A) memorizing strengthens the memory function of the brain

    (B) learning is never instantaneous

    (C) acquiring facts is useful

    (D) memorizing disciplines the student

    (E) children enjoy reciting from memory

106. The non-graded school concept is significant chiefly because it provides for

    (A) flexibility in the designation of grade levels
    (B) implementation of the theory of continuous pupil progress
    (C) longer periods of time for achieving certain learnings
    (D) carefully developed subject-matter sequences
    (E) an alternative to annual promotions

107. A teacher interested in stimulating creative writing might use which of the following stimuli?

    (A) music
    (B) the weather report
    (C) the business section of a newspaper
    (D) scientific experiments
    (E) all of the above

108. A French teacher was constructing a test for first-year students. She consulted courses of study, textbooks, and experts in the field in order to determine what areas to include. She was attempting to ensure that the test would have

    (A) predictive validity
    (B) reliability
    (C) concurrent validity
    (D) content validity
    (E) construct validity

109. Children need the daily routines of nursery school and kindergarten because young children

    (A) want teacher-direction during the school day
    (B) need a feeling of security and knowledge of what is expected of them
    (C) enjoy a change of pace from the play period
    (D) easily become overstimulated in the play period and lose all sense of control
    (E) can neither make decisions nor act independently

110. In which of the following activities should pupil assistance *not* be utilized?

    (A) writing notes on the chalkboard
    (B) giving class demonstrations
    (C) planning advanced lessons
    (D) choosing a place for a class field trip
    (E) preparing term ratings

111. Miss Jones made up a new test in fourth-grade arithmetic, and took the time to determine the reliability, which she discovered was quite high. Fred achieved a score of 82 on the test. If Miss Jones were to test Fred again, soon after the first test, and before any further arithmetic lessons, what prediction would you make about his score?

    (A) He would score higher than 82.
    (B) He would score lower than 82.
    (C) He would score somewhere near 82, but you can't tell if he would be higher or lower.

(D) No matter what his score, he would improve his percentile rank.

(E) You can't predict anything about his score.

112. In Miss W's class pupils are required to follow definite procedures for checking attendance, distributing supplies, etc. From the standpoint of modern class management, such requirements are

(A) undesirable, chiefly because they are excessively routinized and not adaptable to changing situations

(B) undesirable, chiefly because they do not provide for individual differences and increased growth

(C) desirable, chiefly because they enable the teacher to maintain effective control over the classroom situation

(D) desirable, chiefly because they make possible more efficient use of class time

(E) obsolete, because these tasks are now done by the central office

113. A teacher who uses "values clarification" techniques in the classroom is helping the learner develop in

(A) content areas

(B) psychomotor areas

(C) intelligence

(D) affective areas

(E) religious beliefs

114. Creativity is said to involve thinking that is called

(A) convergent

(B) divergent

(C) impulsive

(D) reflective

(E) accommodative

115. A curriculum committee recommends that children in the primary grades begin their social studies program with the consideration of relatively simple cultures, such as that of Eskimos. In later grades they would advance to the study of our own complex, industrial culture. Which one of the following statements most correctly evaluates this suggested program?

(A) The proposal is good, because it takes into consideration the relationship between interest and motivation.

(B) The proposal is good, because it provides for intercultural education at the child's own level.

(C) The proposal is poor, because the so-called "simple" cultures are foreign to the child in our society and actually present many complexities.

(D) The proposal is poor, because most primary grade teachers have little background in anthropology and tend to overstress the odd or "quaint" factors in such studies.

(E) The proposal is good, because children already know by experience the culture around them.

116. A reinforcement

(A) strengthens a stimulus by occurring in conjunction with it
(B) signals the end of a response
(C) is necessary for learning
(D) increases the likelihood of the occurrence of a certain response following a certain stimulus again
(E) must occur before the stimulus to be fully effective

117. If a high-school class of 30, evenly divided between boys and girls, arrives in a classroom with 30 seats, which of the arrangements below is the preferred plan for seating the students?

(A) All should be seated alphabetically.
(B) First separate the boys and girls, then seat alphabetically.
(C) Seat by size, assigning the smallest students to the front seats and then assigning progressively larger students to seats farther from the front.
(D) Ask the students if there are any friends who wish to sit together, seat those who respond, and then permit the others to sit where they wish.
(E) Be certain that students who have sight or hearing deficiencies are seated in front, and then permit the others to choose their seats.

118. The teachers' association and the local Board of Education cannot agree on a new contract. They agree to submit the dispute to three people, one to be selected by the teachers, one by the Board, and the third jointly. This process is called

(A) mediation
(B) striking
(C) hearings
(D) arbitration
(E) negotiation

119. A teacher who discusses the enjoyable aspects of completing a project well, rather than grading it, is a believer in

(A) intrinsic motivation
(B) extrinsic motivation
(C) spiral motivation
(D) hierarchical motivation
(E) Skinnerian principles of motivation

120. Joan cannot take the qualifying examination for the Music Award because of a religious holiday celebrated by her religion, but not by the school system. The result of this is that

(A) Joan loses her chance to compete
(B) Joan must be given another opportunity
(C) Joan should come to school just for the examination
(D) the music teacher must use other criteria to select a winner
(E) everyone must take the examination again, when Joan can take it

121. The learning of principles or rules is required for

(A) devising mnemonic devices
(B) advance organizers
(C) problem-solving
(D) discrimination

(E) response chains

122. The daily homework assignment should usually

    (A) not include exercises on any new work
    (B) have part devoted to review and part based on new work
    (C) require at least one hour of intensive work
    (D) consist mainly of working ahead to prepare better for the next day's lesson
    (E) prepare students to take standardized tests on the material involved

123. When a child is referred to the Child Study team for a comprehensive evaluation, that evaluation must include which of the following?

    I. a health appraisal by the school physician or school nurse
    II. a psychological examination by a school psychologist
    III. an evaluation of dexterity and coordination by the physical education teacher
    IV. a social assessment by the social worker

The required combination is

    (A) I and II only
    (B) I, II, and III only
    (C) II and IV only
    (D) I, II, and IV only
    (E) I, II, III, and IV

124. The concept that schoolchildren have the same kinds of legal and constitutional rights as adults do is referred to as

    (A) civil rights
    (B) individualization
    (C) due process
    (D) habeus corpus
    (E) de jure integration

125. Which of the following is usually the final phase of linear instructional planning?

    (A) designing the evaluation of student performance
    (B) stating the behavioral objectives
    (C) selecting the goals for the instructional unit
    (D) determining the learning activities
    (E) choosing the materials needed

126. To an Essentialist, *how* students study a subject is as important as

    (A) who is teaching
    (B) where they are studying
    (C) what they are studying
    (D) why they are studying it
    (E) what they learn

127. In the years since 1960, American education has been characterized by the increasing importance of

(A) centralization and lay control
(B) centralization and professional control
(C) decentralization and professional control
(D) decentralization and lay control
(E) none of the above

128. The estimated annual cost of vandalism in American public schools is now

(A) $1,000,000
(B) $10,000,000
(C) $50,000,000
(D) $100,000,000
(E) $500,000,000

129. In his work on alternative educational possibilities, Ivan Illich maintains that access to the fruits of science is largely impeded by the professional structure established and maintained by

(A) teacher organizations
(B) professional organizations in the sciences
(C) the way we select curricula
(D) sexism and racism
(E) traditional schooling

130. Skinner suggests that educators must accept which of the following responsibilities?

(A) deciding what skills most students need
(B) selecting subjects that can be taught easily
(C) making value judgments about educational policy
(D) establishing a system that permits students to have free choice of their areas of study
(E) all of the above

Stop

End of section. If you have any time left, go over your work in this section only. Do not work in any other section of the test.

Answer Key
Section 1: Professional Knowledge

Use this Key to score your Examination by circling the number of each item you answered correctly. To be certain you have scored your examination accurately, take an extra few minutes to rescore it and so verify your first scoring.

1. A	27. D	53. C	79. E	105. D
2. D	28. B	54. C	80. A	106. A
3. B	29. B	55. E	81. B	107. E
4. B	30. D	56. B	82. A	108. D
5. A	31. D	57. D	83. B	109. B
6. A	32. B	58. A	84. D	110. E
7. E	33. D	59. C	85. D	111. C
8. A	34. C	60. B	86. C	112. D
9. D	35. E	61. B	87. A	113. D
10. B	36. C	62. A	88. C	114. B
11. E	37. C	63. B	89. D	115. C
12. B	38. A	64. A	90. B	116. A
13. E	39. A	65. D	91. B	117. E
14. A	40. D	66. C	92. B	118. D
15. D	41. E	67. A	93. C	119. A
16. D	42. B	68. A	94. D	120. B
17. A	43. C	69. C	95. C	121. C
18. B	44. E	70. C	96. A	122. A
19. A	45. C	71. C	97. C	123. D
20. D	46. C	72. C	98. A	124. C
21. B	47. A	73. C	99. A	125. A
22. C	48. B	74. D	100. E	126. C
23. B	49. A	75. E	101. D	127. D
24. D	50. B	76. C	102. A	128. D
25. C	51. C	77. D	103. B	129. C
26. A	52. B	78. E	104. C	130. A

Diagnostic Table for the Professional Knowledge Examination

The table below is intended to provide you with a detailed insight into your performance on the Professional Knowledge section on the second Diagnostic Core Battery. The score sheet will provide you with separate scores in the thirteen different content areas tested.

To use the table, first score your performance on the Professional Knowledge Examination. Then circle the number of each item you answered correctly on the table. After you have done this, simply count the number of circles in each row and enter that number in the column headed "Number Correct." A perfect score in any one area would be ten; therefore, any time you achieved fewer than six correct, you have identified an area in need of further study. A score lower than four identifies an area needing major review.

Area Covered	Question Numbers	Number Correct
1. Historical, Philosophical Foundations	1, 16, 26, 31, 41, 86, 96, 126, 129, 130	
2. Social and Cultural Foundations	51, 56, 61, 66, 71, 77, 82, 124, 127, 128	
3. Child and Adolescent Development	3, 27, 32, 37, 42, 47, 52, 57, 62, 67	
4. Application of Child/Adolescent Development	29, 34, 39, 44, 49, 54, 59, 64, 69, 74	
5. Learning Theories and Principles	2, 7, 12, 17, 22, 87, 91, 94, 114, 121	
6. Application of Learning Theory, Principles	4, 9, 14, 19, 24, 81, 95, 100, 105, 109	
7. Test Development, Evaluation, and Assessment Principles	5, 10, 15, 20, 25, 80, 85, 88, 89, 90	
8. Understanding Test and Measurement Concepts, Grading	58, 68, 78, 83, 93, 98, 101, 108, 111, 116	
9. Research and Statistical Concepts	30, 35, 40, 45, 50, 55, 60, 65, 70, 75	
10. Teaching Principles, Practices	13, 18, 23, 28, 33, 38, 107, 113, 119, 122	
11. Classroom Management	8, 92, 97, 102, 103, 106, 110, 112, 117, 125	
12. Curriculum Development and Supervision	43, 48, 53, 63, 72, 73, 84, 99, 104, 115	
13. Professional Awareness	6, 11, 21, 36, 46, 76, 79, 118, 120, 123	

Answer Sheet
Section 2: General Knowledge

SOCIAL STUDIES

1 Ⓐ Ⓑ Ⓒ Ⓓ Ⓔ	6 Ⓐ Ⓑ Ⓒ Ⓓ Ⓔ	11 Ⓐ Ⓑ Ⓒ Ⓓ Ⓔ	16 Ⓐ Ⓑ Ⓒ Ⓓ Ⓔ	21 Ⓐ Ⓑ Ⓒ Ⓓ Ⓔ	26 Ⓐ Ⓑ Ⓒ Ⓓ Ⓔ	31 Ⓐ Ⓑ Ⓒ Ⓓ Ⓔ
2 Ⓐ Ⓑ Ⓒ Ⓓ Ⓔ	7 Ⓐ Ⓑ Ⓒ Ⓓ Ⓔ	12 Ⓐ Ⓑ Ⓒ Ⓓ Ⓔ	17 Ⓐ Ⓑ Ⓒ Ⓓ Ⓔ	22 Ⓐ Ⓑ Ⓒ Ⓓ Ⓔ	27 Ⓐ Ⓑ Ⓒ Ⓓ Ⓔ	32 Ⓐ Ⓑ Ⓒ Ⓓ Ⓔ
3 Ⓐ Ⓑ Ⓒ Ⓓ Ⓔ	8 Ⓐ Ⓑ Ⓒ Ⓓ Ⓔ	13 Ⓐ Ⓑ Ⓒ Ⓓ Ⓔ	18 Ⓐ Ⓑ Ⓒ Ⓓ Ⓔ	23 Ⓐ Ⓑ Ⓒ Ⓓ Ⓔ	28 Ⓐ Ⓑ Ⓒ Ⓓ Ⓔ	33 Ⓐ Ⓑ Ⓒ Ⓓ Ⓔ
4 Ⓐ Ⓑ Ⓒ Ⓓ Ⓔ	9 Ⓐ Ⓑ Ⓒ Ⓓ Ⓔ	14 Ⓐ Ⓑ Ⓒ Ⓓ Ⓔ	19 Ⓐ Ⓑ Ⓒ Ⓓ Ⓔ	24 Ⓐ Ⓑ Ⓒ Ⓓ Ⓔ	29 Ⓐ Ⓑ Ⓒ Ⓓ Ⓔ	34 Ⓐ Ⓑ Ⓒ Ⓓ Ⓔ
5 Ⓐ Ⓑ Ⓒ Ⓓ Ⓔ	10 Ⓐ Ⓑ Ⓒ Ⓓ Ⓔ	15 Ⓐ Ⓑ Ⓒ Ⓓ Ⓔ	20 Ⓐ Ⓑ Ⓒ Ⓓ Ⓔ	25 Ⓐ Ⓑ Ⓒ Ⓓ Ⓔ	30 Ⓐ Ⓑ Ⓒ Ⓓ Ⓔ	35 Ⓐ Ⓑ Ⓒ Ⓓ Ⓔ

LITERATURE

1 Ⓐ Ⓑ Ⓒ Ⓓ Ⓔ	6 Ⓐ Ⓑ Ⓒ Ⓓ Ⓔ	11 Ⓐ Ⓑ Ⓒ Ⓓ Ⓔ	16 Ⓐ Ⓑ Ⓒ Ⓓ Ⓔ	21 Ⓐ Ⓑ Ⓒ Ⓓ Ⓔ
2 Ⓐ Ⓑ Ⓒ Ⓓ Ⓔ	7 Ⓐ Ⓑ Ⓒ Ⓓ Ⓔ	12 Ⓐ Ⓑ Ⓒ Ⓓ Ⓔ	17 Ⓐ Ⓑ Ⓒ Ⓓ Ⓔ	22 Ⓐ Ⓑ Ⓒ Ⓓ Ⓔ
3 Ⓐ Ⓑ Ⓒ Ⓓ Ⓔ	8 Ⓐ Ⓑ Ⓒ Ⓓ Ⓔ	13 Ⓐ Ⓑ Ⓒ Ⓓ Ⓔ	18 Ⓐ Ⓑ Ⓒ Ⓓ Ⓔ	23 Ⓐ Ⓑ Ⓒ Ⓓ Ⓔ
4 Ⓐ Ⓑ Ⓒ Ⓓ Ⓔ	9 Ⓐ Ⓑ Ⓒ Ⓓ Ⓔ	14 Ⓐ Ⓑ Ⓒ Ⓓ Ⓔ	19 Ⓐ Ⓑ Ⓒ Ⓓ Ⓔ	24 Ⓐ Ⓑ Ⓒ Ⓓ Ⓔ
5 Ⓐ Ⓑ Ⓒ Ⓓ Ⓔ	10 Ⓐ Ⓑ Ⓒ Ⓓ Ⓔ	15 Ⓐ Ⓑ Ⓒ Ⓓ Ⓔ	20 Ⓐ Ⓑ Ⓒ Ⓓ Ⓔ	25 Ⓐ Ⓑ Ⓒ Ⓓ Ⓔ

FINE ARTS

1 Ⓐ Ⓑ Ⓒ Ⓓ Ⓔ	6 Ⓐ Ⓑ Ⓒ Ⓓ Ⓔ	11 Ⓐ Ⓑ Ⓒ Ⓓ Ⓔ	16 Ⓐ Ⓑ Ⓒ Ⓓ Ⓔ
2 Ⓐ Ⓑ Ⓒ Ⓓ Ⓔ	7 Ⓐ Ⓑ Ⓒ Ⓓ Ⓔ	12 Ⓐ Ⓑ Ⓒ Ⓓ Ⓔ	17 Ⓐ Ⓑ Ⓒ Ⓓ Ⓔ
3 Ⓐ Ⓑ Ⓒ Ⓓ Ⓔ	8 Ⓐ Ⓑ Ⓒ Ⓓ Ⓔ	13 Ⓐ Ⓑ Ⓒ Ⓓ Ⓔ	18 Ⓐ Ⓑ Ⓒ Ⓓ Ⓔ
4 Ⓐ Ⓑ Ⓒ Ⓓ Ⓔ	9 Ⓐ Ⓑ Ⓒ Ⓓ Ⓔ	14 Ⓐ Ⓑ Ⓒ Ⓓ Ⓔ	19 Ⓐ Ⓑ Ⓒ Ⓓ Ⓔ
5 Ⓐ Ⓑ Ⓒ Ⓓ Ⓔ	10 Ⓐ Ⓑ Ⓒ Ⓓ Ⓔ	15 Ⓐ Ⓑ Ⓒ Ⓓ Ⓔ	20 Ⓐ Ⓑ Ⓒ Ⓓ Ⓔ

SCIENCE

1 Ⓐ Ⓑ Ⓒ Ⓓ Ⓔ	6 Ⓐ Ⓑ Ⓒ Ⓓ Ⓔ	11 Ⓐ Ⓑ Ⓒ Ⓓ Ⓔ	16 Ⓐ Ⓑ Ⓒ Ⓓ Ⓔ	21 Ⓐ Ⓑ Ⓒ Ⓓ Ⓔ	26 Ⓐ Ⓑ Ⓒ Ⓓ Ⓔ
2 Ⓐ Ⓑ Ⓒ Ⓓ Ⓔ	7 Ⓐ Ⓑ Ⓒ Ⓓ Ⓔ	12 Ⓐ Ⓑ Ⓒ Ⓓ Ⓔ	17 Ⓐ Ⓑ Ⓒ Ⓓ Ⓔ	22 Ⓐ Ⓑ Ⓒ Ⓓ Ⓔ	27 Ⓐ Ⓑ Ⓒ Ⓓ Ⓔ
3 Ⓐ Ⓑ Ⓒ Ⓓ Ⓔ	8 Ⓐ Ⓑ Ⓒ Ⓓ Ⓔ	13 Ⓐ Ⓑ Ⓒ Ⓓ Ⓔ	18 Ⓐ Ⓑ Ⓒ Ⓓ Ⓔ	23 Ⓐ Ⓑ Ⓒ Ⓓ Ⓔ	28 Ⓐ Ⓑ Ⓒ Ⓓ Ⓔ
4 Ⓐ Ⓑ Ⓒ Ⓓ Ⓔ	9 Ⓐ Ⓑ Ⓒ Ⓓ Ⓔ	14 Ⓐ Ⓑ Ⓒ Ⓓ Ⓔ	19 Ⓐ Ⓑ Ⓒ Ⓓ Ⓔ	24 Ⓐ Ⓑ Ⓒ Ⓓ Ⓔ	29 Ⓐ Ⓑ Ⓒ Ⓓ Ⓔ
5 Ⓐ Ⓑ Ⓒ Ⓓ Ⓔ	10 Ⓐ Ⓑ Ⓒ Ⓓ Ⓔ	15 Ⓐ Ⓑ Ⓒ Ⓓ Ⓔ	20 Ⓐ Ⓑ Ⓒ Ⓓ Ⓔ	25 Ⓐ Ⓑ Ⓒ Ⓓ Ⓔ	30 Ⓐ Ⓑ Ⓒ Ⓓ Ⓔ

MATHEMATICS

1 Ⓐ Ⓑ Ⓒ Ⓓ Ⓔ   6 Ⓐ Ⓑ Ⓒ Ⓓ Ⓔ   11 Ⓐ Ⓑ Ⓒ Ⓓ Ⓔ   16 Ⓐ Ⓑ Ⓒ Ⓓ Ⓔ   21 Ⓐ Ⓑ Ⓒ Ⓓ Ⓔ

2 Ⓐ Ⓑ Ⓒ Ⓓ Ⓔ   7 Ⓐ Ⓑ Ⓒ Ⓓ Ⓔ   12 Ⓐ Ⓑ Ⓒ Ⓓ Ⓔ   17 Ⓐ Ⓑ Ⓒ Ⓓ Ⓔ

3 Ⓐ Ⓑ Ⓒ Ⓓ Ⓔ   8 Ⓐ Ⓑ Ⓒ Ⓓ Ⓔ   13 Ⓐ Ⓑ Ⓒ Ⓓ Ⓔ   18 Ⓐ Ⓑ Ⓒ Ⓓ Ⓔ

4 Ⓐ Ⓑ Ⓒ Ⓓ Ⓔ   9 Ⓐ Ⓑ Ⓒ Ⓓ Ⓔ   14 Ⓐ Ⓑ Ⓒ Ⓓ Ⓔ   19 Ⓐ Ⓑ Ⓒ Ⓓ Ⓔ

5 Ⓐ Ⓑ Ⓒ Ⓓ Ⓔ   10 Ⓐ Ⓑ Ⓒ Ⓓ Ⓔ   15 Ⓐ Ⓑ Ⓒ Ⓓ Ⓔ   20 Ⓐ Ⓑ Ⓒ Ⓓ Ⓔ

Diagnostic Core Battery II
Section 2.   General Knowledge

1 Hour 35 Minutes — 131 Questions

SOCIAL STUDIES

25 Minutes — 35 Questions

Directions: Each question is followed by five choices. Select the choice that is correct or most nearly correct.

1. In the early 1980's, one of the major factors weakening the power of OPEC, the oil cartel, was the emergence of which of the nations below, as an oil producer?

    (A) United States
    (B) Great Britain
    (C) Canada
    (D) Iran
    (E) Saudi Arabia

2. Which one of the following occurred after the fall of Constantinople?

    (A) the Battle of Tours
    (B) the Crusades
    (C) the Model Parliament
    (D) the Hegira
    (E) the expulsion of the Moors from Spain

3. The Constitution of the United States forbids any amendment that would

    (A) deprive a state, without its consent, of equal suffrage in the Senate
    (B) permit the formation of a new state within the jurisdiction of another state without the consent of its legislature
    (C) authorize a state to enter into a treaty with a foreign power
    (D) change the procedure for amendment set forth in the Constitution
    (E) affect interstate contracts

4. New Deal economic policies most closely reflected the principles of

    (A) Arthur F. Burns
    (B) Alfred Hayek
    (C) John M. Keynes
    (D) David Stockman
    (E) Paul Samuelson

5. The Treaty of Guadalupe-Hidalgo was concerned with the

    (A) land ceded by Mexico to the United States
    (B) Panama Canal Zone
    (C) intervention of the United States in Cuba
    (D) Venezuelan boundary question
    (E) building of the Southern Pacific Railroad

195

Questions 6 and 7 are based on the following data for cotton:

Quantity Demanded (Bales)	Price ($)	Quantity Supplied
450	50	770
500	40	730
560	30	680
610	20	610
670	10	570

6. Equilibrium price is

   (A) 10
   (B) 30
   (C) 40
   (D) 20
   (E) indeterminable from given data

7. Assuming that the government imposes a minimum price of $40 per bale,

   (A) a shortage of cotton will result
   (B) producers of the cotton will not be able to sell all of their cotton
   (C) purchasers would prefer to buy more cotton than is being supplied
   (D) producers of the cotton will make a reduction in the factors of production employed in the production of cotton
   (E) either A or C will be true

8. Which one of the following statements is *incorrect* concerning the process of amending the United States Constitution?

   (A) Of the two methods of proposing amendments to the Constitution, only one — proposal by Congress — has ever been employed.
   (B) If a state rejects an amendment, it cannot reverse its action.
   (C) Congress may fix a time limit of seven years in which the necessary number of states must ratify an amendment if it is to go into effect.
   (D) Of the two methods of ratifying amendments, ratification by conventions has been the more popular.
   (E) Petition of two-thirds of the state legislatures is necessary.

9. The loss of Chicago's claim to the title "Hog Butcher of the World" is due mainly to the

   (A) growth of major cities on the west coast and development of super highways for trucks
   (B) automation in the meat industry
   (C) increase in importation of meat from other countries
   (D) increase in the consumption of meat products
   (E) decrease in American consumption of beef

10. President Cleveland dealt with the question of the annexation of Hawaii by

    (A) restoring Queen Liliuokalani to the throne
    (B) urging the Senate to ratify the treaty of annexation
    (C) offering to buy Hawaii from the Queen
    (D) withdrawing the treaty of annexation from the Senate
    (E) ordering fleet units to oppose European landings

11. Which one of the following statements regarding the position of the serf in sixteenth-century western Europe is correct?

   (A) He was required to work for his lord at all times.
   (B) He could not be deprived of the right to cultivate land for his own benefit.
   (C) He lacked security, because he could be sold to another master.
   (D) He was like a tenant farmer in his relationship to the lord.
   (E) He was without standing in the Church courts.

12. The idea of Ptolemy that the sun revolved around the earth was disproved by

   (A) Sir Isaac Newton
   (B) Nicolaus Copernicus
   (C) Galileo Galilei
   (D) Roger Bacon
   (E) Tycho Brahe

13. The term "savanna" best describes large

   (A) forest areas of central Africa
   (B) swamp areas in the southern part of the United States
   (C) grassland regions of Brazil
   (D) constellations in the Milky Way
   (E) cotton-growing areas in the American south

14. Which one of the following does not require the President's signature?

   (A) a joint resolution
   (B) a pardon
   (C) a private bill
   (D) a public bill
   (E) a proposed amendment to the Constitution

15. Presidential electors in the United States must vote for their party's presidential candidate

   (A) because of recent federal legislation
   (B) as the result of a Supreme Court decision
   (C) if legislation of their state so prescribes
   (D) since the adoption of the Twelfth Amendment
   (E) at all times

16. Hoover Dam is located on the

   (A) Colorado River
   (B) Tennessee River
   (C) Missouri River
   (D) Columbia River
   (E) Mississippi River

17. New York ranks among the first ten states in the production of

   (A) dairy products, fruit, potatoes
   (B) dairy products, wheat, sugar beets
   (C) corn, wheat, sugar beets

(D) fruit, corn, potatoes

(E) beef and hog products

Questions 18 and 19 refer to the graph below.

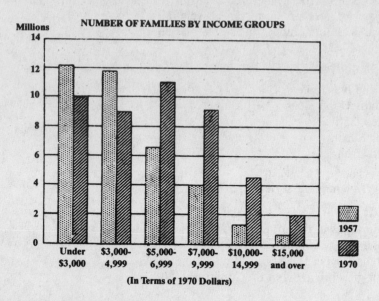

NUMBER OF FAMILIES BY INCOME GROUPS

Millions

(In Terms of 1970 Dollars)

1957

1970

18. Which trend is indicated during the period 1957–1970?

(A) The average family income increased.

(B) The number of families with incomes over $15,000 declined.

(C) The number of families earning between $3,000 and $4,999 increased.

(D) In 1970, 35% of the families in the United States earned $10,000–$15,000 per year.

(E) In 1957, more than half of United States families earned less than $3,000.

19. In which income group was there the greatest increase in the number of families?

(A) $3,000–$4,999

(B) $5,000–$6,999

(C) $7,000–$9,999

(D) $10,000–$14,999

(E) $15,000 and over

20. The outcome of the Whiskey Rebellion demonstrated the

(A) effectiveness of the doctrine of nullification

(B) authority of the central government

(C) popular acceptance of excise taxes

(D) growing approval of Federalist Party policies

(E) persuasive ability of Hamilton

21. Which one of the following was the first official step taken by the United States in support of resistance to Communist aggression?

(A) joint action with the Allies in support of Italy's claims against Yugoslavia

(B) Secretary of State Marshall's plan to strengthen Western Europe
(C) President Truman's plan to aid Greece and Turkey
(D) signing of the North Atlantic Alliance
(E) breaking of the Berlin blockade

22. In which pair is the first item an immediate cause of the second?

(A) assassination of James Garfield—Pendleton Act
(B) election of John Quincy Adams—Twelfth Amendment
(C) assassination of Alexander Hamilton—end of the Federalist Party
(D) sinking of the Lusitania—entry of the United States into World War I
(E) Hitler's attack on Poland—United States entry into World War II

23. The difference between the rigorous climate of Labrador and the relatively salubrious climate of Norway is due chiefly to

(A) prevailing winds and latitude
(B) latitude and altitude
(C) altitude and atmospheric pressure
(D) water currents and prevailing winds
(E) water currents and air flow

24. The Rules Committee of the House of Representatives is the most powerful committee of that branch of Congress by virtue of the fact that

(A) the Speaker of the House is chairperson of the Rules Committee
(B) it is the only committee of Congress composed exclusively of members of the majority party
(C) it ordinarily decides when to call up or to reject bills for consideration by the House
(D) it includes the floor leaders of both major parties
(E) it has unlimited delaying power

25. Which one of the following was *not* a result of the Commercial Revolution?

(A) The domestic system of production was introduced.
(B) Europe started on her career of world conquest.
(C) Some European merchants became wealthy enough to live like princes.
(D) The power of absolute monarchs decreased.
(E) Feudalism continued to disintegrate on the Continent.

26. Which one of the following was the primary issue in the decision in *Marbury* v. *Madison*?

(A) Could the Supreme Court hear an appeal from a state court?
(B) Could a defeated President appoint "midnight judges"?
(C) Could the federal government tax a state agency?
(D) Was Section 13 of the Judiciary Act of 1789 constitutional?
(E) Could a justice participate in a case in which he was an interested party?

27. "We hold these truths to be self-evident, that all men are created equal, that they are endowed by their Creator with certain inalienable rights . . ." This sentence is from which of the following?

(A) Albany Plan of Union
(B) Gettysburg Address

(C) Declaration of Independence
(D) Mayflower Compact
(E) United States Bill of Rights

28. The theory of "manifest destiny" is best illustrated in the

   (A) Good Neighbor Policy
   (B) slogan "Fifty-four forty or fight"
   (C) selection of the parallel 36° 30′ in the Missouri Compromise
   (D) granting of independence to the Philippines
   (E) Emancipation Proclamation

29. The role of the cabinet in American government is

   (A) defined in the Constitution
   (B) based on the ideas of Alexander Hamilton
   (C) an example of a practice that developed through custom
   (D) analogous to the system of government prevailing in England in the eighteenth century
   (E) a concept unique to American government

30. Two international agencies of the United Nations that did not exist under the League of Nations are

   (A) a Trusteeship Council and an International Labor Office
   (B) an Economic and Social Council and an International Court of Justice
   (C) an International Court of Justice and a Trusteeship Council
   (D) an International Labor Office and an Educational, Scientific, and Cultural Council
   (E) an Educational, Scientific, and Cultural Council and an Economic and Social Council

31. The Supreme Court of the United States

   (A) has the right to reverse decisions previously handed down by the Court
   (B) may deal directly with a problem even before it is faced with it in the tangible form of a legal controversy
   (C) must avoid passing judgment on federal laws that state courts have declared contrary to the Constitution
   (D) must muster a two-thirds vote of its membership to declare a law unconstitutional
   (E) has no original jurisdiction in cases with a state as one of the parties

32. "Dependent on outside sources for iron ore, recent development of hydroelectric power, large consumption of wheat products, rainfall scarce in southern portion . . ."— This description applies chiefly to

   (A) West Germany
   (B) Italy
   (C) Sweden
   (D Soviet Union
   (E) England

33. The British government differs from that of the United States in that its powers cannot be expanded by

    (A) laws passed by Parliament
    (B) customs and practices
    (C) judicial decisions
    (D) a specific process of amending the Constitution
    (E) administrative usage

34. The following problems were common to the post-war settlements of World War I and World War II *except*

    (A) the Italo-Yugoslav boundary
    (B) the Polish boundaries
    (C) Russian intransigence at post-war conferences
    (D) reparations from the defeated countries
    (E) realization of nationalistic sentiment

35. The most important factor in England's rise to power in the sixteenth century was the

    (A) riches brought home through expeditions to the New World
    (B) destruction of the Spanish naval power
    (C) world trip of Sir Francis Drake
    (D) conquest of New Amsterdam
    (E) discovery of gold in the West Indies

Stop

End of section. If you have any time left, go over your work in this section only. Do not work in any other section of the test.

LITERATURE

15 Minutes—25 Questions

Directions: Each question is followed by five choices.
Select the choice that is correct or most nearly correct.

1. Which playwright shocked his audiences by championing the cause of women's rights in the mid-nineteenth century?

    (A) Ibsen
    (B) Strindberg
    (C) Chekhov
    (D) Congreve
    (E) Synge

2. Which of the following writers is out of chronological order?

    (A) Chaucer
    (B) Shakespeare
    (C) Joyce
    (D) Milton
    (E) Dickens

3. The central theme of *The Yearling* is a

    (A) boy's distrust of his friends
    (B) boy's growing up
    (C) parent's lack of consideration for his child
    (D) boy's resentment against his environment
    (E) rescue of an abused horse

4. Jupiter was the

    (A) father of the gods
    (B) god of the sea
    (C) god of light
    (D) god of the lower world
    (E) god of war

5. The sirens were creatures that

    (A) warned people of their impending deaths
    (B) signalled the outbreak of war to alarm the population
    (C) sang for people in love and put them under a spell
    (D) sang for sailors, beguiling them towards the rocks where they were ship-wrecked
    (E) sang for the drowned as they went under

6. Which two persons were unwilling witnesses to a murder?

   (A) Jody and Penny Baxter
   (B) Jim Hawkins and Squire Trelawney
   (C) Tom Sawyer and Huckleberry Finn
   (D) Penrod and Sam
   (E) Wendy and John

7. "It was the best of times, it was the worst of times." This is the first sentence of

   (A) "The Collar" by Herbert
   (B) *A Tale of Two Cities* by Dickens
   (C) *The Rape of the Lock* by Pope
   (D) *Orlando Furioso* by Ariosto
   (E) "The Open Window" by Saki

8. Which of the following is an allegory?

   (A) *Joseph Andrews* by Fielding
   (B) *Don Quixote* by Cervantes
   (C) *Saint Joan* by Shaw
   (D) *Pilgrim's Progress* by Bunyan
   (E) *The Forsyte Saga* by Galsworthy

9. Rachel Carson's *Silent Spring* is about the

   (A) change of the seasons in England
   (B) erosion of the Continental Shelf on the Atlantic seaboard
   (C) effects of man's war against insects
   (D) exploration of the bottom of the sea
   (E) changes in migratory bird patterns

10. The archetype of desire on the part of the male child to replace the father in the affections of the mother is called

    (A) the Oedipus complex
    (B) libido
    (C) the myth of Narcissus
    (D) the Christ complex
    (E) the myth of Sisyphus

11. The author of the epic the hero of which, Gargantua, has become an archetype of gigantism and excess is

    (A) Swift
    (B) Rabelais
    (C) Cervantes
    (D) Chaucer
    (E) Tasso

12. Occasionally, comic strip characters originally produced for children gain literary acceptance because of the universal truths they expound. One such character is

    (A) Charlie Brown
    (B) Moon Mullins

(C) Popeye
(D) Red Ryder
(E) Blondie

13. "I believe a leaf of grass is no less than the journey-work of the stars" was written by

(A) Thoreau
(B) Dickinson
(C) Whitman
(D) Freneau
(E) Frost

14. "A children's classic, this book has had perhaps even more impact as a satire of a world of arbitrary and illogical pronouncements where language is used to confuse rather than clarify."
The statement above describes

(A) *Tom Swift*
(B) *The Adventures of Robin Hood*
(C) *Winnie the Pooh*
(D) *Alice in Wonderland*
(E) *The Wind in the Willows*

15. *Ivanhoe,* by Sir Walter Scott, falls in the category of

(A) historical novel
(B) epic poem
(C) sonnet
(D) tragedy
(E) satire

16. Which of the following is a satirical novel, set in the society of the future, in which placards everywhere say: "Big Brother is watching you"?

(A) Robbe-Grillet's *In the Labyrinth*
(B) Huxley's *Brave New World*
(C) Malraux's *Man's Fate*
(D) Orwell's *1984*
(E) Rand's *The Fountainhead*

17. Of the following, the poet whose work is most closely identified with New England is

(A) Vachel Lindsay
(B) Amy Lowell
(C) Carl Sandburg
(D) Robert Frost
(E) e.e. cummings

18. In Greek mythology, which one of the following stole fire from heaven?

(A) Sisyphus

(B) Prometheus
(C) Zeus
(D) Hades
(E) Icarus

19. Two characters who do *not* appear together in a Shakespeare play are

(A) Hamlet and Ophelia
(B) Portia and Othello
(C) Macbeth and Duncan
(D) Mercutio and Tybalt
(E) Falstaff and Henry IV

20. The author of *A Farewell to Arms* also wrote

(A) *Look Homeward, Angel*
(B) *Giant*
(C) *The Old Man and the Sea*
(D) *East of Eden*
(E) *The Naked and the Dead*

21. In the Old Testament, Joseph was

(A) sold by his brothers
(B) disowned by his father
(C) adopted by the queen
(D) betrayed by his wife
(E) tricked by Pharoah

22. *Profiles in Courage,* the Pulitzer Prize-winning biography, was written by a

(A) United States senator
(B) Supreme Court justice
(C) mountain climber
(D) pioneer in aviation
(E) World War I veteran

23. Keats' "Ode on a Grecian Urn" expresses the author's belief that

(A) all men are basically good
(B) beauty is a fleeting quality
(C) truth and beauty are inseparable
(D) only the art of the past is worthwhile
(E) poetry is the purest art

24. A line of poetry *not* taken from *A Child's Garden of Verses* is

(A) "Tiger, tiger, burning bright"
(B) "We built a ship upon the stairs"
(C) "Boats of mine a-boating"
(D) "The rain is raining all around"
(E) "I have a little shadow"

25. The name Walden is associated with

   (A) Emerson
   (B) Thoreau
   (C) Hawthorne
   (D) Alcott
   (E) Wordsworth

Stop

End of section. If you have any time left, go over your work in this section only. Do not work in any other section of the test.

FINE ARTS

10 Minutes—20 Questions

Directions: Each question is followed by five choices.
Select the choice that is correct or most nearly correct.

1. In accordance with the painter's wishes,

   (A) Picasso's *Guernica* was returned to Spain in the 1980's
   (B) Warhol's *Nude Descending a Staircase* was donated to the Guggenheim
   (C) Several late DeChirico works were auctioned off for charity
   (D) A Chagall window was installed at the United Nations
   (E) Wyeth's *Silent Spring* was returned to the Wyeth family collection

2. The words "I looked over Jordan, and what did I see" are found in the spiritual

   (A) "Steal Away"
   (B) "Deep River"
   (C) "Were You There"
   (D) "Swing Low, Sweet Chariot"
   (E) "He Has the Whole World in His Hands"

3. Considerable controversy raged over performances of Wagner's *Der Ring des Nibelungen*, marking the centenary of the Bayreuth Opera House. The performances were conducted by

   (A) Pierre Boulez
   (B) Herbert von Karajan
   (C) James Levine
   (D) Karl Bohm
   (E) Sarah Caldwell

4. Albrecht Dürer is best known for his use of which of the following media?

   (A) oils
   (B) water colors
   (C) woodcuts and engravings
   (D) charcoal and pastels
   (E) pen and ink

5. Of the following, the one in which Figaro is a character is

   (A) *Pagliacci*
   (B) *The Barber of Seville*
   (C) *Madame Butterfly*
   (D) *La Tosca*
   (E) *Aida*

6. Which of the following explains why it is often misleading to refer to a painting of Peter Paul Rubens as "genuine"?

   (A) Most are modern forgeries.
   (B) Most were begun by Rubens but detailed or completed by others.
   (C) He never actually painted anything but only managed a painting workshop.
   (D) Only copies of his work by his pupils now exist.
   (E) "Rubens" was one of Rembrandt's pseudonyms.

7. Of the following, the song *not* composed by Stephen Foster is

   (A) "Nelly Bly"
   (B) "Jeanie with the Light Brown Hair"
   (C) "Beautiful Dreamer"
   (D) "Carry Me Back to Old Virginny"
   (E) "Swanee River"

8. A "casting" in sculpture refers to the use of which of the following materials?

   (A) stone
   (B) wood
   (C) metal
   (D) ivory
   (E) papier-mâché

9. A "concerto" is a(n)

   (A) musical instrument
   (B) composition for solo instrument with orchestral accompaniment
   (C) kind of vocal solo with organ accompaniment
   (D) composition for chorus
   (E) instrumental concert

10. The addition of a quaver or "flag" on the stem of a quarter note

    (A) doubles its time value
    (B) halves its time value
    (C) has no effect on its time value
    (D) is related to correct phrasing
    (E) is related to volume

11. A "frieze" is best associated with which of the following terms?

    (A) bas-relief
    (B) pediment
    (C) caryatid
    (D) free-standing
    (E) entablature

12. Who of the following is *not* a twentieth-century sculptor?

    (A) Giacometti
    (B) Moore
    (C) Brancusi
    (D) Donatello
    (E) Arp

13. Which of the following kinds of scenes is *most* often associated with Paul Cezanne?

   (A) still life
   (B) formal portrait
   (C) informal portrait
   (D) action study
   (E) architectural rendering

14. Of the following terms, the one opposite in meaning to "pianissimo" is

   (A) bravissimo
   (B) glissando
   (C) fortissimo
   (D) pretissimo
   (E) diminuendo

15. Which one of the following terms is *not* a term used in music?

   (A) crescendo
   (B) sotto voce
   (C) finale
   (D) key
   (E) innuendo

16. A woodwind section of an orchestra would include all but which of the following instruments?

   (A) flute
   (B) clarinet
   (C) trumpet
   (D) oboe
   (E) bassoon

17. Music for string quartets is an example of

   (A) chamber music
   (B) orchestral music
   (C) symphonic music
   (D) oratorios
   (E) scherzos

18. Which of the paintings on the following page is by Diego Rivera?

   (A)
   (B)
   (C)
   (D)
   (E)

19. Which of the paintings on the following page is a futurist painting?

   (A)
   (B)
   (C)
   (D)
   (E)

(B)

(A)

(C)

(D)

(E)

20. American composers of the twentieth century include all but which one of the following:

(A) Charles Ives
(B) Aaron Copland
(C) Virgil Thomson
(D) Leonard Bernstein
(E) Alexander Scriabin

Stop

End of section. If you have any time left, go over your work in this section only. Do not work in any other section of the test.

SCIENCE

25 Minutes — 30 Questions

Directions: Each question is followed by five choices.
Select the choice that is correct or most nearly correct.

1. Of the planets below, which has the largest number of satellites?

   (A) Jupiter
   (B) Mercury
   (C) Neptune
   (D) Pluto
   (E) Earth

2. Which of the following items could best be called biodegradable?

   (A) phosphate detergents
   (B) polystyrene cups
   (C) polyvinylchloride pipes
   (D) cellulose
   (E) aluminum

3. Organisms in temperate zones are able to time their activities by cues given by the photoperiod, since

   (A) all organisms need time to rest
   (B) light is a limiting factor
   (C) all organisms have a biological clock
   (D) day length is always constant for a specific locality and season
   (E) some plants need long days in order to bloom

4. Which of the following statements best distinguishes electrolytes from non-electrolytes?

   (A) Electrolytes are always ionic compounds while non-electrolytes are always covalent compounds.
   (B) Electrolytes are usually covalent compounds while non-electrolytes are usually ionic compounds.
   (C) Electrolytes and non-electrolytes are really both covalent compounds.
   (D) Non-electrolytes are usually insoluble in water while electrolytes are usually soluble.
   (E) Electrolytes can be covalent or ionic compounds but must be ionic in solution.

5. The Beaufort Scale indicates

   (A) temperature
   (B) air pressure
   (C) humidity
   (D) wind direction
   (E) wind force

6. Consider the following chemical formulae: CH_4, CCl_4, $CHCl_3$. These formulae show that

   (A) the carbon atom has four combining sites
   (B) many compounds contain carbon
   (C) carbon is important to living things
   (D) ionic bonds have been formed
   (E) carbon is a very complex element

7. The existence of microorganisms in the human gastric system is an example of

   (A) mutualism
   (B) parisitism
   (C) meiosis
   (D) phylesis
   (E) variance

8. The time that it takes for the earth to complete a 60° rotation is

   (A) one hour
   (B) four hours
   (C) six hours
   (D) 24 hours
   (E) 12 hours

9. Which of the following is a balanced chemical equation?

   (A) $H_2 + Br_2 \rightarrow HBr$
   (B) $P_4 + O_2 \rightarrow P_4O_{10}$
   (C) $C_3H_8 + 5O_2 \rightarrow 3CO_2 + 4H_2O$
   (D) $H_2 + O_2 \rightarrow 2H_2O$
   (E) $H_2O + CO_3 \rightarrow H_2CO_3 + 2OH$

10. A piece of copper wire is cut into ten equal parts. These parts are connected in parallel. The joint resistance of the parallel combination will be equal to the original resistance of the single wire, multiplied by a factor of

    (A) .01
    (B) .10
    (C) 10
    (D) 100
    (E) 120

11. The condition known as goiter is best described by which of the following statements?

    (A) It is caused by a deficiency of iron.
    (B) It is an enlarged thyroid gland.

(C) It is caused by a deficiency of insulin.

(D) It is caused by an excess of sugar.

(E) It is an abnormally small pineal gland.

12. People who advocate fluoridation of water do so in the interest of

(A) prevention of the spread of typhus

(B) prevention of dental caries

(C) whitening the teeth of the people in the area

(D) improvement of the potability of the water supply

(E) helping ease the threat of a water shortage

13. Of the following planets, the one that has the shortest revolution around the sun is

(A) Earth

(B) Mercury

(C) Jupiter

(D) Venus

(E) Saturn

14. Of the following, the lightest element known on earth is

(A) hydrogen

(B) helium

(C) chalcopyrite

(D) pitchblende

(E) lead

15. A 1,000-ton ship must displace a weight of water equal to

(A) 500 tons

(B) 1,000 tons

(C) 1,500 tons

(D) 2,000 tons

(E) one ton

16. Of the following organisms, the one that has an incomplete but functional digestive system is

(A) lumbricus

(B) lobster

(C) clam

(D) grasshopper

(E) planaria

17. What is the name of the negative particle that circles the nucleus of the atom?

(A) neutron

(B) proton

(C) meson

(D) electron

(E) cyclotron

18. Of the following kinds of clouds, the ones that occur at the greatest height are called

   (A) cirrus
   (B) cumulus
   (C) nimbus
   (D) stratus
   (E) cirro-nimbus

19. Of the following, who explained the retrograde motion of the planets by the use of epicycles?
   I. Ptolemy
   II. Galileo
   III. Kepler

   (A) I only
   (B) II only
   (C) III only
   (D) I and II only
   (E) I, II, and III

20. The living material comprising the bulk of a cell is called the

   (A) chloroplast
   (B) protoplasm
   (C) cytochrome
   (D) genes
   (E) hormones

21. The Schick test indicates whether or not a person is probably immune to

   (A) tuberculosis
   (B) diphtheria
   (C) poliomyelitis
   (D) scarlet fever
   (E) measles

22. Of the following instruments, the one that can convert light into an electric current is the

   (A) radiometer
   (B) dry cell
   (C) electrolysis apparatus
   (D) photoelectric cell
   (E) sphygmomanometer

23. In the production of sounds, the greater the number of vibrations per second, the

   (A) greater the volume
   (B) higher the tone
   (C) lower the volume
   (D) lower the tone
   (E) greater the volume and lower the tone

24. Which of the following statements is not true, according to Dalton's Atomic Theory?

    (A) All material is made of atoms.
    (B) All atoms are basically the same.
    (C) Atoms are indivisible.
    (D) Atoms are basically solid.
    (E) Atoms of the same element are exactly the same.

25. Of the following, the only safe blood transfusion would be

    (A) group A blood into a group O person
    (B) group B blood into group A person
    (C) group O blood into a group AB person
    (D) group AB blood into a group B person
    (E) group B blood into a group A person

26. Of the following, the scientist who originated and developed the system of classifying the plants and animals of the earth was

    (A) Linnaeus
    (B) Darwin
    (C) Mendel
    (D) Agassiz
    (E) Galileo

27. A dry cell is safe for children's experimentation because it

    (A) is small and easily carried
    (B) is leakproof
    (C) has low voltage
    (D) is fireproof
    (E) can't be turned on accidentally

28. It is probable that a mammal smaller than a shrew could not exist because it would

    (A) not get sufficient oxygen
    (B) reproduce too rapidly
    (C) have to eat at too tremendous a rate
    (D) not be able to defend itself
    (E) be unable to bear live young

29. The half-life of radium is 1,600 years. After a period of 3,200 years, a given quantity of radium will be

    (A) one-quarter disintegrated
    (B) one-half disintegrated
    (C) three-quarters disintegrated
    (D) completely disintegrated
    (E) less radioactive, but unchanged in size

30. Antibodies are found in

    (A) vaccines
    (B) plasma
    (C) red blood cells
    (D) platelets
    (E) mycin drugs

Stop

End of section. If you have any time left, go over your work in this section only. Do not work in any other section of the test.

MATHEMATICS

20 Minutes—21 Questions

Directions: Select the correct answer to each of the following questions.

1. How many twelfths of a pound are equal to $83\frac{1}{3}\%$ of a pound?

    (A) 5
    (B) 10
    (C) 12
    (D) 14
    (E) 16

2. A rectangular flower bed with the dimensions 16 yards by 12 yards is surrounded by a walk 3 yards wide. The area of the walk is

    (A) 93 square yards
    (B) 396 square yards
    (C) 204 square yards
    (D) 165 square yards
    (E) none of these

3. If 15 cans of food are needed for seven men for two days, the number of cans needed for four men for seven days is

    (A) 10
    (B) 15
    (C) 20
    (D) 25
    (E) 30

4. In the accompanying figure, ACB is a straight angle and DC is perpendicular to CE. If the number of degrees in angle ACD is represented by x, the number of degrees in angle BCE is represented by

    (A) 90–x
    (B) x–90
    (C) 90 + x
    (D) 180–x
    (E) 45 + x

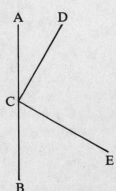

5. A taxi charges 75 cents for the first quarter of a mile and 15 cents for each additional quarter of a mile. The charge in cents for a trip of d miles is

   (A) $75 + 15d$
   (B) $75 + 15(4d - 1)$
   (C) $75 + 75d$
   (D) $75 + 4(d - 1)$
   (E) $75 + 75(d - 1)$

6. Four quarts of a certain mixture of alcohol and water is at 50% strength. To it is added a quart of water. The alcoholic strength of the new mixture is

   (A) 12.5%
   (B) 20%
   (C) 25%
   (D) 40%
   (E) 45%

7. What is $\frac{3}{4}$ in decimal form?

   (A) .75
   (B) 7.5
   (C) .075
   (D) .0075
   (E) 75.00

8. The net price of a $25 item after successive discounts of 20% and 30% is

   (A) $11
   (B) $12.50
   (C) $14
   (D) $19
   (E) $21

9. How many gallons of paint must be purchased to paint a room containing 820 square feet of wall space, if one gallon covers 150 square feet?

   (A) 4
   (B) 5
   (C) 6
   (D) 7
   (E) 8

10. A recent "educational bulletin" states that if you were to eat each meal in a different restaurant in New York City, it would take you more than 19 years to cover all of New York City's eating places, assuming that you eat three meals a day. On the basis of this information, the number of restaurants in New York City presumably

   (A) is between 20,500 and 20,999
   (B) is between 21,000 and 21,499
   (C) is between 21,500 and 22,000
   (D) exceeds 22,000
   (E) is exactly 20,000

11. Based on the graph below, which of the following statements is most probably true?

   (A) The number of Bachelor's and First Professional degrees given out each year was approximately equal to the number of higher degrees given out that year.
   (B) The ratio between Master's and Ph.D.'s remained fairly constant between 1950 and 1965.
   (C) The number of Ph.D.'s given out has increased every year since 1940.
   (D) The number of Bachelor's and First Professional degrees conferred in 1951 was about 110% of the number in 1946.
   (E) In 1946, only two Ph.D.'s were conferred.

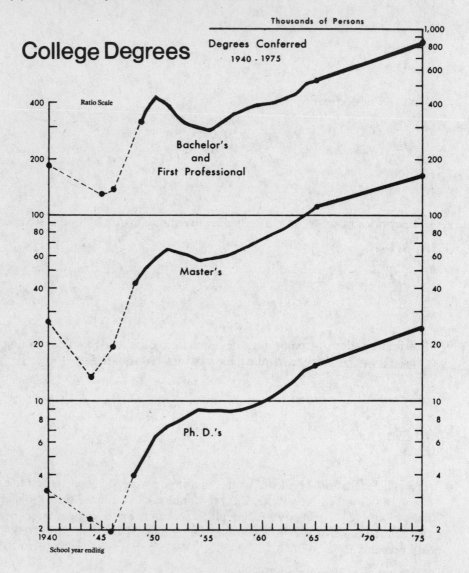

12. By the distributive property of multiplication over addition, which of the following is equivalent to 9×123?

   (A) $9 \times 120 + 3$
   (B) $(9 \times 100) + (20 \times 3)$

(C) $(9 \times 100) + (9 \times 20) + (9 \times 3)$

(D) $900 + 9 + 23$

(E) $920 + 9 \times 3$

13. Which of the following is equal to 3.63×10^5?

(A) 363,000

(B) 363

(C) 3,630

(D) 3,630,000

(E) 36,300

14. The 13th term of the progression 7, 4, 1, __ is

(A) 28

(B) −28

(C) 29

(D) −29

(E) impossible to determine

15. If the standard time in London is five hours later than in New York, what time is it in London when it is 10:00 A.M. in New York?

(A) 5 A.M.

(B) 6 A.M.

(C) 4 P.M.

(D) 3 P.M.

(E) 2 P.M.

16. If a map has a scale of 1 inch equals 50 miles, how many miles apart are two towns separated on the map by $6\frac{3}{4}$ inches?

(A) $187\frac{1}{2}$

(B) $337\frac{1}{2}$

(C) 300

(D) $366\frac{2}{3}$

(E) $37\frac{1}{2}$

17. The number of square tiles, each 8 inches on a side, needed to cover a rectangular area 12 feet by 16 feet is

(A) 36

(B) 3

(C) 432

(D) 864

(E) 960

18. The circumference of a circle whose area is 16π is

(A) 8π

(B) 4π

(C) 16π

(D) 8

(E) 16

19. If clerk A can type 50 letters in ten minutes, whereas clerk B can type only 40 letters in ten minutes, in how many minutes can they type 360 letters together?

(A) 35

(B) 38

(C) 39

(D) 40

(E) 90

20. The cost for developing and printing a roll of film is c cents for processing the roll and d cents for each print. How much will it cost, in cents, to develop and print a roll of film with 20 exposures?

(A) $20c + d$

(B) $20(c + d)$

(C) $c + 20d$

(D) $c + \dfrac{d}{20}$

(E) $\dfrac{c + d}{20}$

21. What is the numerical equivalent of the Roman number DCCCLXXIX?

(A) 879

(B) 549

(C) 1499

(D) 249

(E) 839

Stop

End of section. If you have any time left, go over your work in this section only. Do not work in any other section of the test.

Answer Key
Section 2:   General Knowledge

SOCIAL STUDIES

1. B	8. D	15. C	22. A	29. C
2. E	9. A	16. A	23. D	30. E
3. A	10. D	17. A	24. C	31. A
4. C	11. D	18. A	25. D	32. B
5. A	12. B	19. C	26. D	33. D
6. D	13. C	20. B	27. C	34. C
7. B	14. E	21. B	28. B	35. B

LITERATURE

1. A	6. C	11. B	16. D	21. A
2. C	7. B	12. A	17. D	22. A
3. B	8. D	13. C	18. B	23. C
4. A	9. C	14. D	19. B	24. A
5. D	10. A	15. A	20. C	25. B

FINE ARTS

1. A	5. B	9. B	13. A	17. A
2. D	6. B	10. B	14. C	18. A
3. D	7. D	11. E	15. E	19. E
4. C	8. C	12. D	16. C	20. E

SCIENCE

1. A	8. B	15. B	22. D	29. C
2. D	9. C	16. E	23. B	30. B
3. B	10. A	17. D	24. D	
4. E	11. B	18. A	25. C	
5. E	12. B	19. A	26. A	
6. A	13. B	20. B	27. C	
7. A	14. A	21. B	28. C	

MATHEMATICS

1. B	6. D	11. B	16. B	21. A
2. C	7. A	12. C	17. C	
3. E	8. C	13. A	18. A	
4. A	9. C	14. D	19. D	
5. B	10. A	15. D	20. C	

Answer Sheet
Section 3: Communication Skills
Listening Ability

Tear out this sheet. Have it ready to use with the Answer Options on page 231.

1. LISTENING TO SINGLE SENTENCES

1 Ⓐ Ⓑ Ⓒ Ⓓ　　6 Ⓐ Ⓑ Ⓒ Ⓓ　　11 Ⓐ Ⓑ Ⓒ Ⓓ

2 Ⓐ Ⓑ Ⓒ Ⓓ　　7 Ⓐ Ⓑ Ⓒ Ⓓ　　12 Ⓐ Ⓑ Ⓒ Ⓓ

3 Ⓐ Ⓑ Ⓒ Ⓓ　　8 Ⓐ Ⓑ Ⓒ Ⓓ　　13 Ⓐ Ⓑ Ⓒ Ⓓ

4 Ⓐ Ⓑ Ⓒ Ⓓ　　9 Ⓐ Ⓑ Ⓒ Ⓓ　　14 Ⓐ Ⓑ Ⓒ Ⓓ

5 Ⓐ Ⓑ Ⓒ Ⓓ　　10 Ⓐ Ⓑ Ⓒ Ⓓ　　15 Ⓐ Ⓑ Ⓒ Ⓓ

2. LISTENING TO CONVERSATIONS

Conversation 1

1 Ⓐ Ⓑ Ⓒ Ⓓ　　2 Ⓐ Ⓑ Ⓒ Ⓓ　　3 Ⓐ Ⓑ Ⓒ Ⓓ

Conversation 2

1 Ⓐ Ⓑ Ⓒ Ⓓ

2 Ⓐ Ⓑ Ⓒ Ⓓ

Conversation 3

1 Ⓐ Ⓑ Ⓒ Ⓓ

2 Ⓐ Ⓑ Ⓒ Ⓓ

3. LISTENING TO BRIEF PASSAGES

Passage 1

1 Ⓐ Ⓑ Ⓒ Ⓓ　　　　2 Ⓐ Ⓑ Ⓒ Ⓓ

Passage 2

1 Ⓐ Ⓑ Ⓒ Ⓓ　　　　2 Ⓐ Ⓑ Ⓒ Ⓓ

Diagnostic Core Battery II
Section 3. Communication Skills

1 Hour 45 Minutes — 95 Questions

LISTENING ABILITY

20 Minutes — 26 Questions

SCRIPT (Detach for Speaker)

Directions: To simulate the actual NTE Listening Ability test, you need a second person (the speaker) to assist you. Detach the pages of this script for the speaker and have the speaker read you the stimulus material (the entire script). When the conversations are read, the speaker should indicate to you which person is speaking.

You should have both Question and Answer Sheets in front of you. Go through the entire Listening Ability test without repeating anything and without pausing. Answer options begin on page 231.

1. LISTENING TO SINGLE SENTENCES

(Speaker should read and pause as noted in script.)

1. *Read*
   When did you move into this apartment?
   > *Pause for answer*

2. *Read*
   Where did you go last weekend?
   > *Pause for answer*

3. *Read*
   Although the trip lasted several months, we had to leave out several important sites.
   > *Pause for answer*

4. *Read*
   Is the furniture all yours?
   > *Pause for answer*

5. *Read*
   The third shelf is reserved for history texts, since the collection is so large.
   > *Pause for answer*

6. *Read*

   In spite of his optimistic predictions, output proved to be far below our expectations.

   Pause for answer

7. *Read*

   I hope he gets through to the trapped miners despite the flood waters in the mineshaft.

   Pause for answer

8. *Read*

   Designing a test of creativity has been extremely difficult.

   Pause for answer

9. *Read*

   In highly technical areas, publications more than five or ten years old are almost useless.

   Pause for answer.

10. *Read*

    The building had been designed by a professional, but he forgot to include adequate storage space.

    Pause for answer

11. *Read*

    Do you visit your relatives often?

    Pause for answer

12. *Read*

    Did the doctor advise you to have an operation?

    Pause for answer

13. *Read*

    For the first time, most of the students scored over 80 percent.

    Pause for answer

14. *Read*

    Where did you complete your degree?

    Pause for answer

15. *Read*

    Student performance on these tests depends on many factors, only one of which is ability.

    Pause for answer

2. LISTENING TO CONVERSATIONS

(Speaker should read entire conversation and indicate who is speaking. Pause and ask questions as indicated in script.)

Conversation 1

Read

Man: The students have submitted a list of courses they would like to see offered next semester. Do you think we should present it to a department meeting?

Woman: Since they don't know the restrictions on budget and scheduling that we face, I don't see how their list could be very useful.

Man: It would still be of interest to the faculty, and might suggest some modifications in the syllabus.

Woman: That's true, but it might be dangerous to appear to give in so easily to student pressure. We should see what the chairman thinks fits in best.

Pause 5 seconds and ask

1. Why does the woman doubt the usefulness of bringing the students' list to the faculty?

Pause for answer, then ask

2. What conclusion can be drawn about the man's attitude?

Pause for answer, then ask

3. What conclusion can be drawn about the woman's attitude?

Conversation 2

Read

Woman: Is this the current reservations desk? I'd like two tickets for tonight.

Man: This number only handles advance sales. You'll have to call back after 3 o'clock to extension thirty-four.

Woman: Can you tell me when the concert starts?

Man: The overture begins exactly at 8:05, and latecomers will not be seated until the first act is over.

Pause 5 seconds and ask

1. The woman is trying to contact the reservations desk by

Pause for answer, then ask

2. What time is it?

Conversation 3

Read

Man: The survey results are in, and I'm afraid we're going to have to answer some very serious charges soon.

Woman: Are the parents against the changes we introduced last year?

Man: Overall, they seem to be against them.

Woman: Maybe we didn't explain our reasons clearly enough to them.

Pause 5 seconds, and ask

1. The two teachers are concerned about complaints from whom?

Pause for answer, then ask

2. What do we know about the changes?

3. LISTENING TO BRIEF PASSAGES

(Speaker should read each passage. Pause and ask questions as indicated.)

Passage 1
Read

Most people who are visually impaired do have some vision, even if they are classified as legally blind. While many people today prefer to use the word "blind" only when talking about total blindness, which is the complete absence of vision or light perception, the term "legally blind" is still in use because of its value in identifying those individuals eligible for specialized services or economic assistance.

Pause 5 seconds, then ask

1. According to the speaker, how could most visually impaired people be described?

Pause for answer, then ask

2. Why is the term "legally blind" still used separately from the simple word "blind"?

Passage 2
Read

The task of the poet or novelist is to convey states of mind and of being, as immediately as possible, through language. Immediacy of language is not always or necessarily simplicity, although simplicity is a highly desirable and immensely difficult literary instrument. Valery says that of two words, we should always choose the lesser. But we don't always have a lesser word that meets our need—although it can be said that truth tends to express itself with eminent simplicity in art as in life, just as talkativeness can often be an index of falsehood.

Pause 5 seconds and then ask

1. What is the speaker concerned with?

Pause for answer, and then ask

2. What does the speaker claim?

Answer Options for Listening Ability Questions

These are the answer options for the Listening Ability test. On the NTE the questions will be printed in your question booklet. Keep these questions in front of you as you listen; when you hear a basis for selecting an answer, fill in the answer blank corresponding to that answer on your answer sheet. Be certain you fill in the answer space corresponding to the question-number you are answering.

1. LISTENING TO SINGLE SENTENCES

Select the option most consistent with the statement made by the speaker.

1. (A) The view of the park from here is wonderful.
   (B) We used to live in the suburbs.
   (C) About six months ago.
   (D) It used to belong to a friend of mine.

2. (A) The beaches are deserted at this time of year.
   (B) I prefer some place with an exciting nightlife.
   (C) Long car trips make me sick.
   (D) We went to my sister's home in New Jersey.

3. (A) The weather proved worse than usual for the summer.
   (B) The countryside has many interesting villages.
   (C) We didn't get to some of the places we had hoped to see.
   (D) Government officials proved very difficult to handle.

4. (A) Most of it is in American Colonial style.
   (B) I've always been passionately fond of antique lamps.
   (C) My husband enjoys hunting for surprises at garage sales, and we've acquired dozens of fine pieces that way.
   (D) I've borrowed a few things from my sister, but all the paintings and artwork are my own.

5. (A) Students here show little interest in history.
   (B) There are many history books in the collection.
   (C) The other texts in the library treat related topics.
   (D) The problems of selecting display methods have finally been solved.

6. (A) Weather conditions proved to be the deciding factor.
   (B) His mood was based on expert advice.

(C) The results spread through related industries.

(D) We had shared his positive hopes.

7. (A) Flooding in the mine is hampering rescue efforts.

(B) When human lives are at stake, no expense should be spared.

(C) There's been a long history of underground flooding.

(D) No one else could find a solution either.

8. (A) Creative students can be held back, for example, by their environment.

(B) One difficulty is that there is no universally accepted definition of creativity.

(C) Such a test would be most valuable to a teacher in planning.

(D) Students often react adversely to unorthodox tests.

9. (A) Writing about research results is always difficult.

(B) It's important to have complete coverage of any topic, back to the earliest stages, no matter how long ago.

(C) As a result, many libraries store older materials in out-of-the-way areas and give priority to new journals.

(D) The high cost of printing works against the need to have the latest results.

10. (A) Our needs are growing at a tremendous rate.

(B) There's no way to tell how much space you really need.

(C) Everything else was fine.

(D) We had more material to store than he knew about.

11. (A) We're not that fond of them, and prefer to stay at home.

(B) Since they moved away, we only see them once a month.

(C) Children of our families have become close friends.

(D) The breakdown of the family is a factor in the growth of crime.

12. (A) He thought my knee could be restored with minor surgery, and said yes.

(B) Doctors' fees are becoming ridiculously expensive.

(C) Operations unheard of a few years ago are now routine.

(D) I can't decide whether or not to take the chance.

13. (A) The majority of last year's results were below that figure.

(B) The students seem to be working harder nowadays.

(C) This was one of many encouraging signs.

(D) Different scoring methods must have been used.

14. (A) Most of my family attended a small community college.

(B) I won a scholarship to a major East Coast university.

(C) Small colleges, I'm sure, provide a better education.

(D) I got my B.A. from Columbia two years ago.

15. (A) Scores have risen in recent years.

(B) There is a movement to replace tests with interviews.

(C) Students seem to enjoy taking them, however.

(D) The student's state of health, for example, can affect his score.

2. LISTENING TO CONVERSATIONS

Conversation 1

1. (A) She feels the present curriculum meets their needs.
   (B) Students don't always know what's best for them.
   (C) Students would not ordinarily know about teachers' workloads and department budgets.
   (D) Earlier lists were rejected as impractical.

2. (A) He doesn't think the list is a practical one.
   (B) He is afraid of student pressure.
   (C) He is not really interested in the woman's reaction.
   (D) He sees real value in the students' initiative, and is trying to present it in the best way.

3. (A) She is on the students' side from the start.
   (B) She is fearful of student pressure.
   (C) She has seen earlier lists like this ridiculed.
   (D) She is not receptive to the idea of student input into department decision-making.

Conversation 2

1. (A) letter
   (B) telephone
   (C) telegram
   (D) in person

2. (A) Exactly 3 o'clock
   (B) Before 3 o'clock
   (C) After 3 o'clock
   (D) Can't tell from the conversation.

Conversation 3

1. (A) parents
   (B) students
   (C) other teachers
   (D) central budget office

2. (A) They were accompanied by explanations, and followed by a survey.
   (B) They were superficial, and required no real explanations.
   (C) They will be initiated next semester.
   (D) They were in response to results of a survey last month.

3. LISTENING TO BRIEF PASSAGES

Passage 1

1. (A) Most of them have some vision.
   (B) They have no light perception at all.

(C) They have vision which deteriorates with time.

(D) They deserve our assistance.

2. (A) It is a polite way of referring to an embarrassing condition.

(B) It describes different degrees of blindness.

(C) It is used to separate those who need further examination to determine whether or not they have light perception.

(D) It is used to describe those who are entitled to special services and assistance legally.

Passage 2

1. (A) The writer—poet or novelist—and his use of language.

(B) The formation of new words to meet the writer's needs.

(C) The distinction between truth and falsehood.

(D) The distinction between visual arts and literature.

2. (A) Truth is often clear and simple, while lies are elaborate and wordy.

(B) The communication of states of mind is simple.

(C) Our vocabulary is inadequate to convey new experiences.

(D) The choosing of a "lesser" word at all times is the mark of a poet.

Stop

End of section. If you have any time left, go over your work in this section only. Do not work in any other section of the test.

Answer Key
Section 3: Communication Skills
Listening Ability

1. LISTENING TO SINGLE SENTENCES

1. C	6. D	11. B
2. D	7. A	12. A
3. C	8. B	13. A
4. D	9. C	14. D
5. B	10. D	15. D

2. LISTENING TO CONVERSATIONS

Conversation 1
1. C
2. D
3. D

Conversation 2
1. B
2. B

Conversation 3
1. A
2. A

3. LISTENING TO BRIEF PASSAGES

Passage 1
1. A
2. D

Passage 2
1. A
2. A

Answer Sheet
Section 3: Communication Skills
Reading Ability

1 Ⓐ Ⓑ Ⓒ Ⓓ Ⓔ   6 Ⓐ Ⓑ Ⓒ Ⓓ Ⓔ   11 Ⓐ Ⓑ Ⓒ Ⓓ Ⓔ   16 Ⓐ Ⓑ Ⓒ Ⓓ Ⓔ   21 Ⓐ Ⓑ Ⓒ Ⓓ Ⓔ

2 Ⓐ Ⓑ Ⓒ Ⓓ Ⓔ   7 Ⓐ Ⓑ Ⓒ Ⓓ Ⓔ   12 Ⓐ Ⓑ Ⓒ Ⓓ Ⓔ   17 Ⓐ Ⓑ Ⓒ Ⓓ Ⓔ   22 Ⓐ Ⓑ Ⓒ Ⓓ Ⓔ

3 Ⓐ Ⓑ Ⓒ Ⓓ Ⓔ   8 Ⓐ Ⓑ Ⓒ Ⓓ Ⓔ   13 Ⓐ Ⓑ Ⓒ Ⓓ Ⓔ   18 Ⓐ Ⓑ Ⓒ Ⓓ Ⓔ   23 Ⓐ Ⓑ Ⓒ Ⓓ Ⓔ

4 Ⓐ Ⓑ Ⓒ Ⓓ Ⓔ   9 Ⓐ Ⓑ Ⓒ Ⓓ Ⓔ   14 Ⓐ Ⓑ Ⓒ Ⓓ Ⓔ   19 Ⓐ Ⓑ Ⓒ Ⓓ Ⓔ

5 Ⓐ Ⓑ Ⓒ Ⓓ Ⓔ   10 Ⓐ Ⓑ Ⓒ Ⓓ Ⓔ   15 Ⓐ Ⓑ Ⓒ Ⓓ Ⓔ   20 Ⓐ Ⓑ Ⓒ Ⓓ Ⓔ

Diagnostic Core Battery II
Section 3: Communication Skills

READING ABILITY

50 Minutes — 23 Questions

Directions: Each of the following passages is followed by one or more questions. The questions following each passage refer to that passage only, and are to be answered using only the information presented in the passage. If you prefer, you may read the questions before reading the passage, or you may read the passage, read the questions, re-read the passage, and then answer the questions. Use these practice passages to decide on the style which is most efficient for you.

There is only one answer to each question. In some instances more than one answer may seem to be reasonable; thus, you should select the answer which is most consistent with the material presented in the passage.

Questions 1 and 2 refer to the following passage.

Many of the sciences, physical and social, can provide us with insights into why people have different attitudes, personalities, and points of view, but no science can provide a basis for preferring one attitude to another. Science can and does provide information that can be deeply involved in ethical issues, but in and of itself, it does not answer the question of which is right and which is wrong. Thus the scientist can give us a great deal of information about possible actions and their outcomes, but cannot tell us what we should do.

1. The underlying assumption of this statement is that

    (A) value judgments are not appropriate subjects of scientific inquiry
    (B) biology is of little use in understanding human behavior
    (C) differences of opinion cannot be proven scientifically
    (D) psychology and biology are based on different theories of personality
    (E) ethics and science are unrelated

2. The author of this article would most probably advise scientists to

    (A) *not* engage in ethical disputes
    (B) study individual differences
    (C) exercise caution in reporting their findings
    (D) explain the potential risks and benefits of their experiments to human subjects
    (E) make it clear that because something is scientifically possible does not necessarily mean that it is good or desirable

Questions 3 and 4 refer to the following passage.

Pedagogue was the Greek word for a kind of slave, but to us it means teacher. Although no rational person contends that the conditions of teachers in the United States of America today are like those of slaves, until very recently teachers were certainly second-class citizens.

3. The author suggests that the word "pedagogue"

    (A) indicates that teachers were not respected in ancient Greece
    (B) came into English because slaves were used as free labor in schools
    (C) reflected, at one time, the conditions of teachers in the United States
    (D) was misunderstood by those who adopted it for use in English
    (E) is a poor choice for teachers

4. The author implies that conditions for teachers in the United States today

    (A) are similar to those in ancient Greece
    (B) are better than they were a few years ago
    (C) are like those of second-class citizens
    (D) are intolerable to any rational person
    (E) have not changed much over the last hundred years

Questions 5 and 6 refer to the following passage.

Knowledge of precedent and authority opinion through reference to the literature is the basic foundation of sound research planning. This use of the literature in research in education is in sharp contrast to the almost total avoidance of the literature by the practitioner in education. For example, how many teachers faced with a new and difficult problem will turn to the literature to see what others before them have done? The typical teacher will try some idea which comes to mind (trial and error) or ask some colleague down the hall what he has done in a similar situation (verbally transmitted precedent). In this use of precedent, one could argue that the practicing teacher functions almost as if teachers were a preliterate primitive culture without a written record!

5. The author suggests that teachers behave like preliterate cultures because they

    (A) make little use of the educational literature
    (B) do not do serious research
    (C) do not know how to solve problems
    (D) avoid solving their own problems
    (E) make no use of precedent and authority

6. Which of the following is assumed by the author of this passage?

    (A) Trial and error solutions never work.
    (B) Asking colleagues for help is unprofessional.
    (C) Solutions to practical problems appear in the literature.
    (D) Every generation of teachers must develop its own solutions.
    (E) Every school should have a professional library.

Questions 7 and 8 refer to the following passage.

Marriage serves other purposes for primitive societies for, through the customs which developed around it, decisions were automatically made about where people lived, who counted as whose descendants, and subsequently whom a child was named after. Historically, there have been all possible combinations in reckoning descent through the male (patrilineal) and female (matrilineal) as well as deciding whether a newly formed family should live with the family of the male (patrilocal) or that of the female (matrilocal). Societies have existed (and still do) in which the male goes to live with the wife's group, but descent is nevertheless figured through the male line. There are examples of other possibilities as well.

7. "Patrilineal" is used in this passage to mean

    (A) tracing descent through the female
    (B) tracing descent through the biological parents
    (C) tracing descent through the male
    (D) living with the male's family
    (E) assuring that the child's parents are married

8. According to the author's definitions, a society in which the married couple want to live with the family of the bride, but traced descent through the male, would be

    (A) matrilocal and patrilineal
    (B) patrilocal and patrilineal
    (C) matrilocal and matrilineal
    (D) patrilocal and matrilineal
    (E) unusual and not seen today

Questions 9 and 10 refer to the following passage.

Perceptual learning refers to acquiring knowledge or understanding through the senses. It means experience involving seeing, hearing, tasting, smelling, feeling, handling, and manipulating things in different ways. It applies particularly to experience by means of which we get our interpretations of the fundamental characteristics of particular and material things. A child learns that certain effects upon his physical organism are called hard and soft. These are abstract terms, but hard recalls one type of experience, and soft, another. In turn, the qualities of chalk are described in terms of hardness and softness, together with such characteristics as weight, color, texture, etc. All of these characteristics are in terms of sense experiences.

9. A preschool teacher, if he or she followed this author's views on learning, should make certain to

    (A) label each object in the room as hard or soft
    (B) have children describe chalk as best they can
    (C) use descriptive terms when a child picks up an object
    (D) have a science corner where children can weigh objects
    (E) make certain children color each day

10. Which of the following experiences would this author consider examples of perceptual learning?

    I. taking the class to the zoo to pet different animals
   II. bringing in various fruit and vegetables to class
  III. teaching the names of parts of the body

(A) I and II
(B) I, II, and III
(C) I only
(D) II only
(E) III only

Questions 11 and 12 refer to the following passage.

Referring to the distinction between pure and applied research makes it sound as if we were dealing with a dichotomy, but in reality it is a continuum being treated as a dichotomy. The terms pure and applied research refer to the extent to which the research is directed toward, or has relevance for, the solution of a currently existing problem. At one end of the continuum is pure research which, in its extreme form, is research motivated solely by intellectual interest and directed toward the acquisition of knowledge for knowledge's sake. In this extreme form, there is no known or intended practical application of the findings, even if the research is successfully completed. In contrast, applied research in its extreme form would be directed toward solving a specific practical problem, even though no new knowledge was acquired in the process.

11. According to this author, which of the following projects would be the best example of pure research?

(A) an inquiry into the familial background of Pestalozzi
(B) a study of the attitudes towards school taxes in a community of 2,500
(C) a study of why college seniors avoid teaching as a career
(D) a review of contemporary educational philosophers
(E) an experiment on ways of teaching mathematics to fourth graders

12. The author is using the term "research" to refer to

(A) only those studies which yield new information
(B) studies which are experimental in nature
(C) only studies which have a practical application immediately
(D) a variety of studies
(E) studies which deal with reality

Question 13, 14, and 15 refer to the following passage.

The United States Supreme Court, in a major decision, *Tinker* v. *Des Moines Independent School District*, held that students do not lose their right to free expression under the First Amendment to the Constitution when they enter school. The Court explicitly rejected the position taken by some officials that, once inside the gates of the schools, students may be prevented from expressing themselves whether on school policies or national events—unless the school wishes to permit such expression. The

Court said that, on the contrary, students may be prevented from expressing their views only when they (the students) "materially and substantially" disrupt the work and discipline of the school.

13. The main idea of this passage is that

   (A) the First Amendment protection of freedom of expression applies to students in public school
   (B) the U.S. Constitution only guarantees students' rights to express their opinions about school matters
   (C) public school principals have a constitutional right to determine on what issues students may express themselves
   (D) students have an unlimited right under the Constitution to express their views while they are in school
   (E) the First Amendment guarantees students' rights to express their opinions about school policies but only while they are on school grounds

14. According to the Supreme Court decision discussed in this passage,

   (A) teachers cannot discipline disruptive students
   (B) students have to be given an opportunity to express their opinion about school policies before they are adopted
   (C) students must participate in political rallies held at the school
   (D) members of the school board cannot forbid students from peacefully protesting the nuclear arms race
   (E) a student wishing to publish an article in the school newspaper must get the prior consent of the principal.

15. According to this passage, which of the following activities would probably *not* be protected by the First Amendment?

   (A) distribution of leaflets announcing a political rally to be held on the football field
   (B) wearing of armbands to protest the federal government's sale of arms to El Salvador
   (C) an editorial in the school newspaper criticizing the school's dress regulations
   (D) an announcement over the public address system encouraging students to boycott classes as a protest against the curriculum
   (E) wearing buttons in support of a national political candidate with unpopular views

Questions 16 and 17 refer to the following passage.

One interesting development is the increasing use of children as witnesses in court, despite the fact they are not defined as competent witnesses in most of the United States. However, in some courts, they are permitted, provided that the presiding judge is convinced that they know the difference between right and wrong, between lying and telling the truth, and that it is reasonable to assume they remember the events about which they are to testify. This development is in keeping with the general belief among psychologists, sociologists, and child-care specialists that children now mature earlier than in previous generations, and the practical fact that cases involving abused children are reaching the courts in greater numbers.

16. According to the passage, why are children being accepted as witnesses in court?

     I. Most states have changed their laws regarding such testimony.
    II. Judges are more easily satisfied now of their competence.
   III. Children reach sufficient maturity earlier these days.
   IV. There are more prosecutions in cases involving child abuse, and their testimony is needed.

    (A) I and IV
    (B) III and IV
    (C) II and IV
    (D) III only
    (E) I, II, III, and IV

17. Which of the following seems to be assumed by the writer?

    (A) The use of children as witnesses is a positive development.
    (B) It is an undesirable development because of the pressure placed on children, a pressure they were earlier spared.
    (C) Child abuse seems to be rising as a phenomenon.
    (D) Children have been reluctant to cooperate in the past.
    (E) Psychologists, sociologists, and child-care workers bring children into court as witnesses.

Questions 18, 19, and 20 refer to the following passage.

Analyzing the patterns of business failures is a complex phenomenon, but recent data indicate that the overall level of business activity, the money available, and the general prosperity have an effect on different regions of the United States. For example, business failures were higher in 1981 than in 1980 throughout the country, but not consistently. Failure rates were relatively low in New England, the Middle Atlantic states, but much higher in areas such as the Pacific and Mountain areas. The cities did relatively well, with a failure rate a third lower than the surrounding suburban and rural areas, and in several large cities the rate of business failure was stable.

18. Based on the information given in this passage, which of the following *cannot* be said?

    (A) New England experienced more severe business failures in 1981 than did the Mountain and Pacific states.
    (B) There were more business failures in 1981 than in 1980 nationwide.
    (C) Metropolitan areas suffered a lower rate of business failures between 1980 and 1981 than did non-metropolitan areas.
    (D) Fewer new businesses were started in 1981 than in 1980.
    (E) Regional trends in business failure are also an indication of the level of economic activity in the country.

19. According to this passage, the causes of the failure trends are

    (A) related to the recent population shift from the Northeast to other parts of the country
    (B) the result of changes in the corporate tax structure

(C) due to the fact that more people live in metropolitan than in rural areas
(D) not made clear in the information given
(E) a function of poor management

20. The information presented in this passage is most likely to be used by

(A) the Internal Revenue Service
(B) big city mayors
(C) economists
(D) manufacturers of automobile parts
(E) state governments

Questions 21, 22, and 23 refer to the following passage.

As we talk about "the good old days" in politics, we often mention the New England town meeting as an example of public participation in the process of government. One reason the town meeting was important was the greater level of local responsibility for the affairs of government, since neither the federal nor state governments had assumed the powers they have today. While the town meeting system was hardly perfect, for social or economic equality was no more typical then than now, it did assure a level of participation greater than we now have, when half or fewer even vote. One reason was that people had the sense that the decisions to be made were theirs to make, and so they were anxious to become involved and participate.

21. The main idea of this passage is that

(A) the government failed, on the whole, in the early days of the republic to meet its obligations to the people
(B) the obligation of the people in a democracy to actively participate in government was hampered by the town meeting
(C) life was simpler in the eighteenth century than it is today
(D) there was no need for the election of local representative in the early days of the Republic because the people governed themselves at town meetings
(E) the value of the town meeting was that it ensured equal representation of all the people in government

22. If the author of this passage were to run for local election today, with which of the following statements would he be most likely to agree?

(A) The problem with the country today is that the people don't fulfill their obligation to vote.
(B) The survival of democracy depends upon the revitalization of town meetings in every community.
(C) The solutions to today's problems require that we return to a simpler way of life.
(D) We must find new ways to promote ongoing citizen participation in the affairs of government.
(E) We need to recognize that self-government is no longer truly possible.

23. In the opinion of the author of this passage, a symbol of American democracy today would most probably be

(A) a city councilman
(B) the Supreme Court
(C) a lobbying group
(D) the U.S. Congress
(E) a school board election

Stop

End of section. If you have any time left, go over your work in this section only. Do not work in any other section of the test.

Answer Key
Reading Ability

1. A		13. A
2. E		14. D
3. C		15. D
4. B		16. B
5. A		17. A
6. C		18. A
7. C		19. D
8. A		20. C
9. C		21. D
10. A		22. D
11. A		23. E
12. D		

Answer Sheet
Section 3: Communication Skills
Writing Ability

ENGLISH USAGE

1 Ⓐ Ⓑ Ⓒ Ⓓ Ⓔ   5 Ⓐ Ⓑ Ⓒ Ⓓ Ⓔ   9 Ⓐ Ⓑ Ⓒ Ⓓ Ⓔ   13 Ⓐ Ⓑ Ⓒ Ⓓ Ⓔ   17 Ⓐ Ⓑ Ⓒ Ⓓ Ⓔ

2 Ⓐ Ⓑ Ⓒ Ⓓ Ⓔ   6 Ⓐ Ⓑ Ⓒ Ⓓ Ⓔ   10 Ⓐ Ⓑ Ⓒ Ⓓ Ⓔ   14 Ⓐ Ⓑ Ⓒ Ⓓ Ⓔ   18 Ⓐ Ⓑ Ⓒ Ⓓ Ⓔ

3 Ⓐ Ⓑ Ⓒ Ⓓ Ⓔ   7 Ⓐ Ⓑ Ⓒ Ⓓ Ⓔ   11 Ⓐ Ⓑ Ⓒ Ⓓ Ⓔ   15 Ⓐ Ⓑ Ⓒ Ⓓ Ⓔ   19 Ⓐ Ⓑ Ⓒ Ⓓ Ⓔ

4 Ⓐ Ⓑ Ⓒ Ⓓ Ⓔ   8 Ⓐ Ⓑ Ⓒ Ⓓ Ⓔ   12 Ⓐ Ⓑ Ⓒ Ⓓ Ⓔ   16 Ⓐ Ⓑ Ⓒ Ⓓ Ⓔ   20 Ⓐ Ⓑ Ⓒ Ⓓ Ⓔ

SENTENCE CORRECTION

1 Ⓐ Ⓑ Ⓒ Ⓓ Ⓔ   6 Ⓐ Ⓑ Ⓒ Ⓓ Ⓔ   11 Ⓐ Ⓑ Ⓒ Ⓓ Ⓔ   16 Ⓐ Ⓑ Ⓒ Ⓓ Ⓔ   21 Ⓐ Ⓑ Ⓒ Ⓓ Ⓔ

2 Ⓐ Ⓑ Ⓒ Ⓓ Ⓔ   7 Ⓐ Ⓑ Ⓒ Ⓓ Ⓔ   12 Ⓐ Ⓑ Ⓒ Ⓓ Ⓔ   17 Ⓐ Ⓑ Ⓒ Ⓓ Ⓔ   22 Ⓐ Ⓑ Ⓒ Ⓓ Ⓔ

3 Ⓐ Ⓑ Ⓒ Ⓓ Ⓔ   8 Ⓐ Ⓑ Ⓒ Ⓓ Ⓔ   13 Ⓐ Ⓑ Ⓒ Ⓓ Ⓔ   18 Ⓐ Ⓑ Ⓒ Ⓓ Ⓔ   23 Ⓐ Ⓑ Ⓒ Ⓓ Ⓔ

4 Ⓐ Ⓑ Ⓒ Ⓓ Ⓔ   9 Ⓐ Ⓑ Ⓒ Ⓓ Ⓔ   14 Ⓐ Ⓑ Ⓒ Ⓓ Ⓔ   19 Ⓐ Ⓑ Ⓒ Ⓓ Ⓔ   24 Ⓐ Ⓑ Ⓒ Ⓓ Ⓔ

5 Ⓐ Ⓑ Ⓒ Ⓓ Ⓔ   10 Ⓐ Ⓑ Ⓒ Ⓓ Ⓔ   15 Ⓐ Ⓑ Ⓒ Ⓓ Ⓔ   20 Ⓐ Ⓑ Ⓒ Ⓓ Ⓔ   25 Ⓐ Ⓑ Ⓒ Ⓓ Ⓔ

Diagnostic Core Battery II
Section 3: Communication Skills
Writing Ability

35 Minutes—45 Questions

ENGLISH USAGE

15 Minutes—20 Questions

Directions: The sentences below contain errors in grammar, usage, word choice, and idiom. Parts of each sentence are underlined and lettered. Decide which underlined part contains the error and mark its letter on your answer sheet. If the sentence is correct as it stands, mark (E) on your answer sheet. No sentence contains more than one error.

1. If the manager would have planned more carefully, bankruptcy might have been
   A   B   C   D
   avoided. No error.
              E

2. The prisoners were accused of robbery, assault, embezzlement, and forging.
                  A   B   C   D
   No error.
   E

3. Since there was no evidence to indicate who's ring it was, the presiding magis-
                                          A   B   C
   trate dismissed the case. No error.
         D   E

4. Offer the nomination to whoever commands the respect of the people. No error.
   A   B   C   D   E

5. Two astronauts were disappointed because they had hoped to have made the
       A   B   C
   first trip to the moon. No error.
         D   E

6. If you want me to express my opinion, I think that Report A is equally as good as
   A   B   C   D
   Report B. No error.
             E

251

7. "Frank's dog is still in the yard," my father said, "perhaps he <u>had better stay</u>
          <u>A</u>   B   C
  <u>there until we have finished</u> our dinner." No error.
              D   E

8. I know that you <u>will enjoy</u> <u>receiving</u> flowers that <u>smell</u> so <u>sweetly.</u> No error.
                 A   B   C   D   E

9. The snow fell <u>during the night</u> so that it was <u>laying</u> in big drifts <u>on the highway</u>
                  A   B   C
  <u>the next morning.</u> No error.
        D   E

10. The <u>coach</u> with <u>his</u> entire team <u>are</u> traveling <u>by plane.</u> No error.
         A   B   C   D   E

11. By his <u>perserverance,</u> he succeeded in <u>overcoming</u> the <u>apathy</u> of <u>his</u> pupils.
             A   B   C   D
  No error.
    E

12. <u>This</u> is <u>one</u> of those <u>tricky</u> questions that <u>has</u> two answers. <u>No error.</u>
   A   B   C   D   E

13. She <u>did</u> the work very <u>well, however,</u> she showed <u>no interest</u> in anything <u>beyond</u>
         A   B   C   D
  her assignment. <u>No error.</u>
             E

14. Roberts, a man <u>whom</u> we trusted with the <u>most difficult</u> task of <u>all proved</u> loyal
     A   B   C   D
  to his country. <u>No error.</u>
             E

15. It was <u>hard</u> to believe that <u>conscientious</u> pupils could <u>misspell</u> so many words in
        A   B   C
  their <u>quizzes.</u> <u>No error.</u>
       D   E

16. The <u>mayor</u> <u>expressed</u> concern about the large <u>amount</u> of people injured at street
         A   B   C
  <u>crossings.</u> <u>No error.</u>
    D   E

17. "<u>Leave</u> <u>us</u> face the fact that <u>we're</u> in <u>trouble!</u>" he shouted. <u>No error.</u>
    A   B   C   D   E

18. Jones seems <u>slow</u> on the track, but you will find few boys <u>quicker</u> <u>than</u> <u>him</u> on
           A   B   C D
the basketball court. <u>No error.</u>
                     E

19. We had <u>swam</u> <u>across</u> the lake <u>before</u> the sun <u>rose.</u> <u>No error.</u>
        A   B   C   D   E

20. The <u>loud noise</u> of the cars and trucks <u>annoys</u> those <u>who</u> live <u>near the road.</u>
        A   B   C   D
<u>No error.</u>
 E

Stop

**End of section. If you have any time left, go over your
work in this section only. Do not work in any other section of the test.**

SENTENCE CORRECTION

20 Minutes—25 Questions

Directions: The sentences below contain problems in grammar, sentence construction, word choice, and punctuation. Part or all of each sentence is underlined. Select the lettered answer that contains the best version of the underlined section. Answer (A) always repeats the original underlined section exactly. If the sentence is correct as it stands, select (A).

1. Whoever the gods wish to destroy, they first make mad.

   (A) Whoever
   (B) Whoever,
   (C) Whomever
   (D) Whomever,
   (E) Whosoever

2. She is one of those girls who are always complaining.

   (A) who are
   (B) who is
   (C) whom are
   (D) whom is
   (E) whose

3. We buy only cherry plums since we like those kind best.

   (A) those kind
   (B) these kind
   (C) that kind
   (D) that kinds
   (E) them kind

4. Making friends is more rewarding than to be antisocial.

   (A) to be antisocial.
   (B) us being anti-social.
   (C) being anti social.
   (D) to be anti-social.
   (E) being antisocial.

5. The man spoke polite and sensible, belying his bizarre and menacing appearance.

   (A) polite and sensible
   (B) polite and made sense
   (C) polite and sensitively
   (D) politely and in a sensible way
   (E) politely and sensibly

6. They invited my whole family to the cookout—my father, my mother, <u>my sister and I.</u>

   (A) my sister and I.
   (B) my sister and me.
   (C) I and my sister.
   (D) me and my sister.
   (E) both my sister and I.

7. As they drifted silently downstream, <u>the paddles were hardly used.</u>

   (A) the paddles were hardly used.
   (B) the paddles were used hard.
   (C) the paddles weren't hardly used.
   (D) they used the paddles hardly at all.
   (E) they hardly used the paddles.

8. Her brother <u>never has</u> and never will be dependable.

   (A) never has
   (B) hardly never has
   (C) never had
   (D) not ever has
   (E) never has been

9. <u>Walking into the dimly lit</u> restaurant, her eyes took a moment to adjust.

   (A) Walking into the dimly lit
   (B) Walking dimly lit into the
   (C) When she walked into the dimly lit
   (D) While walking into the dimly lit
   (E) As she walks into the dim lit

10. His tone <u>clearly implied</u> that he was bitterly disappointed.

    (A) clearly implied
    (B) clearly inferred
    (C) inferred clearly
    (D) implied a clear inference
    (E) made a clear implication

11. Now kick your feet in the water <u>like Gregory just did.</u>

    (A) like Gregory just did.
    (B) as Gregory just did.
    (C) like Gregory just done.
    (D) as Gregory just done.
    (E) like Gregory's.

12. Macy's sells merchandise of equal quality and <u>having a lower price.</u>

    (A) having a lower price.
    (B) having lower prices.
    (C) having lower price.

(D) has a lower price.

(E) with a lower price.

13. After I had sucked the lemon, the apple tasted sweetly.

(A) tasted sweetly.

(B) tasted sweet.

(C) tasted sweetened.

(D) tastes sweetly.

(E) had a taste that was sweet.

14. The reason Frank is going to Arizona is because he needs a dry climate.

(A) is because he needs

(B) is that he needs

(C) is because he needed

(D) is on account of he needs

(E) is that he has a need for

15. We can't assist but one of you at a time, so try to be patient.

(A) We can't assist but one

(B) We can assist but one

(C) We can't assist only one

(D) We can't only assist one

(E) We can assist not one

16. If you would have been prompt, we might have arrived in time for the first act.

(A) If you would have been prompt,

(B) If you were to have been prompt,

(C) If you would've been prompt,

(D) If you had been prompt,

(E) If you'd of been prompt,

17. After he graduated high school, he went to Dartmouth.

(A) After he graduated high school,

(B) When he graduated high school,

(C) After he had graduated from high school,

(D) After he graduated from high school,

(E) Having graduated high school,

18. The recurrence of identical sounds help to awaken the emotions.

(A) help to awaken

(B) help to wake up

(C) will help to have awakened

(D) assist in awakening

(E) helps to awaken

19. Oliver Wendell Holmes decided to become a writer <u>being that</u> his father was a successful author.

   (A) being that
   (B) on account of
   (C) because
   (D) in view of
   (E) in that

20. Nothing would satisfy him <u>but that</u> I bow to his wishes.

   (A) but that
   (B) although that
   (C) when that
   (D) that
   (E) but

21. <u>Our teacher won't leave us come</u> into the room after the gong sounds.

   (A) Our teacher won't leave us come
   (B) Our teacher won't let us come
   (C) Our teacher refuses to leave us come
   (D) Our teacher won't leave us enter
   (E) Our teacher won't allow that we come

22. <u>Being an intelligent person, the slur was disregarded by him.</u>

   (A) Being an intelligent person, the slur was disregarded by him.
   (B) Being that he was an intelligent person, the slur was disregarded by him.
   (C) Being an intelligent person, he disregarded the slur.
   (D) Being that he was an intelligent person, he disregarded the slur.
   (E) As an intelligent person, the slur was disregarded by him.

23. I prefer <u>him singing his own material</u> to his performances of other people's songs.

   (A) him singing his own material
   (B) him when he is singing his own material
   (C) him to sing his own material
   (D) him singing his own material himself
   (E) his singing his own material

24. <u>If the parent would have shown more interest,</u> her daughter would have been in college today.

   (A) If the parent would have shown more interest,
   (B) If the parent had shown more interest,
   (C) If the parent would have showed more interest,
   (D) If the parent would have been showing more interest,
   (E) Should the parent have shown more interest,

25. <u>Everyone except Ruth and I knows her.</u>

   (A) Everyone except Ruth and I knows her.
   (B) Everyone except Ruth and I know her.

(C) Everyone besides Ruth and me knows her.
(D) Everyone except I and Ruth knows her.
(E) Everyone except Ruth and me knows her.

Stop

End of section. If you have any time left, go over your work in this section only. Do not work in any other section of the test.

Answer Key
Section 3: Communication Skills
Writing Ability

ENGLISH USAGE

1. A	5. C	9. B	13. B	17. A
2. D	6. D	10. C	14. D	18. D
3. A	7. B	11. A	15. E	19. A
4. E	8. D	12. E	16. C	20. E

SENTENCE CORRECTION

1. C	6. B	11. B	16. D	21. B
2. B	7. E	12. E	17. C	22. C
3. C	8. E	13. B	18. E	23. E
4. E	9. C	14. B	19. C	24. B
5. E	10. A	15. B	20. A	25. E

Part Eight

WRITING ABILITY DIAGNOSTIC SCORE SHEET

WRITING ABILITY DIAGNOSTIC SCORE SHEET

To Use With Tests in Written English Expression to Identify Problems in Communication in Writing

HOW TO USE THE SCORE SHEET

On the left, nine different aspects of written English expression are listed. In the other four columns we have listed the items in each Diagnostic Examination which test each aspect. After taking each practice examination and correcting your answer sheet, transfer the information for the English Usage and Sentence Correction subtests to this Diagnostic Score Sheet by circling the number of the items you answered *correctly*. Any aspect missing more than one circle is worth reviewing.

This aspect is reviewed in these items:

Aspect	On Diagnostic Core Battery I in the subtest on:		On Diagnostic Core Battery II in the subtest on:	
	English Usage	Sentence Correction	English Usage	Sentence Correction
1. Expressing ideas precisely		1,6,8,11, 14,15,21	5,9	7,9,15,22,24
2. Sentence Structure	4,10,20	18,25		
3. Vocabulary, word usage	1,15	20	2,6,11,15,16	
4. Use of Adjectives, adverbs, comparative, superlative	12	10,13,19,22		5,10,13
5. Use of pronouns	5,7,8,18	5,9,12,23,24	3,4,18	1,3,6,23
6. Agreement of subject and verb	2,3,9,14	7,17	10,12,20	2,18,25
7. Using the correct form of verbs	6,11,13,16,17	2,3,4,16	1,8,17,19	4,8,12,16,17,21
8. Use of conjunctions, prepositions				11,14,19,20
9. Punctuation	19		7,13,14	

263

Part Nine

REVIEW TESTS FOR SPECIALTY AREAS

ART EDUCATION

After reading each question, circle the answer you think is correct, and score your examination using the Answer Key that appears after the questions. You should plan for intensive review if you answer fewer than 15 correctly. Give yourself 15 minutes to answer the 20 questions in this examination.

1. Of the following activities, the one that is *least* desirable at the elementary level is

   (A) making mobiles
   (B) doing cut-paper sculpture
   (C) making three-dimensional abstractions from scrap materials
   (D) copying pictures in order to learn drawing techniques
   (E) learning about different media

2. An inexpensive and useful material for modeling in elementary school is

   (A) kaolin and water
   (B) tile cement
   (C) a mixture of salt, flour, and water
   (D) wax
   (E) Play-Doh®

3. In the elementary grades, art education is used primarily

   (A) to provide relief from intensive intellectual experiences
   (B) as play therapy
   (C) as an end in itself
   (D) as a means to an end
   (E) to allow regular teachers a "prep" period

4. In the early grades, clay modeling is closely related to block building principally because

   (A) both use inexpensive materials
   (B) both involve space, proportion, and volume
   (C) color choices are not involved
   (D) the building process is similar
   (E) both help develop fine muscle control

5. As a tool of child growth in the elementary school, art education is best employed when

   (A) the teacher provides good art reproductions for study
   (B) the teacher shows the children how to copy or trace scenes

267

(C) the children are left to their own devices

(D) provision is made for guided first-hand experiences

(E) only a certified art teacher provides the instruction

6. Of the following materials, the one *least* appropriate for use with children in the primary grades is

(A) colored paper
(B) crayon
(C) charcoal
(D) finger paint
(E) poster paint

7. Rottenstone, rouge, and whiting are used for

(A) polishing
(B) filling porous wood surfaces
(C) sterilizing
(D) coloring
(E) cleaning

8. Reference is often made to Stonehenge, a prehistoric monument in England, as an example of primitive architecture that embodied use of

(A) post and lintel
(B) buttress architecture
(C) arch
(D) dome
(E) Ionic columns

9. The most famous of all portraits of Washington was painted by

(A) Charles Wilson Peale
(B) Thomas Sully
(C) Benjamin West
(D) Gilbert Stuart
(E) Edward Hopper

10. Of the following, the one who is noted for work in the field of art education is

(A) Richard Avedon
(B) Aaron Copland
(C) Sherwood Anderson
(D) Victor Lowenfield
(E) Sarah Caldwell

11. Tempera paint is best diluted with

(A) turpentine
(B) vinegar
(C) oil
(D) water
(E) alcohol

12. Of the following schools of painting, the one associated with the technique of "broken color" is

    (A) Surrealism
    (B) Color Field
    (C) Purism
    (D) Cubism
    (E) Pointillism

13. The primary colors are

    (A) red, yellow, green
    (B) red, green, yellow, purple, blue, orange
    (C) red, yellow, blue
    (D) red, yellow, green, black, white
    (E) red, white, blue

14. In developing the concept of three-dimensional design in art with children, we deal chiefly with

    (A) forms and sense of space
    (B) design on a flat surface
    (C) the interaction of all visual elements
    (D) each dimension separately
    (E) the relationship of art, music, and the dance

15. One of the principal and unique psychological advantages of finger painting is that the activity

    (A) provides evidence of emotional disturbance in children
    (B) is a source of satisfaction and release for all children
    (C) permits the child to obliterate his design with a few sweeping movements and start anew
    (D) provides a challenging medium of expression while at the same time satisfying the overly aggressive child
    (E) allows children to get dirty without punishment

16. The architectural style that influenced the Capitol at Washington is

    (A) Byzantine
    (B) Gothic
    (C) Renaissance
    (D) Classical
    (E) Victorian

17. Intaglio printing is

    (A) cutting away film to create printing stencils
    (B) engraving or cutting into a surface to leave relief
    (C) a process that excludes drypoint
    (D) etching a design on a lithographic stone
    (E) a way to add color to silk-screen prints

18. Buckminster Fuller is associated with the

    (A) concepts of pure plastic art and cubism

(B) development of the geodesic dome
(C) designing of the biomorphic home
(D) open plan and loose environmental planning
(E) lacy and decorative architectural rendering

19. The cracking of many nineteenth-century paintings was most likely caused by

(A) inferior brushes
(B) eucaustic
(C) bitumen
(D) restorers
(E) poor-quality canvas

20. The discovery of the oil painting technique is usually associated with

(A) Jan Van Eyck
(B) Leonardo Da Vinci
(C) Giotto
(D) Albrecht Dürer
(E) Michaelangelo

BIOLOGY AND GENERAL SCIENCE

After reading each question, circle the answer you think is correct. Then score your examination using the Answer Key that appears after the questions. You should plan for intensive review if you answer fewer than 18 correctly. Give yourself 20 minutes to answer the 25 questions on this examination.

1. The classification of animals is usually done on the basis of

   (A) physical characteristics
   (B) functional use
   (C) geographic location
   (D) kinds of food eaten
   (E) size

2. In using tap water to set up an aquarium, the water must

   (A) be treated with chemicals to destroy the bacteria present in tap water
   (B) be allowed to stand for a period of approximately 24 hours to allow dissolved chlorine to escape
   (C) have calcium sulfate crystals added to prevent formation of algae
   (D) be changed daily
   (E) be hard rather than soft water

3. Blood leaving the left ventricle of the human heart goes directly to the

   (A) left auricle
   (B) pulmonary arteries
   (C) right ventricle
   (D) aorta
   (E) capillaries

4. Hematite is an ore of

   (A) aluminum
   (B) uranium
   (C) copper
   (D) titanium
   (E) iron

5. A few drops of iodine on a slice of bread will turn the bread

   (A) red-orange
   (B) brick-red

    (C) yellow
    (D) blue-black
    (E) black

6. One of the major breakthroughs in the development of gene splicing was the

    (A) isolation of the *E. coli* bacteria
    (B) discovery of the cancer-fighting properties of SV 40
    (C) use of plasmids to ''transport'' new genes
    (D) improvement in the resolution power of the electron microscope
    (E) discovery of interferon

7. Bile is used in the human body in the digestion of

    (A) starch
    (B) fats
    (C) carbohydrates
    (D) protein
    (E) sugars

8. Almost all weather phenomena are associated with which of the following?

    (A) lithosphere
    (B) stratosphere
    (C) mesosphere
    (D) ionosphere
    (E) troposphere

9. The amount of light entering the eye is controlled by the

    (A) optic nerve
    (B) cornea
    (C) iris
    (D) retina
    (E) lens

10. Of the foods below, the one that produces the quickest heat energy per pound is

    (A) lettuce
    (B) spinach
    (C) bread
    (D) butter
    (E) roast beef

11. The statement that a buoyant force on a floating body is equal to the weight of fluid displaced is known as the principle or law of

    (A) Newton
    (B) Boyle
    (C) Bernoulli
    (D) Galileo
    (E) Archimedes

12. You can extract chlorophyll from a leaf by

    (A) covering it with iodine solution

(B) electrolysis
(C) boiling it in alcohol
(D) soaking it in water
(E) photosynthesis

13. In most flowers pollen is produced in the

(A) corolla
(B) sepal
(C) stamen
(D) pistil
(E) ovary

14. Which lists the life cycle of the butterfly in correct order?

(A) egg, nymph, pupa, adult
(B) egg, pupa, larva, adult
(C) larva, egg, pupa, adult
(D) egg, larva, pupa, adult
(E) larva, pupa, egg, adult

15. Cheese is a good source of

(A) water
(B) sugar
(C) starch
(D) protein
(E) minerals

16. Alcoholic fermentation is a process involved in

(A) anaerobic metabolism
(B) transpiration
(C) aerobic respiration
(D) intracellular digestion
(E) cell growth

17. Potassium and sodium are necessary nutrients because they are used to

(A) form hydrochloric acid in the stomach
(B) form hemoglobin for red blood cells
(C) maintain healthy condition of the skin
(D) maintain water balance in body fluids
(E) aid in tooth and bone development

18. An example of sedimentary rock is

(A) mica
(B) pumice
(C) sandstone
(D) gneiss
(E) granite

19. Acidity in the soil can be tested with

(A) limewater

(B) Benedict's solution
(C) filter paper
(D) pH paper
(E) Lugol's solution

20. A substance needed for the proper functioning of the thyroid gland is

(A) chlorine
(B) iodine
(C) phosphorus
(D) starch
(E) dextrose

21. Flowers that have no fragrance are usually pollinated by

(A) wind
(B) human beings
(C) insects
(D) birds
(E) small mammals

22. Next to oxygen, the most abundant element in the earth's crust is

(A) aluminum
(B) carbon
(C) iron
(D) silicon
(E) uranium

23. A steep-walled basin in a mountainside at the head of a glacial valley is called a

(A) cirque
(B) pothole
(C) caldera
(D) drumlin
(E) crater

24. An area on a weather map marked "high" means high

(A) temperature
(B) relative humidity
(C) air pressure
(D) wind speed
(E) altitude

25. Comparison of the freezing temperature of water and the melting temperature of ice shows that

(A) melting is almost one degree colder
(B) they are the same
(C) freezing is almost one degree colder
(D) freezing is four degrees colder
(E) freezing is one degree warmer

CHEMISTRY, PHYSICS, AND GENERAL SCIENCE

After reading each question, circle the answer you think is correct. Then score your examination using the Answer Key that appears after the questions. You should plan for intensive review if you answer fewer than 18 correctly. Give yourself 20 minutes to answer the 25 questions on this examination.

1. Sound waves of middle "C" produced on a triangle and a trumpet would

   (A) have the same wavelength
   (B) sound the same
   (C) have different wavelengths
   (D) have waves one octave apart
   (E) differ in amplitude

2. Billowy white clouds with flat bases are called

   (A) altocumulus
   (B) cumulus
   (C) stratus
   (D) cirrus
   (E) nimbus

3. A *distinctive* characteristic of protein compounds is that they are always associated with molecules of

   (A) nitrogen
   (B) hydrogen
   (C) oxygen
   (D) carbon
   (E) sulphur

4. Gastric juice aids in the digestion of

   (A) protein
   (B) fats
   (C) dextrose
   (D) starch
   (E) minerals

5. The poles of an armature are reversed by the arrangement of the

   (A) magnets
   (B) windings

(C) armature
(D) split rings
(E) generator

6. The sun has a direct effect on the heating of

    (A) land
    (B) air
    (C) water
    (D) deserts
    (E) all of the above

7. Isotopes of the same element have different numbers of

    (A) atoms
    (B) electrons
    (C) neutrons
    (D) protons
    (E) pions

8. Chemical combining power expressed in small whole numbers is

    (A) valence
    (B) atomic weight
    (C) atomic number
    (D) molecular weight
    (E) molarity

9. One of the more surprising findings of Voyager I's trip past Saturn is

    (A) the absence of any canals
    (B) the lack of biological life
    (C) how many rings there are
    (D) how few moons there are
    (E) a volcanic eruption on the moon Io

10. The loudness of a sound depends on its

    (A) frequency
    (B) wavelength
    (C) amplitude
    (D) pitch
    (E) velocity

11. In order to build body tissues, a person needs plenty of

    (A) minerals
    (B) fats
    (C) carbohydrates
    (D) proteins
    (E) vitamins

12. If bubbles are formed when hydrochloric acid is dropped on a rock specimen, it is most probably

    (A) marble

(B) mica
(C) sandstone
(D) quartz
(E) slate

13. Granite is a rock that resulted from the

(A) cementing of sand
(B) cooling of molten minerals
(C) eruption of a volcano
(D) pressure on clay
(E) sedimentation

14. The symbol for the element californium is

(A) C
(B) Co
(C) Ca
(D) Cf
(E) Cn

15. A large weight is placed at one end of a lever and a small weight on the other end. To make the two weights balance, the fulcrum must be

(A) at the center of the lever
(B) between the center and the large weight
(C) between the center and the lighter weight
(D) directly under the heavy weight
(E) between the heavy weight and the end of the lever

16. A new era in the treatment of disease is expected as a result of

(A) tamper-proof packaging
(B) revised curricula in medical education
(C) research in birth defects
(D) genetic engineering
(E) improved federal standards for drug safety

17. The pressure on the curved top surface of an airplane wing is less than on the bottom surface because

(A) the air is moving faster on top
(B) the top is at a greater altitude
(C) there is less air on bottom
(D) there is less air on top
(E) the air is moving faster on the bottom

18. When 5 grams of water freeze at $0°$ C., the amount of heat liberated is

(A) 80 calories
(B) 288 calories
(C) 400 calories
(D) no calories
(E) 5 calories

19. Ohm's Law can be expressed as

    (A) $R = \frac{I}{E}$

    (B) $RE = I$

    (C) $\frac{R}{I} = E$

    (D) $R = \frac{E}{I}$

    (E) $R = E \times I$

20. Soil that characteristically has colloidal structure and has been derived from feldspathic rock is

    (A) clay
    (B) sand
    (C) granite
    (D) loam
    (E) coal

21. Energy is often defined as

    (A) the amount of difficulty encountered in attempting to move an object
    (B) the ability to do work
    (C) a force acting through a distance
    (D) the total velocity of the molecules in an object
    (E) the work required to resist the pull of gravity

22. The smallest possible number of atoms in a molecule is

    (A) one
    (B) two
    (C) three
    (D) four
    (E) none

23. Tallness is dominant and dwarfness is recessive. Td is crossed with Td. Of 1,000 offspring, approximately how many will be phenotypically tall?

    (A) 250
    (B) 333
    (C) 500
    (D) 750
    (E) cannot be determined without additional data

24. The boiling point of water in degrees Kelvin (absolute) is

    (A) 100°
    (B) 212°
    (C) 273°
    (D) 373°
    (E) 32°

25. A one-molal solution contains

  (A) one gram of solute in 100 grams of solvent
  (B) six ounces of solute in 100 grams of solvent
  (C) 6.02×10^{23} grams solute in one gram of solvent
  (D) one gram of solute in one gram of solvent
  (E) Avogadro's number of particles of solute in one kilogram solvent

EARLY CHILDHOOD EDUCATION

After reading each question, circle the answer you think is correct. Then score your examination using the Answer Key that appears after the questions. You should plan for intensive review if you answer fewer than 29 correctly. Give yourself 35 minutes to answer the 40 questions on this examination.

1. Between the first and second birthdays, the vocabulary of most children

   (A) doubles
   (B) expands from 20 to 30 words
   (C) expands from 300 or 400 words to about 1,000 words
   (D) acquires adult grammatical structure
   (E) depends on the number and ages of siblings

2. A typical three-year-old will not believe you if you tell him that

   (A) it will rain if you wear a blue shirt
   (B) his father can make it rain
   (C) you keep a tiger in the cellar
   (D) there is a man who comes to take away naughty children
   (E) his father is a child of his grandmother

3. In a group dramatic play, young preschool children

   (A) resist taking on roles of the opposite sex
   (B) change roles quickly
   (C) prefer to take on the powerful roles of professional, white-collar workers
   (D) acquire a sense of power that can be readily transferred to real situations
   (E) can learn complex plots and dialogue

4. A beneficial preschool program must

   (A) last at least six hours per day to allow for enough intellectual bombardment
   (B) prohibit parental involvement so that children can develop a sense of independence
   (C) include a substantial number of routine activity sequences
   (D) have a fixed schedule of activities that does not vary from day to day
   (E) emphasize emotional development over all other aspects of development

5. The idea of the kindergarten originated in

   (A) France
   (B) England

(C) Germany
(D) Austria
(E) New England

6. Which of the following behaviors is characteristic of three- and four-year-old children?

   (A) drawing a single straight line when attempting to fill in the missing corner of a geometric figure
   (B) grouping color in order of the solar spectrum
   (C) tracing a looping line across the intersection of the line without changing direction or detouring around the loop
   (D) memorizing material in a well-organized and systematic manner
   (E) preferring the company of their peers over adults

7. Which one of the following was *not* stressed by Montessori in her method for young children?

   (A) Children should become increasingly independent of the teacher.
   (B) Children should have many experiences with form, number, and touch.
   (C) Children should be taught predominantly in small groups.
   (D) Children should have appropriate responsibilities.
   (E) Children's muscles, coordination, and physical development are of particular concern.

8. Creative children tend to

   (A) show flexibility in perceptual tasks
   (B) have highly structured thought systems
   (C) produce few but very good ideas
   (D) prefer symmetry over asymmetry
   (E) be most free in highly structured situations

9. The grammatical errors made by the four- and five-year-old child result chiefly from his

   (A) inability to distinguish phonemes
   (B) articulatory difficulties
   (C) inadequate vocabulary
   (D) faith in the lawfulness of language rules
   (E) inability to pronounce morphemes

10. The chief aim of a desirable social environment in the preschool classroom should be to encourage the child to

    (A) develop self-reliance
    (B) converse freely with other children
    (C) solve his own social problems
    (D) choose his own activity
    (E) relate well to the adults about him

11. In the formation of learning sets, the young child must

    (A) be able to use symbols
    (B) respond to a number of problems according to the same principle

(C) have had some drill in modern math
(D) all of the above
(E) none of the above

12. To provide worthwhile science experiences in the kindergarten and primary grades, it is important for the teacher to

(A) give every child in the class some experience with plant and animal life
(B) plan for and set up opportunities for the observation of experiments
(C) help children to establish new facts through observing the relatedness of known facts
(D) provide every child with experience in reducing an immediate problem to such simple form that deductions can be made
(E) provide each child with the opportunity to manipulate equipment

13. Which of the following kinds of school is more common in England than in the United States?

(A) day-care centers
(B) private nursery schools
(C) public nursery schools
(D) cooperative nursery schools
(E) all of the above

14. Which of the following is the *least* significant for the development of perceptual sensitivity in young children?

(A) seeing likeness and difference
(B) seeing bigness and littleness
(C) seeing patterns of color
(D) seeing many details
(E) being exposed to a wide variety of stimuli

15. The nursery school and kindergarten provide time for free play chiefly in order that the child may have opportunities to

(A) establish both self-confidence and self-control
(B) meet concrete, problem-solving situations
(C) plan and carry out individual or group projects
(D) choose activities and experiment freely with materials
(E) burn up excessive energy

16. Children with learning disabilities are usually characterized by which of the following behaviors?
   I. hyperactivity
  II. lack of physical coordination
 III. talkativeness
 IV. forgetfulness

(A) IV only
(B) I and III
(C) I, III, and IV
(D) II and III
(E) I, II, and IV

17. Which of the following statements about materials for early childhood education is *incorrect?*

    (A) Montessori provided materials that would teach children through sense perception.
    (B) Pestalozzi emphasized through his mazes and games the importance of problem-solving.
    (C) Froebel's small manipulative equipment was intended to help the child learn joyfully and uncoercively.
    (D) Patty Hill's large blocks were a result of deepened understanding of children and their needs.
    (E) Cuisinaire rods help the child concretize abstract arithmetic functions.

18. The meaning of play most acceptable to early-childhood educators today is that play is

    (A) a means of using surplus energies not needed in the struggle for survival
    (B) an expression of the natural urge of all living things to be active
    (C) a basic need of all higher forms of life
    (D) best explained as the demand of the higher cerebral centers for relaxation
    (E) basically work for the young child

19. Pictures created by combining materials of different textures, patterns, and colors are called

    (A) paste pictures
    (B) collages
    (C) montages
    (D) stabiles
    (E) mobiles

20. The typical pre-primers in a modern basal reading series contain a total of about

    (A) 50 different words
    (B) 100 different words
    (C) 150 different words
    (D) 250 different words
    (E) 300 different words

21. Which of the following offers the *best* illustration of the principle of gravity at the kindergarten and primary school level?

    (A) suspending a weight from a piece of string and setting it in motion as a pendulum
    (B) making a parachute using the four corners of a handkerchief attached to a single weight and throwing the parachute in the air
    (C) opening a milkweed case and tossing it into the air
    (D) tying a basket containing heavy blocks onto one end of a see-saw, and going to the other end and trying to make the basket go up in the air
    (E) pouring oil on water and seeing it float

22. The nursery school, kindergarten, and primary grades include a variety of activities in which there is an opportunity for the child to manipulate materials. The *primary* reason for including this type of activity is that it

    (A) develops perceptual skills

(B) develops a positive attitude towards work

(C) provides concrete experiences that form the basis for conceptual thinking

(D) introduces children to a variety of creative materials

(E) forces the child to pay attention to the lesson

23. Teachers who are concerned with developing a strong sense of responsibility for self-care would most sensibly do which of the following?

(A) provide carefully structured situations so children know what is expected of them

(B) provide direct instruction in how to handle all the simple life-situations, such as dressing

(C) make certain that children are dressed appropriately for the weather

(D) let the children choose between two cookies at milk and cookie time

(E) provide activities that help children learn how to choose between several alternatives

24. Children's capacity to evaluate their own behavior is a basic factor in the development of

(A) social awareness

(B) knowledge

(C) sexual identification

(D) personal experiences

(E) self-esteem

25. Among the Piagetian stages of cognitive development listed below, the one that most closely applies to children's mental activities at the preschool level is

(A) sensory-motor

(B) conservation

(C) preoperational

(D) concrete operations

(E) formal operations

26. The concept that intelligence can be modified by environmental conditions and that the best time for modification is with young children, was part of the theoretical rationale for

(A) kindergarten

(B) the Madison project

(C) Environmental Education

(D) the Head Start Program

(E) day care programs

27. Several characterisics have an identified half-development period, which is the age by which the individual has achieved about half of the characteristics he or she will exhibit between the ages of eighteen to twenty. Which of the following will have been half-developed by the age of five?

   I. weight

  II. height

 III. general intelligence

IV. vocational interests

V. general school achievement

(A) I and II

(B) I, II, III, and V

(C) I, II, and V

(D) III, IV, and V

(E) I and III

28. When Piaget discusses the development of intelligence, he describes three stages before age seven:

I. extract concepts from experience

II. preconceptual and intuitive thought

III. acquire sensorimotor control

The chronological development order he states is:

(A) I, II, III

(B) I, III, II

(C) II, III, I

(D) III, I, II

(E) III, II, I

29. The British Infant School enrolled children in which of the following age spans?

(A) birth to age 2

(B) 2–4

(C) 4–7

(D) 5–8

(E) 7–11

30. The notion that the importance of a child's self-concept lies in its contribution towards self-actualizing and becoming a fully functioning person is associated with

(A) Maslow and Rogers

(B) Guilford

(C) Freud

(D) Almy and Piaget

(E) Jung

31. A method of identifying gifted children is described as "good for screening, may not identify those with reading difficulties, emotional or motivational problems, or cultural impoverishment." The method referred to is probably

(A) teacher observation

(B) an individual intelligence test

(C) a group intelligence test

(D) a creativity test

(E) a reading test

32. A teacher concerned with the concept development as described by Piaget and others would accept which of the following as true?

    I. On any given concept, a child's attitudes and understandings are either correct or incorrect.

   II. Concepts gradually evolve and develop more precisely.

  III. New concepts evolve from questioning previous concepts.

  IV. Opportunities for observation and experimentation are necessary for concept development.

(A) I and II

(B) II and III

(C) III and IV

(D) I, II, and III

(E) I, II, III, and IV

33. The perception of intelligence as consisting of several sub-aspects rather than one general factor was put forward by

(A) Binet

(B) Guilford

(C) Wechsler

(D) Skinner

(E) Thorndike

34. Children who sort materials by color, shape, size, brightness, and weight are illustrating the mathematical process of

(A) counting

(B) making comparisons

(C) geometric forms

(D) spatial relations

(E) classification

35. Of the following aspects of scientific process, which are appropriate for an Early Childhood class?

    I. identifying problems

   II. formulating hypotheses

  III. making generalizations

(A) all of the above

(B) none of the above

(C) only I

(D) only III

(E) only II and III

36. A teacher concerned with teaching reading to young children will provide which of the following experiences?

    I. oral communication experiences

   II. visual discrimination experiences

  III. auditory discrimination experiences

(A) I only

(B) II only

(C) III only

(D) II and III

(E) I, II, and III

37. Which of the following concepts will be the most difficult to introduce into a social studies class at the Early Childhood level?

(A) communication

(B) ownership and sharing

(C) transportation

(D) celebrations

(E) anger and joy

38. Of the following which would be the most dangerous piece of play equipment for young children?

(A) wheeled toys

(B) cardboard packing boxes

(C) a slide

(D) rubber balls

(E) a wooden swing

39. The housekeeping area of an Early Childhood classroom is conducive to which of the following?

   I. practicing language skills

  II. providing opportunities for social interaction

 III. developing problem solving skills

 IV. making scientific observations

(A) I, II, and III

(B) II, III, and IV

(C) I, III, and IV

(D) I and II

(E) I, II, III, and IV

40. A method for teaching beginning reading which involved developing symbols for forty-three sounds in English was

(A) the phonics method

(B) the initial teaching alphabet

(C) Flesch's critical sound approach

(D) Bloomfield's "Let's Read"

(E) the sound-it-out approach

EDUCATION OF
THE MENTALLY RETARDED

After reading each question, circle the answer you think is correct. Then score your examination using the Answer Key that appears after the questions. You should plan for intensive review if you answer fewer than 22 correctly. Give yourself 25 minutes to answer the 30 questions on this examination.

1. On the whole, severely mentally retarded children

   (A) are placid and withdrawn
   (B) are aggressive and dangerous
   (C) are outgoing and friendly
   (D) are responsible for a very high percentage of delinquency
   (E) manifest a variety of personality patterns

2. Mongolism was first described by

   (A) Kretschmer
   (B) Binet
   (C) Bender
   (D) Downs
   (E) Jervis

3. If a group of mentally retarded children read at the second-grade level, functional reading material should be at

   (A) first-grade level
   (B) second-grade level
   (C) third-grade level
   (D) levels from first grade to third grade
   (E) any level, as long as vocabulary is simple

Questions 4 through 8 use the following information.

Kevin is a tall, slender boy who is 10 years old, with blond hair, blue eyes, and fair skin. His parents have swarthy complexions. Kevin is poorly coordinated, walks with a stiff gait, and has difficulty dressing himself. During the examination, Kevin preferred looking out of the window, but could, on pressure, be brought back to the task at hand. His Stanford-Binet results were: IQ = 48, Basal = 4, Terminal = 6.

4. Kevin's mental age is rounded at

   (A) two years
   (B) four years
   (C) five years
   (D) six years
   (E) ten years

5. Kevin's looking out of the window is probably due to

   (A) epilepsy
   (B) a visual defect
   (C) curiosity
   (D) fear
   (E) short attention-span

6. Kevin's reading expectancy level is

   (A) pre-primer
   (B) first grade, first few months
   (C) first grade, end of year
   (D) reading readiness
   (E) a non-reader

7. A possible explanation for Kevin's retardation would be

   (A) Marfan's syndrome
   (B) galactosemia
   (C) cretinism
   (D) phenylketonouria
   (E) impossible to tell from the information given

8. If an individualized educational program is developed for Kevin, how often is that program to be reviewed?

   (A) weekly
   (B) monthly
   (C) twice a year, after each semester
   (D) every three months
   (E) annually

9. The term "Down's syndrome" describes a(n)

   (A) chromosomal difference
   (B) dominant-gene transmission
   (C) single recessive-gene transmission
   (D) thymus gland malfunction
   (E) Rh factor problem

10. The due-process rights provided in P.L. 94–142 provide protection to which of the following in relation to the exceptional child?
    I. parents, in their right to make decisions related to their child
    II. related professionals' right to determine children's needs
    III. the school's right to make educational decisions

(A) I only
(B) I and III
(C) I and II
(D) II and III
(E) I, II, and III

11. "Least restrictive environment" is used in P.L. 94–142 to refer to

(A) intermediate educable classes
(B) the need to redesign schools and other community institutions to make them readily accessible
(C) the need to reorganize schools to be certain that handicapped children are placed in normal curricular and extracurricular settings at all times
(D) the assurance that handicapped children are in regular classes in the non-academic components of their education
(E) handicapped children receiving specialized services, as needed and appropriate, through special instructional placement

12. An assessment program for special education programs should be which of the following?
   I. structured so that every child receives the same tests
  II. continuous
 III. non-discriminatory

(A) I only
(B) II only
(C) I and III
(D) II and III
(E) I, II, and III

13. An important development in identifying the mentally retarded child was the development of the

(A) Rorschach Test
(B) Stanford Achievement Test
(C) Stanford-Binet Test
(D) Peabody Picture Vocabulary Test
(E) Lorge-Thorndike Intelligence Test

14. Rubella may cause which of the following?

(A) neurological defects
(B) deafness
(C) mental retardation
(D) cataracts and glaucoma
(E) all of the above

15. Especially crucial for the mildly retarded person in today's culture are

(A) community-living skills
(B) self-care skills
(C) literacy skills
(D) sheltered workshops
(E) psychological services

16. You have been given responsibility for establishing an extracurricular program for a mentally retarded group. Which of the following is (are) appropriate?

    (A) music
    (B) art
    (C) drama
    (D) Scouting
    (E) all of the above

17. Which of the following is a rating system to determine the indicators of normalcy a child exhibits at birth?

    (A) Vineland Social Maturity Scale
    (B) Apgar Test
    (C) Infant Rating Scale
    (D) Seguin Scale
    (E) Amniocentesis

18. The first historical era that can be said to have exhibited some sensitivity towards the mentally retarded is the

    (A) Greco-Roman period
    (B) Middle Ages
    (C) Renaissance
    (D) nineteenth century
    (E) twentieth century

19. Present estimates of the extent of mental retardation in the total population place the extent at
    (A) less than 1%
    (B) about 1%
    (C) 2 to 3%
    (D) about 5%
    (E) not precise, but at least 5%

20. All of the following are arguments for mainstreaming *except* that

    (A) special classes are a way of shunting children who are different out of the regular classroom
    (B) labeling children causes more damage in addition to their original problem
    (C) separate-but-equal facilities lead to inequality of opportunity
    (D) it ensures that a great deal of time will be devoted to student evaluation, conferences, planning, and paperwork
    (E) students in special classes do no better than similarly disabled students in regular classes

21. Which is the correct chronological order for the following events?

    I. The National Society for the Study of Education devoted a yearbook to the education of exceptional children.
    II. The Stanford Binet Scale of Intelligence was published.
    III. The U.S. Office of Education formed a section on exceptional children.
    IV. The Elementary and Secondary Education Act was passed.

(A) I, II, III, IV
(B) IV, III, II, I
(C) II, I, III, IV
(D) III, II, I, IV
(E) II, I, IV, III

22. The majority of federal legislation and court action in special education has ignored which of the following groups?

(A) the severely retarded
(B) the gifted and talented
(C) the physically handicapped
(D) the multiply handicapped
(E) the educable retarded

23. Which of the following cases resulted in extension of educational rights to handicapped children?

(A) *Goss* vs. *Lopez*
(B) *Brown* vs. *Kansas*
(C) Aspira decision
(D) *PARC* vs. *Pennsylvania*
(E) P.L. 94–142

24. There are many ways in which experts estimate the number of children requiring special education services. If one were to estimate this by determining the proportion of children who, between kindergarten and grade six, require some kind of supplementary help and/or display disturbed learning problems, that proportion would be about

(A) 10 percent
(B) 25 percent
(C) 40 percent
(D) 65 percent
(E) 85 percent

25. Which of the following would be consistent with the philosophy on the education of the mentally retarded which began to evolve in the 1980's?

I. Education is a right
II. Grading should be non-competitive and relate to individual goals
III. Learning difficulties are seen as coming from the children and the environment as an interacting pair

(A) all of the above
(B) I only
(C) II only
(D) III only
(E) I and II only

26. The research on mainstreaming through 1980 indicated which of the following arrangements was preferable?

(A) Fully integrate children beginning in kindergarten or first grade.
(B) Begin to integrate in kindergarten and first grade, but only in certain areas.

(C) Segregate children until grade three or four, then gradually integrate.

(D) Segregate children until grade three or four, then fully integrate.

(E) No one arrangement is preferable.

27. Which of the following is *not* an aspect of the Individual Educational Plan developed to meet the requirements of PL 94–142?

(A) It is jointly arrived at by parents and school.

(B) It lists the proposed educational objectives.

(C) It includes a plan for evaluating results.

(D) It indicates how much and which aspects of the program will be mainstreamed.

(E) It is a legally binding document.

28. In the 1980's, the definition below came into use to refer to which of the groups listed?

"Children with special learning disabilities exhibit a disorder in one or more of the basic psychological processes involved in understanding or in using spoken or written languages. These may be manifested in disorders of listening, thinking, talking, reading, writing, spelling, or arithmetic."

(A) exceptional children

(B) educable retarded children

(C) learning disabled children

(D) handicapped children

(E) emotionally disturbed children

29. Of the following, the most important observable phenomenon in recognizing learning disabled children is

(A) low grades

(B) poor achievement test scores

(C) disparity between estimates of potential and achievement

(D) discrepancy between the results of successive IQ tests

(E) conflicts with other children

30. Which of the following is *not* a due process safeguard under PL 94–142?

(A) Parents have full access to relevant school records.

(B) Only natural parents may use the procedure even if the child is a ward of the state.

(C) Prior notice must be given parents before a program is changed.

(D) A parent has a right to bring a lawyer to a hearing.

(E) The parent is entitled to a transcript of any hearing or a copy of any written decision.

ELEMENTARY EDUCATION

After reading each question, circle the answer you think is correct. Then score your examination using the Answer Key that appears after the questions. You should plan for intensive review if you answer fewer than 29 correctly. Give yourself 35 minutes to answer the 40 questions on this examination.

1. Which one of the following situations would most clearly justify subdividing a class into smaller groups (that is, grouping within the classroom)?

   (A) a wide range of individual differences in ability
   (B) differences in academic achievement in basic subjects
   (C) differences in motivational level
   (D) cliques and social-personal conflicts
   (E) the value of a particular pattern of grouping for the attainment of a special goal

2. Which of the following words does *not* follow a phonic principle common to the other four?

   (A) come
   (B) dime
   (C) gene
   (D) same
   (E) cone

3. Probably the greatest waste in spelling instruction is caused by

   (A) using one spelling list for the entire class
   (B) having able spellers study words they already know
   (C) teaching spelling rules
   (D) analyzing each word on the list
   (E) not teaching the 100 most commonly misspelled words

4. The increase in recent years in the number of trade books used in school reading programs in the early grades stems chiefly from the

   (A) greater emphasis upon individualized instruction
   (B) availability of workbook materials related to the trade books
   (C) integration of social studies and science content in these books
   (D) satisfaction children get from reading books to their parents at home
   (E) availability of federal funds

5. Research has shown that the social self-image begins to develop significantly

   (A) as the child grows into adolescence

(B) upon the child's entrance into school

(C) during the beginning of autonomous behavior

(D) as the child recognizes different standards and expectations among his peers

(E) in infancy

6. Of the following teacher strategies, which one is *least* sensible?

(A) being friendly and warm to the children

(B) singling out for special attention maladaptive behavior that you wish to extinguish

(C) arranging conditions so that children experience success rather than failure

(D) not punishing children in front of their classmates

(E) not asking a child to do something you know he/she cannot do

7. Good practices employed in teaching poetry should assure the child a vital contact with the poem as

(A) an intuitive, imaginative conception of experience

(B) a logical arrangement of rhyming words

(C) an arrangement of rhythm patterns

(D) a means of telling a story

(E) an exercise in memorization

8. When a child who is reading a story to the class comes to a word he does not know, the teacher should

(A) have him use phonetic analysis

(B) have him use structural analysis

(C) tell him the word

(D) tell him to look for meaning clues

(E) tell him to move on and see if the word becomes clear

9. A primary-grade teacher could use the book *When We Were Very Young* to enrich his/her pupil's acquaintance with

(A) stories of American childhood

(B) animal stories

(C) whimsical poetry

(D) folk tales of different lands

(E) historical figures

10. According to Piaget, in the usual pattern of development, egocentric speech

(A) increases gradually from three to twelve years of age

(B) is equally characteristic of adults and children

(C) decreases considerably from early childhood to later childhood

(D) remains at the same level until about seven years of age, after which it declines rapidly

(E) reflects a growing self-esteem

11. Correct racial self-identification may occur as early as

(A) three years of age

(B) four years of age

(C) five years of age

(D) seven years of age

(E) infancy

12. In guiding the very impulsive child to develop good thinking habits, the teacher should provide experiences that

(A) require observing, comparing, summarizing

(B) involve following precise direction

(C) are easy enough to provide immediate success

(D) require independent problem-solving

(E) involve working with other children

13. Which of the following are *incorrectly* paired?

(A) Maria Montessori—a prepared environment for learning

(B) Sir James Pitman—the Initial Teaching Alphabet

(C) Jean Piaget—stages in intellectual development

(D) Jerome Bruner—a behavioral theory of learning

(E) Abraham Maslow—a hierarchy of motivation

14. There is consensus that the major reading-study skills should be an important part of the total reading program. Which of the following would *not* be included as a reading-study skill?

(A) locating information

(B) evaluating relevant data

(C) reading from left to right

(D) retention of pertinent material

(E) using context clues

15. According to linguists, the phoneme is identified as a(an)

(A) visual phenomenon of perception

(B) perceived distinctive sound

(C) word or unit of meaning

(D) letter that represents a specific sound

(E) initial consonant

16. In introducing learning tasks, the most important element for success is that the

(A) goals be clearly identified for the class by the teacher

(B) proper materials be readily available

(C) class be organized into interest groups

(D) teacher provide suitable motivation for the children

(E) new learning be paced to the learners' maturation and previous knowledge

17. Research has shown that creativity

(A) correlates very highly with intelligence

(B) does not correlate very highly with intelligence

(C) is possessed in a substantially similar degree by most persons

(D) is usually expressed in only one area by each person

(E) increases as children go up through the grades

18. Developmental norms are *most* useful in the sense that they

    (A) provide useful information about the sequence of development
    (B) are based on representative samples
    (C) provide guidelines for grouping in the classroom
    (D) allow prediction of later intellectual development
    (E) help a teacher to decide how to group for reading

19. All of the following aspects of the readiness program should be completed before systematic instruction in reading is begun *except* the

    (A) keeping of a bulletin board in the classroom with weather reports, special
    events, or messages to the children
    (B) labeling of objects in the classroom such as desks, chairs, and blackboard
    (C) use of a pre-primer as an introduction to a reading series
    (D) composing of little stories by the children that are recorded on a chart by
    the teacher
    (E) teaching the letters of the alphabet

20. When an eight-year-old child understands that two pieces of clay that originally
were equal spheres are still equal after one has been flattened into a pancake, we
say the child is showing

    (A) rote thinking
    (B) intuitive thought
    (C) convergent thinking
    (D) understanding of conservation
    (E) the ability to generalize

21. Which of the following points have been made by critics of individualization in
elementary education?
    I. There is an excessive emphasis on skills that are easily translated into work-
    book exercises.
    II. Individualization limits integration of subject matter.
    III. There is an over-emphasis on spontaneous, personal experiences.

    (A) I, II, and III
    (B) I only
    (C) III only
    (D) I and II only
    (E) II and III only

22. The basic reason for securing more male elementary school teachers is that they

    (A) will provide a wider range of teacher interests, for example, sports and
    hobbies
    (B) function more effectively as authority figures than women teachers
    (C) are more apt to make teaching a permanent career than women teachers
    (D) are needed to serve as models of masculine behavior, especially for boys
    (E) will stabilize salary scales

23. The "experience curriculum" is most likely to face difficulty in

    (A) stimulating group experiences
    (B) developing a meaningful sequence of studies

(C) vitalizing content with current materials

(D) providing for individual differences

(E) the costs associated with implementing it

24. The readability formulas that are currently used to assess reading materials are based chiefly upon measures of the

(A) vocabulary difficulty and sentence complexity

(B) correlation between content and children's interests at each grade level

(C) level of abstractness and unfamiliarity of concepts

(D) proportion of nouns, verbs, and modifiers used

(E) interest level of the material

25. The following pairs are correctly matched with the *exception* of

(A) *Water Babies*—Charles Kingsley

(B) *Just So Stories*—Rudyard Kipling

(C) *Ugly Duckling*—Grimm

(D) *Charlie and the Chocolate Factory*—Roald Dahl

(E) *Rootabaga Stories*—Carl Sandburg

26. Which of the following factors in reading readiness is *not* measured by most reading readiness tests?

(A) experiential background

(B) word-meanings

(C) visual discrimination

(D) interest in reading

(E) understanding initial consonants

27. The main purpose of the summary of a lesson is to

(A) emphasize the key points of the lesson

(B) test pupil attentiveness

(C) evaluate the teaching techniques used

(D) test pupils' skills

(E) establish the foundation for the next lesson

28. The amount and kind of homework assigned by the teacher should be determined by the

(A) difficulty of the subject

(B) behavior of the pupils

(C) length of the class period

(D) amount of time needed to cover the content of the course

(E) contribution the homework can make to learning

29. The notion that play is a central component in the development of children was first emphasized by who among the following?

(A) Froebel

(B) Pestalozzi

(C) Dewey

(D) Rousseau

(E) Montessori

30. Which of the following can be considered to be teaching strategies?
    I. discovery
    II. repetition
    III. explanation
    IV. direct observation

    (A) I and IV
    (B) I, III, and IV
    (C) I only
    (D) III and IV
    (E) all of the above

31. The notion that most American schools in the 1970's could be described as "grim, joyless places," was stated by

    (A) Goodman
    (B) Holt
    (C) Silberman
    (D) Kohl
    (E) Conant

32. Which of the following would be included in a curriculum concerned with affective functions of instruction?

    I. emotions
    II. motives
    III. moral sensibilities
    IV. appreciation
    V. self-image

    (A) None of the above
    (B) all of the above
    (C) V only
    (D) I and V only
    (E) II, III, and IV

33. The classification of educational objectives related to cognitive functioning into the categories of knowledge, comprehension, application, analysis, synthesis, and evaluation was developed by

    (A) Bruner
    (B) Havighurst
    (C) Piaget
    (D) Bloom
    (E) Spencer

34. The primary implication for teachers of the fact that most classes will have children who range over a wide spectrum in intelligence is that teachers should

    (A) be alert to signs of divergent thinking
    (B) realize that a teacher's judgment of children's ability has some degree of bias
    (C) avoid labelling children as slow
    (D) adapt work to individual differences
    (E) realize the importance of providing success experiences for all children

35. Research has shown that as one measures intelligence and separately measures creativity in large groups of children, the proportion of those who will score high on both measures is

    (A) close to zero
    (B) about 10 percent
    (C) about 30 percent
    (D) about 65 percent
    (E) almost 100 percent

36. If a child is in a situation to which he or she responds strongly, research indicates that as feelings intensify, the ability to perceive in the situation narrows. This has been called

    (A) selective perception
    (B) attention span
    (C) retroactive inhibition
    (D) proactive inhibition
    (E) tunnel vision

37. In his survey of research on creative children, Torrance has found which of the following to be characteristic of creative children?

    (A) They diverge from sex norms and prefer to learn in groups.
    (B) They prefer difficult tasks and have different values from those of other children.
    (C) Their friends enjoy their creativity and they become leaders.
    (D) They are extremely well-rounded and have a clear sense of purpose.
    (E) They find it difficult to sustain work but enjoy dangerous tasks.

38. As you observe Fred and Joan in class, you conclude that Fred needs primary reinforcement while Joan responds to intrinsic reinforcement. Which of the following best expresses their reaction to a specific task?

    (A) Fred will need immediate payoff.
    (B) Joan will need immediate payoff.
    (C) Fred will respond better to a delayed gratification.
    (D) There should be no difference in gratification patterns.
    (E) You can't predict anything about gratification patterns.

39. During the 1980's, social studies at the elementary school level has developed a new emphasis on the teaching of

    (A) names and dates in American History
    (B) global education
    (C) the European background of American History
    (D) the importance of the farm in American development
    (E) mercantilism as an economic philosophy

40. Of the following, the most important observable phenomenon in recognizing learning disabled children is

    (A) low grades
    (B) poor achievement test scores
    (C) disparity between estimates of potential and achievement
    (D) discrepancy between the results of successive IQ tests
    (E) conflicts with other children

ENGLISH LANGUAGE AND LITERATURE

After reading each question, circle the answer you think is correct. Then score your examination using the Answer Key that appears after the questions. You should plan for intensive review if you answer fewer than 18 questions correctly. Give yourself 18 minutes to answer the 25 questions on this examination.

1. There are relatively few stressed words in a "typical" English sentence. Many English-as-a-second-language students have to learn to take *strong* stress off words in sentences like

   (A) I'd like a little sugar in it, please.
   (B) But I am not from Mexico.
   (C) That is definitely my pen.
   (D) All of the work must be completed now.
   (E) Don't do that now.

2. The annual award for the most distinguished contribution to children's literature, first presented in 1922, is the

   (A) John Newbery
   (B) Laura Ingalls Wilder
   (C) Hans Christian Andersen
   (D) Elizabeth Peabody
   (E) Randolph Caldecott

3. In developing student awareness and knowledge of levels of language, the term that should be stressed most is

   (A) correct
   (B) standard
   (C) appropriate
   (D) colloquial
   (E) dialectic

4. The 26 letters of the Roman alphabet that we use today are generally represented in American English by which of the following numbers of phonemes and graphemes?

   (A) 44/300
   (B) 37/200
   (C) 40/400
   (D) 35/250
   (E) 26/260

5. Scholars of Black English have identified the characteristic of dropping consonant endings. This phenomenon can result in reading difficulties because of the
greatly increased number of

   (A) morphemes
   (B) graphemes
   (C) homophones
   (D) inflections
   (E) misspellings

6. The term that refers to the principle of reinforcing left-right eye movement is

   (A) dominance
   (B) eyedness
   (C) laterality
   (D) graphemics
   (E) binocular vision

7. It is important when working with children and adults to avoid terms that are
offensive to or denigrate individual backgrounds. The term, therefore, that
would be best to use in talking about the speech the child comes to school with
would be

   (A) school
   (B) street
   (C) slang
   (D) non-standard
   (E) everyday

8. Dialects vary in which of the characteristics listed below?
   I. vocabulary
   II. pronunciation
   III. structure

   (A) II and III
   (B) II only
   (C) III only
   (D) I and II
   (E) I, II, and III

9. In American English, the phoneme often referred to as the "lazy sound" is the

   (A) diphthong
   (B) short e
   (C) the schwa (ə)
   (D) long o
   (E) double consonant

10. The teacher who is concerned about sexism and racism in children's literature
should

   (A) carefully censor the books in the class library and on reading lists
   (B) choose to read books in class without offensive stereotypes
   (C) use a variety of books and wait until children react to the stereotypes
   (D) alert parents to the problem and ask them to watch what their children read
   (E) make children aware of how, as readers, they can be manipulated through
       sexual and racial stereotyping

11. Chaucer derived the story of *Troilus and Criseyde* from

    (A) Dante
    (B) Virgil
    (C) Boccaccio
    (D) Plato
    (E) Shakespeare

12. Swift's modest proposal was concerned with

    (A) cannibalism
    (B) child-rearing practices
    (C) the reconstruction of St. Paul's cathedral
    (D) free love
    (E) the withdrawal of debased currency

13. *Piers Plowman* is a work of the

    (A) Middle Ages
    (B) Victorian age
    (C) eighteenth century
    (D) High Renaissance
    (E) classical period

14. A novel that deals with the decay of a once-powerful family is

    (A) *A Tree Grows in Brooklyn*
    (B) *The Brook Kerith*
    (C) *Gentlemen's Agreement*
    (D) *Buddenbrooks*
    (E) *Shibumi*

15. Hotspur is a character in

    (A) *Henry IV, Part I*
    (B) *Henry VI*
    (C) *Richard III*
    (D) *Richard II*
    (E) *Henry VIII*

16. Harold Ross was associated with

    (A) *The New Yorker*
    (B) *The New York Times*
    (C) *Saturday Review*
    (D) *The New Republic*
    (E) *Commentary*

17. Which of the following is the name of a muse?

    (A) Calliope
    (B) Corydon
    (C) Kallicrates
    (D) Thyrsis
    (E) Clytemnestra

18. If you wanted your class to read an example of a burlesque or parody, which of the following would you use?

    (A) *MacFlecknoe*
    (B) *The Anatomy of Melancholy*
    (C) *A Shropshire Lad*
    (D) *Culture and Anarchy*
    (E) *War and Peace*

19. Which of the following plays was *not* written by Samuel Beckett?

    (A) *Happy Days*
    (B) *Waiting for Godot*
    (C) *Endgame*
    (D) *Krapp's Last Tape*
    (E) *No Exit*

20. All of the following are contemporary American playwrights *except*

    (A) Neil Simon
    (B) Imamu Baraka
    (C) John Osborne
    (D) Carson McCullers
    (E) Edward Albee

21. Which of the following has as its central theme creative evolution and the eternal pursuit of the male by the female?

    (A) O'Neill's *Desire Under the Elms*
    (B) Albee's *Who's Afraid of Virginia Woolf?*
    (C) Shaw's *Man and Superman*
    (D) Williams' *Streetcar Named Desire*
    (E) Genet's *The Maids*

22. The poem entitled "The People, Yes" was written by

    (A) Robert Frost
    (B) e.e. cummings
    (C) Dylan Thomas
    (D) Sara Teasdale
    (E) Carl Sandburg

23. A novel based on the history of South Africa describes

    (A) Michener's *The Covenant*
    (B) Williams' *Masquerade*
    (C) Vidal's *Creation*
    (D) Stewart's *Century*
    (E) Caldwell's *Answer as a Man*

24. A scientist who became a popular non-fiction writer on scientific subjects during the early 1980s is

    (A) Adam Smith
    (B) Ernest Gann
    (C) Robin Cook

(D) Gay Talese
(E) Carl Sagan

25. In 1981, after several decades, the apparently original, uncensored version of which of the novels appeared?

(A) Wolfe's *Look Homeward, Angel*
(B) Miller's *Tropic of Capricorn*
(C) Orwell's *1984*
(D) Dreiser's *Sister Carrie*
(E) Joyce's *Ulysses*

INDUSTRIAL ARTS EDUCATION*

After reading each question, circle the answer you think is correct. Then score your examination using the Answer Key that appears after the questions. You should plan for intensive review if you answer fewer than 18 questions correctly. Give yourself 18 minutes to answer the 25 questions on this examination.

1. You are teaching a class to process film, and you want to teach the following processes:
   I. fixing
   II. washing
   III. stopping
   IV. developing
   The proper sequence of these is:

   (A) I, II, III, IV
   (B) IV, III, I, II
   (C) IV, I, II, III
   (D) III, IV, II, I
   (E) I, IV, II, III

2. Offset lithography is based on the principle that

   (A) ink will print on paper
   (B) grease and water will not mix
   (C) ink will not stick to a rubber blanket
   (D) different paper has different absorption quality
   (E) a fountain solution makes ink unnecessary

3. Pre-sensitized plates have advantages over other metal offset plates, but the major advantage is that they are

   (A) safer to handle for students
   (B) less expensive
   (C) simpler to use
   (D) longer lasting
   (E) usable without platemaking equipment

4. In offset printing, the term "offsetting" refers to

   (A) the diluting of ink
   (B) failure of ink to adhere
   (C) a transparency of printed sheets

*This section is adapted in part from material originally developed by the Bureau of Industrial Arts Education of the New York State Department of Education.

(D) printing of photographs

(E) flow of ink

5. Of the phrases below, the one that best describes the flatbed press is

(A) a small letterpress

(B) a silk-screen press

(C) a cylinder press with type horizontally

(D) a press used to print on round surfaces

(E) a small lithographic press

6. If you wanted to demonstrate how molded plastic cooking-utensil handles were made, the molding process to be demonstrated is

(A) compression

(B) thermoforming

(C) extrusion

(D) encapsulation

(E) injection

7. If your students working on injection molding were troubled by excessive shrinkage, the remedy for the problem would be to

(A) increase the temperature

(B) increase the injection time

(C) decrease the temperature

(D) cool in the mold longer

(E) dry the resin

8. Which plastic resin would be used in the manufacture of plastic raincoats?

(A) polyvinylchloride

(B) acrylic

(C) phenolic

(D) polyester

(E) polyethylene

9. One of the advantages of some plastics is the ability to resist sharp blows or shocks. This physical property is called

(A) viscosity

(B) tensile strength

(C) compressive strength

(D) impact strength

(E) damping

10. The basic building blocks used in making plastics are

(A) atoms

(B) molecules

(C) electrons

(D) compounds

(E) neutrons

11. Which of the following can be considered ceramic products?

   I. acoustical brick

II. china

III. a Pyrex dish

IV. a granite tombstone

(A) I, II, and III

(B) I and II

(C) II and III

(D) I, II, and IV

(E) all of them

12. As your students are working with glass bottles, you notice that the bottles are beginning to sag. You know that the temperature has reached

(A) 500° F (260° C)

(B) 1,000° F (540° C)

(C) 1,500° F (815° C)

(D) 2,000° F (1095° C)

(E) cannot be determined without additional information

13. One of your students decides that she wants to finish a ceramic vase with green and blue glaze. She asks you what material she should use. Which of the following do you advise?

(A) magnesium oxide

(B) copper oxide

(C) nickel oxide

(D) iron oxide

(E) cobalt oxide

14. As you walk around a class that is working on an enameling project, you notice that one student's work has pinholes and blisters. What has the student done wrong?

(A) too thin a layer of enamel

(B) improper cleaning of base metal

(C) object overfired

(D) object underfired

(E) cannot tell without additional information

15. The seam below is an example of which kind of seam?

(A) lap seam

(B) single bottom seam

(C) standing seam

(D) grooved seam

(E) flat lock seam

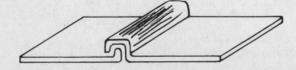

16. Your students have been making clay objects. They have removed the physical and chemical water, but have not yet glazed their work. Their clay objects, at this stage, are called

   (A) bisque
   (B) bone dry
   (C) leather-hard
   (D) plastic
   (E) glostware

17. A metal's ability to be drawn or stretched is called

   (A) fusibility
   (B) elasticity
   (C) malleability
   (D) ductility
   (E) hardness

18. You wish to show your students how to produce a smooth finish by moving their work against a rotating abrasive wheel. This process is called

   (A) milling
   (B) broaching
   (C) drilling
   (D) grinding
   (E) turning

19. One of your students suspects that she has a cracked grinding wheel. Which of the following tests is most commonly used to detect such a problem?

   (A) submerge the wheel in water and look for bubbles
   (B) strike the wheel lightly with a mallet and listen for a ring
   (C) run your hand lightly over the wheel while she turns it slowly
   (D) drop the wheel on the floor and look for chips
   (E) lock the wheel in a vise and bend it back and forth

20. Several methods of sawing lumber are illustrated below. The method in number three is called

   (A) radial
   (B) tangential
   (C) quarter
   (D) combination
   (E) plain

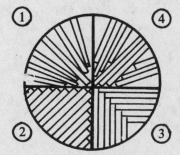

21. The safest way to show students how to remove metal chips from a cutting machine is to use

   (A) an air hose
   (B) a broom

(C) a rag
(D) a brush
(E) any flat-sided object that is not metal

22. Five ways to measure the length of a round-head screw are illustrated below. The correct way is illustrated in which diagram?

(A)   (B)   (C)   (D)   (E)

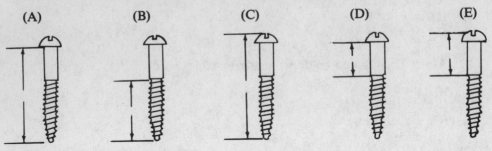

23. What solvent is used for shellac?

(A) alcohol
(B) turpentine
(C) benzene
(D) linseed oil
(E) water

24. All but one of the following woods would be classified as a hardwood. Which one is *not* a hardwood?

(A) walnut
(B) mahogany
(C) birch
(D) elm
(E) fir

25. Mr. Franklin's class is beginning a project on making a cutting board, as sketched in below. Of the tools listed, which would not be needed for this project?

(A) rule
(B) crosscut saw
(C) center punch
(D) coping saw
(E) jig saw

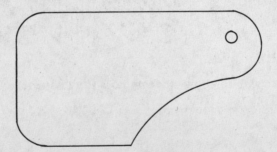

MATHEMATICS EDUCATION

After reading each question, circle the answer you think is correct. Then score your examination using the Answer Key that appears after the questions. You should plan for intensive review if you answer fewer than 18 correctly. Give yourself 20 minutes to answer the 25 questions on this examination.

1. The *chief* way in which programs for arithmetic teaching in most public school systems differ today from those of fifty years ago is in

   (A) rejection of drill and memorization
   (B) use of computers
   (C) integration of arithmetic with other curriculum areas
   (D) stress upon social utility
   (E) emphasis upon mathematical meanings

2. Select from the following number statements the one statement in which the mathematical sign $<$ would be appropriately placed within the circle.

   (A) $4+9$ $\bigcirc$ $8+5$
   (B) $51+40$ $\bigcirc$ $10+80$
   (C) $64-16$ $\bigcirc$ $41+13$
   (D) $20+40$ $\bigcirc$ $30+10$
   (E) $5+16$ $\bigcirc$ $17+4$

3. Of the following four stages in developmental mathematics learning, what is the appropriate order?
   I. developing mathematical skills through computation
   II. generalizing mathematical relationships
   III. perceiving number groups or sets
   IV. objectifying mathematical concepts

   (A) I, II, III, IV
   (B) I, III, IV, II
   (C) III, II, I, IV
   (D) IV, II, III, I
   (E) IV, III, I, II

4. In writing numbers in decimal form, the decimal point

   (A) indicates the position of the hundreds place
   (B) indicates the position of the tens place
   (C) separates units from tens
   (D) separates the integer and the decimal fraction
   (E) is essentially a placeholder

311

5. In mathematics, counting is defined as the

   (A) first operation learned in arithmetic
   (B) decimal system of numeration
   (C) ordered mapping of the objects of a set
   (D) recognition of numbers
   (E) way to arouse interest in numbers

6. The "3" in the upper right-hand corner of a newspaper page denotes the

   (A) ordinal meaning of the number
   (B) cardinal meaning of the number
   (C) total collection at a particular point
   (D) place-value
   (E) fractional part of the total paper

7. Which statement below best describes the relationship between a "number" and a "numeral"?

   (A) A numeral represents an amount; a number is a symbol of a numeral.
   (B) A number represents an amount; a numeral is a symbol of a number.
   (C) Numerals express ordinal values; numbers express cardinal values.
   (D) Numerals express cardinal values; numbers express ordinal values.
   (E) Numerals stem from the decimal system; numbers stem from the metric system.

8. The associative law in the process of multiplication states that

   (A) $a \times a = a^2$
   (B) $(a \times b) \times c = a \times (b \times c)$
   (C) $a \times b = b \times a$
   (D) $a \times (b \times c) = (a \times b) + (a \times c)$
   (E) $a + b \times a = a + a \times b$

9. A student subtracts 3y from 5y and obtains the answer 2. Her error probably stems from the failure to recognize the meaning of the

   (A) additive inverse postulate
   (B) associative postulate
   (C) commutative postulate
   (D) distributive postulate
   (E) generalization postulate

10. On a number line, the sum of a number and its inverse is always

    (A) greater than either number
    (B) a positive number
    (C) zero
    (D) the greater of two numbers
    (E) one

11. The pupils in your class are having difficulty understanding what you are teaching. Of the following, it would be *least* desirable to stress

    (A) the meaning of mathematical concepts
    (B) rigorous proof of mathematical principles
    (C) motivation for mathematical principles

(D) applications of mathematical principles

(E) the need to practice the mathematical processes involved

12. Through an exercise in the reduction of a fraction to lowest terms, a teacher can illustrate a property of which of the following?

(A) multiplicative identity

(B) additive identity

(C) additive inverse

(D) least common multiple

(E) all of the above

13. Of the following, the *best* reason for studying numbers represented by numerals written in bases other than 10 is that such study

(A) helps the student appreciate the structure of the decimal system

(B) provides good materials for problems and recreations in mathematics

(C) trains the mind to a rigorous intellectual discipline

(D) prepares the student for the study of the duodecimal system

(E) prepares the student for the study of the binary and octal systems, important in the study of the digital computer

14. Of the following, the most effective motivation for rationalizing the denominator of a fraction is to

(A) show that the procedure is an application of the principle that the value of a fraction is unchanged if it is multiplied by unity

(B) point out that it is always desirable for the denominator of a fraction to be a rational number

(C) point out the need for practice with irrational numbers

(D) find a four-place approximation for tan 30, using a right triangle the hypotenuse of which has a length of 2 units

(E) point out the need for rational fractions in understanding money systems

15. The best initial introduction to an understanding of decimal fractions is

(A) changing simple fractions to decimals

(B) learning the most common percentages

(C) developing a simplified concept of ratio

(D) teaching the binary system

(E) computing with money

16. Which one of the following topics should be placed on the highest grade level in an appropriate mathematics sequence?

(A) computing the area of a room

(B) recognition of geometric shapes

(C) partioning as a division concept

(D) associative properties of multiplication

(E) computing discount in taxes

17. To which of the following groups of operations can the commutative principle in mathematics *always* be applied?

(A) addition and multiplication

(B) addition, division, and multiplication

(C) division and subtraction
(D) division and multiplication
(E) addition and division

18. Insight into problem-solving is deepest when pupils can arrive at solutions according to

(A) a given structured pattern
(B) a self-developed pattern
(C) several different patterns
(D) patterns based on the analysis and analogy method
(E) trial and error

19. The greatest common divisor of $3x^2 - 3xy$, $6x^2y$, $9x^2y^2$ is

(A) $3xy$
(B) 3
(C) $3x^2y$
(D) $3y$
(E) $3x$

20. Checking the accuracy of an obtained difference involves adding the

(A) minuend and difference
(B) minuend and subtrahend
(C) subtrahend and addend
(D) subtrahend and difference
(E) addend and difference

21. One way to demonstrate to a student that a statement is false is to

(A) prove the converse of the statement is true
(B) prove the inverse of the statement is true
(C) prove the contrapositive of the statement is true
(D) find one counterexample of the statement
(E) have the students attempt to apply the statement

22. In planning the motivation for a mathematics lesson, the most important factor to consider is that it should

(A) not consume more than two minutes of the lesson
(B) be related to the aim of the lesson
(C) involve a mathematical game or puzzle
(D) involve the use of an appropriate visual aid
(E) involve an application to a subject other than mathematics

23. All possible pairings of two factors in multiplication are defined as the

(A) Cartesian product
(B) operation product
(C) inclusion product
(D) solution set
(E) simple product

24. If you wanted to illustrate the partitioning concept of division for your students, which one of the following would be preferred? To

    (A) divide $20 into sets of $4 each
    (B) divide $40 into 4 sets of equal amounts of dollars
    (C) ask how many sets of 4 are there in 20
    (D) ask how many sets of 5 are there in 20
    (E) show that 4 consists of four units of one

25. A student was given an algebraic expression and told to remove the parentheses and combine like terms. He solved the problem in the steps indicated below:
    (a) $x(a + b) + ax$
    (b) $(xa + xb) + ax$
    (c) $ax + ax + bx$
    (d) $2ax + bx$
    Which of the basic laws of arithmetic did he employ?

    (A) distributive only
    (B) commutative only
    (C) associative and distributive
    (D) commutative and distributive
    (E) associative, commutative, and distributive

MUSIC EDUCATION

After reading each question, circle the answer you think is correct. Then score your examination using the Answer Key that appears after the questions. You should plan for intensive review if you answer fewer than 18 correctly. Give yourself 18 minutes to answer the 25 questions on this examination.

1. The music activity in an elementary classroom should ideally be scheduled

   (A) at the same time each day so that proper habits can be developed
   (B) daily, varying in nature and occasionally arising from other activities
   (C) only when a music specialist is present
   (D) only when it can be successfully integrated with another subject
   (E) when it provides a way of relaxing or when the children are bored and tired

2. The teaching of rhythmic notation should be

   (A) approached arithmetically, since numbers are involved
   (B) delayed until fractions are mastered
   (C) coupled with bodily movement
   (D) delayed until rhythm instruments are available
   (E) related to major and minor scales

3. Young children who have trouble singing should be

   (A) encouraged to listen
   (B) classified as "non-singers"
   (C) grouped in a special class
   (D) encouraged to sing
   (E) allowed to take art rather than music

4. Allegro Molto

is basically

   (A) sextuple meter
   (B) triple meter
   (C) duple meter
   (D) compound duple meter
   (E) cut time

5. Permission from the publisher must be obtained to

   (A) make a special arrangement of a popular song for your school group
   (B) make copies of words from a Broadway musical for an assembly sing
   (C) reproduce an extra orchestra part on a duplicating machine
   (D) all of the above
   (E) none of the above

6. The autoharp is *least* useful as a(n)

   (A) melody instrument
   (B) harmony instrument
   (C) rhythmic instrument
   (D) piano substitute
   (E) accompanying instrument

7. The experience of listening to music in school generally should

   (A) be associated with another activity, such as drawing or story-telling
   (B) serve as a restful interlude in the day's work
   (C) involve discussion and direction about what to listen to or listen for
   (D) avoid technical discussion, which tends to destroy the unique appeal of music
   (E) be restricted to cultivating taste for the classics

8. A system of music education currently in wide use in Europe, with a substantial following in the elementary grades of the United States, was devised by

   (A) Hindemith
   (B) Britten
   (C) Dalcroze
   (D) Orff
   (E) Montessori

9. Ideally, instrumental music experience in the first grade should start with

   (A) the use of percussion instruments to explore rhythms
   (B) individual lessons on the piano
   (C) group lessons on the piano
   (D) playing in a rhythm band
   (E) string instruments

10. Classroom work on the recorder is usually begun

    (A) in the second grade
    (B) in the fourth grade
    (C) in the sixth grade
    (D) after the students have learned to read music
    (E) as an introduction to instrumental music

11. In conducting the following example, the *preparatory* motion is associated with the

    (A) down-beat
    (B) up-beat
    (C) third beat

(D) second beat

(E) last beat

12. The standard instrumentation for the piano quartet is

(A) piano, violin, viola, bass

(B) piano, violin, viola, cello

(C) two pianos, two players at each

(D) four pianos, one player at each

(E) piano, violin, cello, bass

13. To which valve on the baritone saxophone does the third position of the trombone correspond?

(A) fourth

(B) second

(C) third

(D) first and second

(E) first

14. In singing, high notes are most easily reached by

(A) dropping the jaw

(B) raising the head

(C) pursing the lips as in saying "oo"

(D) using the chest tones

(E) using the throat tones

15. "Tessitura" refers to

(A) a highly florid vocal line

(B) a high soprano

(C) the prevailing vocal range of a given piece

(D) falsetto singing

(E) the key of a vocal piece

16. Recitative is generally found in

(A) opera only

(B) opera, oratorio, and cantatas

(C) chamber music and art songs

(D) percussion and band music

(E) oratorio only

17. The root of the chord is

(A) C

(B) A

(C) B

(D) F

(E) none of these

18. In an art song the emphasis is on the

(A) vocal line, text, and accompaniment equally

(B) vocal line

(C) words
(D) style of the accompaniment
(E) figure bass

19. "A capella" indicates

(A) with mutes
(B) from the beginning
(C) without accompaniment
(D) harp-like
(E) in choir robes

20. Which sentence most clearly fits the rhythmic implications of the musical passage below?

(A) Jack and Jill went up the hill to fetch a pail of water
(B) Over hill, over dale, we will hit the dusty trail
(C) Tomorrow we all will feel much better than now
(D) Taking tests is easy when one is well prepared
(E) Oh, what a beautiful morning

21.  signifies

(A) A Major
(B) A Major and F# Minor
(C) F# Minor
(D) G# Major and B Minor
(E) C Major

22. The fingering on the B♭ trumpet for the note written below is

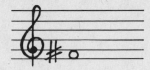

(A) first valve
(B) second valve

(C) third valve
(D) second and third valves
(E) first and second valves

23. In giving the starting note of a song, the first pitch or pitches sounded should be

(A) tonic, then starting note
(B) starting note only
(C) starting note, then tonic
(D) tonic only
(E) selected by the accompanist

24. A "riff" is a(n)

(A) rudimentary drum pattern
(B) short musical pattern constantly repeated in some jazz compositions
(C) accented percussion beat
(D) "refrain"
(E) bridge

25. Numbers such as $2\frac{1}{2}$, 3, and $3\frac{1}{2}$ on clarinet and saxophone reeds refer to the

(A) length of the reed
(B) width of the reed
(C) quality of the reed
(D) brand name of the reed
(E) stiffness of the reed

PHYSICAL EDUCATION

After reading each question, circle the answer you think is correct. Then score your examination using the Answer Key that appears after the questions. You should plan for intensive review if you answer fewer than 22 correctly. Give yourself 22 minutes to answer the 30 questions on this examination.

1. The *least* important qualification of an automobile driver is

   (A) emotional maturity
   (B) intelligence
   (C) hand-foot coordination
   (D) reaction time
   (E) vision

2. Of the following methods of presenting a new skill to a gymnasium class, the *most* effective is

   (A) a demonstration of the skill by pupil leaders
   (B) a filmstrip presenting analytical pictures of the skill followed by group performance
   (C) a demonstration by the teacher followed by group performance as the teacher presents cues
   (D) a description of the action by the teacher together with a blackboard illustration
   (E) observation of a skilled professional

3. Rousseau stated in his novel *Emile* (1762) that the essential thing, up to 12 years of age, is to exercise the body continually. In the light of modern knowledge of child growth and development, this principle

   (A) is invalid, because of the likelihood that children may exercise excessively
   (B) is debatable, because of the relatively small heart and lung capacity of children
   (C) tends to over-emphasize physical development at the expense of intellectual development
   (D) is still acceptable
   (E) is impossible to implement

4. Grades in a physical education activity course should be based to a large degree on

   (A) preparation and attitude
   (B) physical fitness test scores
   (C) achievement in skills

(D) regularity of attendance

(E) improvement

5. As a teacher of physical and health education, your best approach to participation in community affairs would be to serve as a(n)

(A) member of a number of community organizations

(B) active leader in a youth organization such as Boy Scouts or Girl Scouts

(C) active member of the dominant political organization

(D) consultant to community groups interested in health and recreation

(E) organizer of an adult recreational team in a competitive sport

6. Selye's theory of stress postulates three stages of bodily reaction, which are

(A) stress, alarm, and resistance

(B) alarm, resistance, and adaptation

(C) stress, resistance, and adaptation

(D) stress, reaction, and equilibrium

(E) alarm, resistance, and exhaustion

7. Rheumatic fever in childhood is considered serious primarily because it

(A) may lead to arthritis in later life

(B) may cause a crippling joint deformity in childhood

(C) is frequently associated with severe streptococcus infection

(D) may damage the valves of the heart

(E) is difficult to diagnose

8. The most potent factor influencing the pre-college drinking practices of teenagers is the

(A) drinking practices of other teenagers

(B) availability of liquor

(C) drinking practices of their parents

(D) drinking practices of their teachers

(E) liquor advertisements

9. The most widely distributed sense of the body is that of

(A) touch

(B) kinesthesia

(C) dysphoria

(D) temperature change

(E) taste

10. Drug addiction is *least* likely to be associated with

(A) hedonism

(B) inadequacy

(C) dependency

(D) aggressiveness

(E) depression

11. The best method of reducing tooth decay by the use of fluorides is

(A) periodic application of sodium fluoride to children's teeth

(B) inclusion of foods rich in fluorides in the daily diet
(C) regular use of fluoride toothpaste
(D) addition of fluoride to public water supply
(E) doing all of the above simultaneously

12. The greatest single cause of hearing impairment in children is

(A) streptococcus infection
(B) impacted earwax
(C) punctured eardrum, as the result of an accident
(D) congenital defects in the hearing apparatus
(E) exposure to excessive noise

13. The factor with the greatest potential influence upon an individual's eating practice is

(A) knowledge about nutrition
(B) a desire to be healthy
(C) early childhood eating experiences
(D) peer group eating practices
(E) number of siblings

14. Which of the following should be taught first in a unit on tumbling conducted in a high school program?

(A) head stand
(B) shoulder roll
(C) forward roll
(D) backward roll
(E) hand stand

15. Of the following vitamins, the one that is water soluble is

(A) vitamin A
(B) vitamin C
(C) vitamin D
(D) vitamin K
(E) vitamin B_1

16. In the United States, the greatest power in public health matters rests with the

(A) schools
(B) cities
(C) counties
(D) states
(E) federal government

17. The sub group of the United Nations that carries on public health activities is

(A) WHEN
(B) WHO
(C) UNICEF
(D) UNESCO
(E) USPHS

18. Future trends in interscholastic sports indicate that during the 1980s,

    (A) programs will be about the same, but extended to include the handicapped
    (B) club sports and intramurals will replace existing interscholastic sports, because the interscholastics are too expensive
    (C) city-run recreation programs will replace existing school sports programs
    (D) expensive male-only sports such as football will disappear in order to free funds for women's sports
    (E) programs will become more diversified and will be offered to more boys, girls, and handicapped students

19. Physical education includes which of the following domains?
    I. psycho-motor
    II. cognitive
    III. affective

    (A) I and II
    (B) I and III
    (C) I, II, and III
    (D) I only
    (E) II and III

20. The growth in girls' and women's sports resulted largely from

    (A) P.L. 94–142
    (B) Title X
    (C) Title IX
    (D) P.L. 94–145
    (E) Title III

21. Grouping for instruction and competition is desirable because

    (A) competition will be more fair
    (B) instruction will be more scientific
    (C) the program will have more continuity
    (D) the health and safety needs of all students will be met
    (E) all of the above

22. An isometric exercise is best described as the

    (A) shortening of the muscles
    (B) lengthening of the muscles
    (C) building up of tensions in the muscles without any muscle shortening or lengthening
    (D) stretching of a group of muscles
    (E) none of the above

23. Principles of physical education
    I. are based on facts
    II. are never based on philosophical inquiry
    III. are not scientific
    IV. never accept experience as a valid fact
    Which of the above statements is (are) correct?

    (A) I, II, and III
    (B) III and IV

(C) all four
(D) I and IV
(E) I only

24. An example of placing a handicapped student in a flexible plan of instruction would be to

    (A) schedule the student into a regular class that participates in diverse activities
    (B) provide individual instruction
    (C) schedule the student in an integrated class if the student is capable of participating successfully
    (D) schedule the student only on days when his or her class schedule has periods free of academic activities
    (E) schedule the student into two special classes, one of which is recreationally oriented, the other rehabilitative

25. Which of the following statements is true about the preferred food value of the three meals each day?

    (A) The heaviest food value should be at breakfast.
    (B) The heaviest food value should be at lunch.
    (C) The heaviest food value should be at dinner.
    (D) It makes no difference as long as there is one meal heavy in food value.
    (E) They should all be the same or nearly the same in food value.

26. Among the objectives of a drug education program for the elementary grades is (are) to

    (A) explain physiological effects of some of the commonly used drugs
    (B) increase interest in learning about varieties of drugs and their effects on the body
    (C) cite examples of misuse and abuse of drugs
    (D) start to develop the students' practices and habit patterns as a protection against drug abuse
    (E) all of the above

27. Students should be taught to understand that misusers of alcohol include the person who
       I. takes a drink occasionally
      II. gets drunk once or twice a year
     III. always gets drunk at social events where alcohol is served
      IV. always takes one drink before dinner

    (A) III only
    (B) II, III, and IV
    (C) III and IV only
    (D) II and III only
    (E) I, II, III, and IV

28. Marijuana does *not* cause

    (A) an effect on the central nervous system
    (B) emotional dependence
    (C) physical dependence
    (D) an effect on the sense of time
    (E) occasional fear and anxiety

29. Research studies indicate that teenagers most often smoke because

    (A) they see smoking as part of the adolescent rebellion
    (B) they see smoking as a way to achieve peer-group acceptance
    (C) adults encourage them to smoke
    (D) they prefer it to drinking as a way to socialize
    (E) they like the way cigarettes taste

30. A sound program on tobacco use would include which of the following?
    I. consideration of the effects of tobacco on the body
    II. role-playing how to refuse cigarettes from a friend
    III. a test for knowledge of tobacco and smoking
    IV. trying different cigarettes for taste

    (A) all of the above
    (B) I and II only
    (C) I only
    (D) I, II, and III
    (E) I, III, and IV

READING

After reading each question, circle the answer you think is correct. Then score your examination using the Answer Key that appears after the questions. You should plan for intensive review if you answer fewer than 26 correctly. Give yourself 30 minutes to answer the 35 questions on this examination.

1. A child who has only beginning word-analysis skills is most likely to

   (A) miss the beginning part of the word
   (B) blend together only the first and second syllables of a word
   (C) miss the meaning of a word
   (D) miss the middle or ending parts of a word
   (E) have greatest success with consonant blends

2. The most efficient method for locating reading disabilities in a class of children is probably a short

   (A) standardized group-survey test
   (B) selection read silently by each child
   (C) oral diagnostic test for each child
   (D) selection read orally by each child
   (E) questionnaire asking the children to identify their difficulties

3. Which of the following is *not* part of the psychotherapeutic relationship that should be established with the child in the remedial situation?

   (A) giving praise for all work done
   (B) setting limits for the situation
   (C) accepting the child as he is
   (D) convincing the child that he can learn
   (E) interpreting the transference aspects of the teacher-student relationship

4. Fernald's kinesthetic method of teaching reading relies on helping the child to learn by using

   (A) alphabet blocks
   (B) grooved writing trays
   (C) tracing
   (D) all of the above
   (E) none of the above

5. Of the following, the *best* technique for judging the reading difficulty of a primary book is probably

   (A) having the children read the book orally

(B) using the Dale-Chall formula
(C) consulting the Thorndike Word List
(D) employing the Spache formula
(E) using the Cloze procedure

6. If an individual intelligence test cannot be given to estimate the potential reading ability of a poor reader, the best estimate would probably be his/her

(A) level of listening comprehension
(B) reading comprehension score
(C) oral reading level
(D) score on a vocabulary test
(E) ability to learn and retain nonsense syllables

7. In general, the most essential technique the classroom teacher can use to determine whether he/she is achieving goals for reading instruction is

(A) objective, preferably standardized, unit tests
(B) frequent on-the-spot evaluation
(C) informal textbook-like tests
(D) carefully planned written assignments
(E) keeping records of how many books the child reads each month

8. When a child who is reading a story to the class comes to a word he does not know, the teacher should

(A) have him use word-analysis clues
(B) ask another child the word
(C) suggest that he look for context clues
(D) tell him the word and make a note of it
(E) suggest he guess

9. The following pairs are correctly matched with the *exception* of

(A) *Ben and Me*—Robert Lawson
(B) *Just So Stories*—Rudyard Kipling
(C) *Ugly Duckling*—Grimm
(D) *Charlotte's Web*—E.B. White
(E) *Little Women*—Louisa May Alcott

10. Probably the most important diagnostic information derived from the Gray Oral Reading Test is

(A) speed of reading
(B) level of interpretation
(C) facility with phrasing
(D) facility with word recognition
(E) breadth of vocabulary

11. Linguistic scientists, such as the late Leonard Bloomfield and C.C. Fries, have criticized the first-grade programs of "conventional" basal readers because they

(A) do not control vocabulary in terms of word-frequency counts
(B) do not stress decoding of graphic symbols
(C) do not challenge the intellectual ability of children

(D) are not based on children's reading interests

(E) ignore Chomsky's theory of the Language Acquisition Device

12. A major weakness of most reading-readiness tests is that they

(A) are not based on valid concepts of reading readiness
(B) do not measure enough factors essential for reading readiness
(C) are poor predictors of later reading achievement
(D) are not properly standardized
(E) are difficult to score and record

13. Probably the most useful information for a teacher to obtain in making a diagnosis of a child with a reading problem would be

(A) the contributing psychological factors
(B) specific strengths and weaknesses in reading
(C) attitude toward reading
(D) performance in other school subjects
(E) IQ score

14. There is a diphthong in the word

(A) boy
(B) lid
(C) head
(D) teach
(E) saw

15. The eye movement of a good reader

(A) is smooth and continuous across a line of print
(B) has many regressive movements across the line of print
(C) has fewer stops or pauses while reading across a line of print
(D) has several pauses or "fixations" on each line of print
(E) is a series of equal movements and rests

16. A group of two or three consonants that are blended together to make one sound but do not lose their separate identity is called a

(A) consonant blend
(B) diphthong
(C) phonogram
(D) schwa
(E) holophrase

17. Mary makes many errors on small words when she reads orally, but knows these words when she sounds them out in isolation. Mary probably needs

(A) more motivation for learning to read
(B) practice on the words she missed
(C) easier reading material
(D) practice with connected reading
(E) sight-drill practice

18. Ability to use context clues as a device in recognizing unfamiliar words is related chiefly to the pupil's

   (A) perceptual discrimination
   (B) knowledge of consonant sounds
   (C) understanding of language
   (D) word-analysis skills
   (E) ability to blend

19. Which one of the following statements is *incorrect* in regard to handling the reading difficulties of children?

   (A) Poor readers who need training in word recognition should be discouraged from using context clues.
   (B) Most authorities agree that auditory discrimination is a factor to be considered in a child's reading performance.
   (C) Some authorities advocate the use of mirrors in overcoming reversal errors.
   (D) Having the child trace and write words is a technique employed by some remedial-reading teachers.
   (E) Psychological support is a neccessity.

20. In recognizing an unfamiliar word, a competent adult reader uses

   (A) a phonic-meaning approach
   (B) a structural-phonic approach
   (C) a whole-word approach
   (D) any of the above approaches
   (E) none of the above approaches

21. As part of present practice in reading instruction, the teaching of phonics or phonetic analysis should be

   (A) omitted for all children
   (B) taught as the basic approach for all children
   (C) taught at some time to all children
   (D) taught only as part of a remedial reading program for those who need it
   (E) taught in the upper grades only

22. Of the following, the one *not* usually included in a reading-readiness test is

   (A) vocabulary comprehension in written context
   (B) recognition of word similarities
   (C) recognition of rhyming words
   (D) matching of one word of a group with its counterpart
   (E) recognition of initial consonants

23. Free silent reading

   (A) should be reserved for the school library
   (B) is a misuse of valuable class time
   (C) is necessary if the teacher is to have an opportunity for individual correction of compositions
   (D) provides the teacher with an opportunity to observe individual reading interests
   (E) should only be used as a reward for finishing classwork quickly

24. A vowel sound in an unaccented syllable is called a

    (A) schwa
    (B) diphthong
    (C) digraph
    (D) silent vowel
    (E) variable

25. Which of the following does the basal reader program provide?

    (A) a total reading program
    (B) orderly practice of word-recognition skills
    (C) a saving of the teacher's preparation time
    (D) control of the number of words introduced in each lesson
    (E) reading material free of sexism or racism

26. A method for teaching beginning reading which involved developing symbols for forty-three sounds in English was

    (A) the phonics method
    (B) the initial teaching alphabet
    (C) Flesch's critical sound approach
    (D) Bloomfield's "Let's Read"
    (E) the sound-it-out approach

27. In her summary of research projects in reading from 1912 to 1965, Jeanne Chall concluded that for beginning reading,

    (A) some code-emphasis methods are clearly superior
    (B) meaning-emphasis is better than code emphasis
    (C) work on decoding should continue well into the elementary years
    (D) code-emphasis is superior to meaning emphasis
    (E) there are no differences among the methods as long as reading is systematically taught

28. A teacher concerned with teaching reading to young children will provide which of the following experiences?

    I. oral communication experiences
    II. visual discrimination experiences
    III. auditory discrimination experiences

    (A) I only
    (B) II only
    (C) III only
    (D) II and III
    (E) I, II, and III

29. The language experience approach includes all but which of the following?

    (A) experience
    (B) description
    (C) phonics analysis
    (D) writing stories for reading
    (E) reading and word study

30. A teacher is using a reading method which sequences and controls the introduction of new words and fundamental reading skills. The method being used is called

    (A) the basal reader
    (B) phonics analysis
    (C) language experience
    (D) individualized reading
    (E) programmed reading

31. Which of the following is a problem faced by teachers using the individualized reading approach?

    (A) organizing reading groups
    (B) record keeping
    (C) maintaining interest
    (D) allowing for self-expression
    (E) making it possible for rapid learners to progress

32. A teacher using the phonics approach to teach reading has arrived at the study of consonants. Which of the following would *not* be included at this point?

    (A) sounds of consonant blends such as bl and br
    (B) doubling consonants when adding an ending such as ed or er
    (C) consonant digraphs such as ch and sh
    (D) silent consonants
    (E) the schwa sound

33. A child asks you whether we really need all the consonants. You answer "no, we could really read well without"

    (A) b and d
    (B) j and v
    (C) c and h
    (D) k and z
    (E) q and x

34. A reading approach which also has demonstrated its usefulness in teaching English as a second language is the approach known as

    (A) linguistics
    (B) phonics
    (C) basal reader
    (D) diagnostic prescription
    (E) basic English

35. You give a child a standardized normative reading test before and after instruction because you wish to estimate the child's position in relation to his group. Which of the following measures would be the best to consider?

    (A) raw score
    (B) grade equivalent
    (C) normal curve equivalent
    (D) percentile
    (E) stanine

SOCIAL STUDIES

After reading each question, circle the answer you think is correct. Then score your examination using the Answer Key that appears after the questions. You should plan for intensive review if you answer fewer than 18 correctly. Give yourself 15 minutes to answer the 25 questions on this examination.

1. Which of the following topics would usually be introduced earliest in teaching map and globe skills?

   (A) map legends
   (B) latitude and longitude
   (C) rotation of the earth
   (D) relationship between actual distances and distances on a map
   (E) location of the continents

2. In a lesson on climate and climatic changes, which of the following offers the best illustration of the fact that climate may change greatly over a period of time?

   (A) the freezing over of the East River in New York fifty years ago
   (B) the discovery of coal beds in the Arctic region
   (C) the dust storms of the 1930s in the midwest
   (D) the discovery of marine fossils in rocks
   (E) the discovery of glacial rocks in the northeast

3. In a lesson on the nature of historical sources, Samuel Pepys' account of the great fire in London would be an example of

   (A) a secondary conscious source
   (B) a secondary unconscious source
   (C) a primary conscious source
   (D) a primary unconscious source
   (E) primary, but cannot be determined if conscious or unconscious

4. The notion of "supply-side economics," popularized by the administration of President Reagan, is based on the belief that

   (A) the law of supply and demand no longer applies in a technological world
   (B) the supply of money has to be increased steadily
   (C) providing incentives to business is the most effective way to restore economic vitality
   (D) those who supply goods under government contract have to participate actively in economic recovery programs
   (E) we have to stockpile commodities such as oil so as not to be at the mercy of those nations that supply them.

333

5. Which of the following patterns of writing history enjoys the most esteem today?

   (A) geographical
   (B) cultural
   (C) revisionist
   (D) biographical
   (E) chronological

   Questions 6 and 7 refer to the following list of research approaches.

   (A) case study
   (B) participant observation
   (C) ideal-type model
   (D) content analysis
   (E) historical regression

6. Which approach is a preferred approach in sociology?

7. Which approach is the preferred approach in anthropology?

8. The purposes of sociological research include which of the following?

   (A) the consequences of group living
   (B) why groups change
   (C) the relationship among group members and among groups
   (D) all of the above
   (E) none of the above

9. Which of the following is most often used by contemporary historians in synthesizing their data?

   (A) climate and geography
   (B) mutability
   (C) independence
   (D) projection
   (E) multiple causation

10. A teacher assigned readings by Clinton Rossiter, Sidney Heyman, and Richard Neustadt to his class. Which aspect of American society was the class studying? The

    (A) American presidency
    (B) American Congress
    (C) American Supreme Court
    (D) American federal system
    (E) American newspaper

11. Which of the following would be a primary source on the drafting of the American Constitution?

    (A) Van Doren's *The Great Rehearsal*
    (B) De Tocqueville's *Democracy in America*
    (C) Madison's *Notes*
    (D) Beard's *Economic Interpretation of the Constitution*
    (E) White's *Making of the President*

12. Arrange the following events in their correct chronological order.
     I. Meji restoration
     II. arrival of Perry in Japan
     III. Townsend Harris becomes first United States consul to Japan
     IV. Shogunate established in Japan

     (A) I, II, III, IV
     (B) II, III, IV, I
     (C) IV, III, II, I
     (D) IV, II, III, I
     (E) II, III, I, IV

13. Which of the following statements is *not* true of American foreign relations in the post-Civil War period?

     (A) The activities of Fenians along the Canadian border embarrassed our relations with Canada.
     (B) The outbreak of a Cuban rebellion in 1868 threatened to involve the United States in war with Spain.
     (C) Secretary of State Seward pursued a vigorous expansionist policy.
     (D) President Grant showed no interest in an expansionist policy.
     (E) President Cleveland strongly supported a unilateral interpretation of the Monroe Doctrine.

14. Which of the following was *least* in accord with Communist principles?

     (A) Gosplan
     (B) NEP
     (C) Comintern
     (D) Five-year plan
     (E) Collectivization

15. In which of the following are the items regarding the United Nations *incorrectly* paired?

     (A) Uniting for Peace Resolution—right of the General Assembly to act because of a Security Council veto
     (B) UNESCO—rehabilitation of Korea following the Korean War
     (C) Procedural Matters—vote of any seven members of the Security Council
     (D) Trusteeship Council—supervision of designated territories whose people have not attained self-government
     (E) International Development Association—assist backward countries in their economic growth

16. Which one of the following indicators would give the best prediction of a person's probable social-class position in the United States?

     (A) religion
     (B) neighborhood of residence
     (C) interests
     (D) occupation
     (E) ancestry

17. Ethnology can best be described as

     (A) a branch of comparative psychology

(B) a branch of anthropology devoted to comparative and descriptive studies of different cultures

(C) the idealistic (as opposed to materialistic) branch of the sociology of knowledge

(D) the field of social history that attempts to study the *ethos* of a particular field

(E) the branch of sociology concerned with ethnic relations

18. The idea that the federal government is a compact or contract among the states was expressed in

(A) Lee's resolution
(B) the theory of manifest destiny
(C) South Carolina's "Exposition and Protest"
(D) Webster's reply to Hayne
(E) the Freeport Doctrine

Questions 19 and 20 are to be answered with reference to the map below.

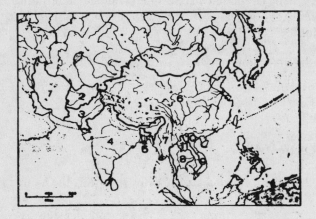

19. Which of the following nations has not been under colonial rule in modern times?

(A) 4
(B) 5
(C) 7
(D) 8
(E) 11

20. The Battle of Dien Bien Phu meant the end of direct French influence in

(A) 8
(B) 9 and 10
(C) 7 and 8
(D) 1
(E) 5

21. The chief reason for the opposition of the South to the election of Abraham Lincoln in 1860 was his

(A) resistance to secession

(B) demand for the immediate abolition of slavery

(C) hostility to the extension of slavery

(D) insistence on equal education for negroes and whites

(E) unsophisticated appearance

22. In the period 1887 to 1890, Congress passed major legislation to regulate abuses in

(A) local government

(B) industrial combinations

(C) union methods

(D) farm credit

(E) governmental hiring practices

Questions 23, 24, and 25 are all to be answered using the data in the table below, and *only* by reference to these data.

NUMBER OF IMMIGRANTS COMING TO THE UNITED STATES EACH TENTH YEAR FROM 1820 TO 1910 AND PERCENTAGE OF TOTAL COMING FROM CERTAIN SELECTED COUNTRIES

YEARS	Total Number of Immigrants	Percentage of Immigrants From					
		United* Kingdom	Germany	Scandinavia	Italy	Austria-Hungary	Russia
1820	12,850	60.7	4.5	0.2	0.3	—	0.1
1830	53,838	45.5	23.2	0.4	0.4	—	0.1
1840	142,733	61.3	27.0	0.9	0.1	—	0.04
1850	281,455	52.6	34.7	4.6	0.3	—	0.02
1860	208,126	46.6	35.2	7.6	0.5	0.2	0.2
1870	274,213	36.5	27.4	12.8	1.7	2.2	1.7
1880	524,856	28.3	27.5	10.6	5.1	6.0	3.8
1890	369,429	19.9	15.7	6.0	16.3	14.5	12.2
1900	820,238	9.9	4.0	3.8	23.5	24.4	18.3
1910	634,738	8.5	2.7	—	19.4	18.2	17.4

*Includes all parts of the former British Empire.

23. The total number of immigrants coming to the United States increased every ten years from 1820 to 1910.

(A) true

(B) probably true

(C) probably false

(D) false

(E) cannot be determined from data in table

24. The marked increase in the total number of immigrants between 1820 and 1910 was due to the increasing leniency of the immigration laws.

(A) true

(B) probably true

(C) probably false

(D) false

(E) cannot be determined from data in the table

25. The percentage of immigrants from Hungary was no greater in the year 1900 than in the year 1860.

   (A) true
   (B) probably true
   (C) probably false
   (D) false
   (E) cannot be determined from data in the table

Answer Key

ART EDUCATION

1.	D	11.	D
2.	C	12.	E
3.	C	13.	C
4.	B	14.	A
5.	D	15.	B
6.	C	16.	D
7.	A	17.	B
8.	A	18.	B
9.	D	19.	C
10.	D	20.	C

BIOLOGY AND GENERAL SCIENCE

1.	A	14.	D
2.	B	15.	D
3.	D	16.	A
4.	E	17.	D
5.	D	18.	C
6.	C	19.	D
7.	B	20.	B
8.	E	21.	A
9.	C	22.	D
10.	C	23.	A
11.	E	24.	C
12.	C	25.	B
13.	C		

CHEMISTRY, PHYSICS, AND GENERAL SCIENCE

1.	A	14.	D
2.	B	15.	B
3.	A	16.	D
4.	A	17.	A
5.	D	18.	C
6.	E	19.	D
7.	C	20.	A
8.	A	21.	B
9.	C	22.	B
10.	C	23.	D
11.	D	24.	D
12.	A	25.	E
13.	B		

Answer Key

EARLY CHILDHOOD EDUCATION

1. B
2. E
3. B
4. C
5. C
6. C
7. C
8. A
9. D
10. A
11. B
12. A
13. C
14. C

15. D
16. E
17. E
18. E
19. B
20. C
21. B
22. C
23. A
24. A
25. C
26. D
27. E
28. D

29. E
30. A
31. C
32. E
33. B
34. E
35. A
36. E
37. B
38. E
39. E
40. B

EDUCATION OF THE MENTALLY RETARDED

1. E
2. D
3. B
4. C
5. E
6. E
7. E
8. E
9. A
10. E

11. E
12. D
13. C
14. E
15. C
16. E
17. B
18. D
19. C
20. D

21. D
22. B
23. D
24. C
25. A
26. A
27. E
28. C
29. C
30. B

ELEMENTARY EDUCATION

1. E
2. A
3. B
4. A
5. E
6. B
7. A
8. E
9. C
10. C
11. A
12. A
13. D
14. C

15. B
16. E
17. B
18. A
19. C
20. D
21. D
22. D
23. B
24. A
25. E
26. A
27. A
28. E

29. A
30. E
31. C
32. B
33. D
34. D
35. C
36. E
37. B
38. A
39. B
40. C

Answer Key

ENGLISH LANGUAGE AND LITERATURE

1. A	10. E	19. E
2. A	11. C	20. C
3. C	12. A	21. C
4. A	13. A	22. E
5. C	14. D	23. A
6. C	15. A	24. E
7. E	16. A	25. D
8. E	17. A	
9. C	18. A	

INDUSTRIAL ARTS EDUCATION

1. B	10. B	19. B
2. B	11. E	20. C
3. C	12. C	21. D
4. B	13. B	22. A
5. C	14. B	23. A
6. A	15. C	24. E
7. B	16. A	25. C
8. A	17. D	
9. D	18. D	

MATHEMATICS EDUCATION

1. E	10. C	
2. C	11. B	19. E
3. E	12. A	20. D
4. D	13. B	21. D
5. A	14. D	22. B
6. A	15. E	23. A
7. B	16. E	24. B
8. B	17. A	25. E
9. D	18. C	

MUSIC EDUCATION

1. B	10. B	19. C
2. A	11. B	20. D
3. A	12. B	21. B
4. E	13. E	22. B
5. D	14. C	23. A
6. D	15. B	24. B
7. C	16. B	25. E
8. C	17. D	
9. A	18. A	

Answer Key

PHYSICAL EDUCATION

1. C	11. D	21. E
2. C	12. A	22. C
3. D	13. C	23. E
4. A	14. C	24. C
5. D	15. C	25. A
6. C	16. D	26. E
7. D	17. B	27. A
8. C	18. E	28. C
9. A	19. C	29. B
10. D	20. C	30. D

READING

1. D	13. B	25. B
2. C	14. A	26. B
3. E	15. A	27. E
4. D	16. A	28. E
5. D	17. D	29. C
6. A	18. C	30. A
7. B	19. A	31. B
8. D	20. D	32. B
9. C	21. C	33. E
10. D	22. A	34. A
11. B	23. D	35. C
12. C	24. B	

SOCIAL STUDIES

1. D	10. A	19. D
2. B	11. C	20. B
3. C	12. D	21. C
4. C	13. E	22. B
5. B	14. B	23. D
6. A	15. B	24. E
7. B	16. D	25. D
8. D	17. B	
9. E	18. C	